DESIRING the BOMB

RHETORIC, CULTURE, AND SOCIAL CRITIQUE

DESIRING the BOMB

COMMUNICATION, PSYCHOANALYSIS, AND THE ATOMIC AGE

Calum L. Matheson

The University of Alabama Press
Tuscaloosa

The University of Alabama Press
Tuscaloosa, Alabama 35487-0380
uapress.ua.edu

Typeface: Garamond and Scala Sans

Cover image and design: Michele Myatt Quinn

Cataloging-in-Publication data is available from the Library of Congress.
ISBN: 978-0-8173-1998-4
E-ISBN: 978-0-8173-9204-8

To the memory of Dr. Lister Malcolm Matheson

Contents

Acknowledgments

I owe debts of gratitude to many people. Lester Olson, Mickey Bannon, Caitlin Bruce, Peter Campbell, Lynn Clarke, Jack Gareis, Meredith Guthrie, Johanna Hartelius, Paul Johnson, Olga Kuchinskaya, John Lyne, Brent Malin, David Marshall, Gordon Mitchell, John Poulakos, Ron Zboray, and the rest of the faculty and staff—part-time, full-time, and administrative—with whom I work have made the University of Pittsburgh an intellectual home. Eric English and Lauri Freund deserve special mention for the hard work they have put into the William Pitt Debating Union, which I could not direct without them.

I am also grateful for my mentors at the University of North Carolina. Chris Lundberg tricked me into getting a PhD, taught me about Lacan, and extensively shaped my thinking about rhetoric and psychoanalysis. Thanks, Oscar. Sarah Sharma taught me about the intersection of media and cultural studies, immeasurably improved my writing, and always rolled her eyes at the right time. She made me feel like I belonged in graduate school, even though I was late to our first meeting and should have already known the importance of time. Carole Blair taught me everything I know about the contemporary field of rhetoric, showed me what excellent rhetorical scholarship is, and made me understand what academic diligence really means. No one taught me more about how to actually *be a professor* than Carole. Ken Hillis introduced me to technology studies with an understated brilliance and seemingly endless well of patience. His thoughtful comments on my work improved this book a great deal. Todd Ochoa introduced me to the study of religion and culture and advised me on the judicious use of Georges Bataille. He is gracious, humble, erudite, and one of the finest young scholars I have met. Finally, Eric King Watts and Bill Balthrop were both sources of wise counsel and positivity throughout my time at Carolina. Geoffrey Wawro, Edward "Duke" Richey, Adrian Lewis, and the late Brigadier General Dr. Alfred Hurley at the University of North Texas gave me invaluable knowledge about military and environmental history on which this book relies.

Two more colleagues deserve special thanks. Jarrod Atchison has helped and encouraged me through every step of my academic career, and was instrumental to the publication of this book. He remains the only person to whom I have lost a substantial bet in which the outcome was entirely in my power to control. I greatly value his friendship. Tim Barouch has offered practical wisdom and perspective as we both navigate our early academic careers. Our ongoing dialogue has put a (small) dent in my misanthropy and made the last few years easier to manage.

I want to thank my family as well. Thanks, Mom and Scott, for tolerating decades of talk about nuclear war. Thanks, Chris, for introducing me to games and speculative fiction and keeping the sand secret . . . kind of. And thanks to Tess Tavormina and my family in Scotland, especially Calum, Katie, Charlotte, John, Calum, and Chuck for reminding me that there's more to life than work. And, of course, Laleh.

This work would also not be possible without the guidance of Dan Waterman and his colleagues at the University of Alabama Press. No one could ask for a better, more generous editor. I also want to thank my reviewers for careful and constructive suggestions, as well as the editors at *Argumentation and Advocacy* and *Games and Culture*, where two earlier articles appeared that have been extensively revised to become elements of chapter 2.

DESIRING the BOMB

Introduction

Enduring Half-Lives of the Bomb

> The problem was simple and terrible: I enjoyed the book. I liked reading about the deaths of tens of millions of people. . . . I liked to think of huge buildings toppling, of firestorms, of bridges collapsing, survivors roaming the charred countryside. . . . I became fascinated by words and phrases like thermal hurricane, overkill, circular error probability, post-attack environment, stark deterrence, dose-rate contours, kill-ratio, spasm war. Pleasure in these words . . . A thrill almost sensual accompanied the reading of this book. What was wrong with me? Had I gone mad? Did others feel as I did? I became seriously depressed. Yet I went to the library and got more books on the subject. . . . I became more fascinated, more depressed, and finally I left Coral Gables and went back home to my room and to the official team photo of the Detroit Lions. It seemed the only thing to do. My mother brought lunch upstairs. I took the dog for walks.
>
> —Don DeLillo, *End Zone*

Why the Bomb?

Although too young to really be a child of the Cold War, I have dim memories of Reagan-era fear. Around fourth grade, I had already been fascinated in school by footage of gray-clad Soviets marching through Red Square with menacing MAZ missile carriers rumbling beside them when the Gulf War started. I thought the Soviets looked cool. I wasn't scared of them. But then I learned that Saddam Hussein had missiles too. Fine distinctions of range were lost on me; circular error probability, the limitations of TEL reliance and the inadequacy of Iraqi EW/GCI were unknown unknowns.[1] I worried that Saddam would kill my parents. For reassurance, someone at school gave me a glossy chart comparing Coalition and Iraqi military equipment. It didn't really work. The pamphlet put all the planes and tanks side by side; it all looked the same to me. Soon after, the August Coup happened in the USSR and my father insisted that I watch all the news coverage about it. I learned that there were good Russians and bad Russians. The one who rode a tank and shelled the Parliament was good. One of the bad ones hanged himself in his office, but there were always more. The world was becoming less certain, but the shadow of nuclear destruction remained.

I attended my first debate tournament as a sophomore in high school. At the time, policy debate was mostly about using block quotations as evidence to weave stories about competing government actions in fast, technical speeches laced with hyperbole. For two days, I argued with other kids, uncomfortable like me, in ill-fitting formal clothes. I had been trained to negate the resolution ("Resolved: That the federal government should establish a program to substantially reduce juvenile crime in the United States") by highlighting its negative consequences for states' rights and federal spending. These things mattered, I was told, because the instability attending to a breakdown in federalism or an economic downturn might cause a nuclear war. A nuclear war would be so awful that it should never be risked, however improbable. I was given excerpts from Jonathan Schell's *The Fate of the Earth*[2] as a resource. I did as I was told and invoked the threat of atomic attack in every debate. After one of my first debates, a young debater from Detroit approached me in the cafeteria. "Are you the nuclear war guy?" he asked. I supposed that I might be. "I heard about you. You're crazy, man. That's awesome." Thus began a lifelong fascination with every aspect of nuclear war—its horrific future landscapes, boundless human toll, and the slick, rarified language of its technical terminology. I was not raised in a religious family. Like the narrator of *End Zone*,[3] ICBM was my tetragrammaton.

A few cults aside, by the late 1990s, apocalypticism had seen better days. Although they would continue to interest me, nuclear issues became gradually less important in American culture more generally. As CIA Director James Woolsey said, once the "dragon" of the Soviet Union was slain, the United States found itself in a "jungle filled with a bewildering variety of poisonous snakes," and of course, "the dragon was easier to keep track of."[4] Following the brief millennial panic of Y2K, popular and academic attention would come to focus more on the George W. Bush administration's "War on Terror" and then the new regime of automatic drone warfare. Just a few decades ago, nearly every public intellectual and prominent academic had something to say about the arms race and the prospect of nuclear extinction. An immense amount of scholarship was produced on all aspects of nuclear weapons and their military, cultural, and philosophical import. With the dragon of superpower nuclear war apparently slain, dull serpents have occupied its lair in the cultural imagination. Non-state nuclear terrorism replaced the once-anticipated Armageddon of Soviet wrath. Climate change supplanted nuclear winter. In popular movies, the devastated postnuclear heartland of *The Day After* (1983) gave way to the gaudy climate chaos of *The Day After Tomorrow* (2004). Cannibalistic mutants have been evicted from their bombed-out ruins to make room for zombies to shamble through broken retail spaces. A legion of horribles still parades, but theirs is an awfully ramshackle apocalypse. For all the fashionable talk about the Anthropocene, not even climate change lays claim to the combination of imminence, plausibility, and finality that once made nuclear war so enthralling. So why write about nuclear weapons now?

We still live in the shadow of the Bomb. I have used the word "we" deliberately. Nearly everyone on Earth is inundated by the cultural apparatuses spawned by the nuclear state. Most English speakers are familiar with nuclear-derived language but not its origins—blonde "bombshells" wearing "bikinis," named for the site of the first hydrogen bomb test; food "nuked" in a microwave oven; pundits threatening to "bomb" our enemies "back to the Stone Age," as Curtis LeMay is supposed to have done. The names Hiroshima and Nagasaki instantly conjure the iconic image of the mushroom cloud. We are aware that Albert Einstein was a genius, but only one equation comes to mind: that which made the Bomb possible. Some public issues are "radioactive," like the "collateral damage" that "war games" should have predicted in various US military interventions. We live in a narrative environment shaped by nuclear stories like *The Road, Mad Max, Manhattan, Jericho, Dr. Strangelove*, the *Fallout* video game series, the 2017 revival of *Twin Peaks*, and hundreds more. An upscale bourgeois bohemian supermarket in my city recently advertised "Atomic Pork Sausages" while the convenience store down the street sold microwave "Bomb" burritos, thus hawking nuclear-themed food to patrician and plebeian alike.

The physical infrastructure of the Atomic Age still persists, as it will for hundreds of millennia. There is a good chance your home is powered in part by nuclear energy, possibly from downblended Soviet nuclear warheads obtained in a defense conversion program. Spent waste accretes; mine tailings remain; test sites are maintained. The traces of the nuclear complex are present as isotopes in our bones and background radiation in the air we breathe. That contamination helps track ivory poachers in Africa, provides isotopes for medical research, powers deep space probes, and reworks the DNA of almost everything living on Earth. The Bomb is not something outside of us, either nature or technology: it is in our hearts and minds and bodies, the words we speak, the fantasies we share and the technologies we use, all the more sly for its gradual exit from public memory. News items about potential nuclear dangers are still reported every day from Iran, the Korean Peninsula, Russia, and the United States.

The most dramatic reactivation of nuclear fear since the end of the Cold War started during the 2016 American presidential campaign. This and the ensuing victory of Donald Trump revived the zeitgeist of doomsday, at least for those who did not support him. Representations of doomsday prepping have had a strong conservative feel since at least the 1950s. Evangelists like Hal Lindsey predicting Armageddon, the anticommunist patriots of *Red Dawn*, gun-toting survivalists in the Rocky Mountains and rural Midwest have dominated this cultural imaginary. American conservatives have often been attacked as fearmongers, but a similar tone is emerging on the "left." Trump has been compared to Adolf Hitler, Benito Mussolini, and Caligula. Concerns about his impetuousness, vindictive character, and lack of experience are often expressed in connection to nuclear weapons. I listened from my office window to Hillary Clinton adopting precisely this left-wing (relative to Trump) apocalyptic discourse, although with a good deal more sophistication and subtlety than is present in other quarters.

A pair of last-minute advertisements run by the Clinton campaign in 2016 highlights this indictment. One features Dr. Bruce Blair, one of the world's foremost experts on nuclear weapon command and control systems. In lieu of his academic credentials, Blair mentions his years as a nuclear missile launch officer. At one point, he is seated in what appears to be a command bunker. Visuals show a silo opening with a Minuteman III missile preparing to launch with harsh electronic noise in the background. "The thought of Donald Trump with nuclear weapons scares me to death," Blair says, and "should scare everyone." The other advertisement is a return to the (in)famous 1964 Daisy Girl ad run by Lyndon B. Johnson. Johnson's original ad featured a young girl pulling petals off a daisy, her counting overtaken by a launch countdown spoken in a harshly amplified voice, ending in the iconic mushroom cloud of a nuclear explosion. The 2016 ad features Monique Corzilius Luiz, the actress from Johnson's original ad, now a concerned adult. Echoing a line from the 1964 ad, Luiz says that "the stakes are too high" not to vote for Hillary Clinton. The middle part of the commercial includes clips of Trump speaking aggressively and media figures noting that he seems to ignore expert opinion. Bookending the ad, Luiz appears again with no credentials other than her casting in the original commercial.[5]

Both commercials focus on Trump, as one would expect from a rival political campaign. Trump is presented as a dangerously unhinged, callous lunatic capable of ending the world at any moment. Although these commercials draw heavily on Cold War disarmament tropes and fears of nuclear war, an important difference is the shift from indictment of the entire nuclear complex and the basic existence of nuclear weapons to the rational capacities of the leader supposedly in charge of them. The possibility of a rogue commander—even a rogue commander in chief—was always a subset of the disarmament movement's critique, but in the case of Trump, it seems to have taken over almost completely. To say that Trump should not be trusted with the Bomb as an endorsement of Clinton without indicting the existence of the weapons themselves enthymematically suggests that Clinton *could* be trusted. The problem, at least in this rhetorical construction, is the individual. A vast technological system forged this nuclear sword, but the primary concern seems to be whether Damocles ("man of the people") will yank on the sword above his new throne, and whether a better technocrat could manage the risks. Trump burns so brightly as a condensation of danger that the quotidian, ever-present hazards of possessing this technology in the first place recede into the background.

A common theme in this discourse is Trump's lack of knowledge. In a lengthy article, Blair detailed some of the procedures for a nuclear launch, then questioned Trump's "brainpower," and "competence."[6] An open letter signed by ten former missile launch officers (including Blair) claimed that Trump "has shown himself time and again to be . . . dismissive of expert consultation and ill-informed of even basic military and international affairs—including, most especially, nuclear weapons."[7] Trump is presented as impulsive and ignorant, constantly making decisions without the adequate knowledge to do so. Many critics have also focused on Trump's frequent use of Twitter to disseminate policy statements. The *Chicago Tribune* published an oft-linked article titled "Could Trump start a nuclear war with a single tweet?" in which Blair expresses trepidation over whether Trump will conduct "nuclear diplomacy by Twitter." President Barack Obama also made the connection between Twitter and the nuclear arsenal in response to reports that Trump's advisors had temporarily taken over control of their candidate's Twitter account. "If your closest advisors don't trust you to tweet," the president said, "how can you trust him with the nuclear codes? You can't."[8]

The image of Donald Trump that emerges is of a man of unrestrained id, a speaking subject announcing demands, threats, and desires without limit. Trump *knows* nothing and favors a medium restricted to 140-character proclamations (280 characters as of late 2017). At the same time, Clinton's advertisements were careful to highlight the everydayness of their stars, not their specialized knowledge. Both Blair and Luiz were presented as having intimate connections to the Bomb, even though Blair is not just a "former launch officer" but also a PhD-holding research scholar at Princeton. Trump becomes the embodiment of Jacques Lacan's master's discourse, a subject speaking, desiring, and demanding, with knowledge located not in him but in the "slave" he subjugates, even when the slave's knowledge is downplayed to fit the present anti-intellectual climate. Trump is the signifier intervening to disrupt an established order. Clinton, on the other hand, represents Lacan's university discourse, privileging the order of law, knowledge, competence, and expertise.[9]

In the context of the larger history of nuclear weapons, Trump is not primarily important due to any internal condition of his mind, no matter how empty or tumultuous we might imagine it to be. Lacan famously argued that the signifier speaks through subjects, not the other way around. Trump's words do not come from a deeply hidden interior psyche to be loosed upon the world. He is a conduit for much bigger things. Concepts and their signifiers lurk unnoticed like shadows beyond the campfire's light: Trump's own shadow is just so large that we see only him. Trump quite literally does not know what he is saying because the signifiers we invoke precede us and stretch far beyond our own personal experience and comprehension. The speaking subject does not know, but it forms an image—an ego—by identifying with a specular image, a seemingly coherent, condensed self that serves to represent it as a signifier to others. Thus the subject is split between the id, speaking, demanding, desiring, and the ego, which is its reflection in which its own lack—and therefore desire—is not perceptible to it. Think of the difference between "I" and "me" in the English language. "I" want, "I" desire, "I" say, "I" demand, that you give to "me," respect "me," love "me," submit to "me." Roughly speaking, the "I" is the id while the "me" is the ego, a split demonstrated graphically in Lacan's Schema L (discussed later in this book).[10] Trump's messages to his predominantly white, working-class voters were less Athena springing from the head of Zeus and more Linda Blair speaking with the devil's voice. His statements about nuclear weapons are not the underlying cause of nuclear war threats, but rather fragments of a larger discourse that represent seventy years of nuclear developments which always raised the possibility of incomprehensible human destruction. As this book will show, in a very real sense, no one *knows* much about nuclear war in any case.

This book is not, however, primarily about Donald Trump. The danger of focusing on the master himself is that the *discourse* will be neglected. Trump's particular characteristics might make him a dangerous leader, but the conditions of nuclear high alert, short warning times, and the antidemocratic structure of what Blair (echoing Elaine Scarry)[11] calls the "nuclear monarchy" all preceded him. Trump steps into a vast cultural, political, and technological complex that created the conditions for his threat and makes a world-rending nuclear catastrophe possible regardless of who holds the authority to authorize a launch. Beyond the tangible infrastructure of the nuclear weapons complex is a set of affective investments, cultural touchpoints, and fantasies that direct meaning and attitudes toward nuclear war in excess of what any one person can determine.

Trump therefore occupies a position within a certain range of possibilities, but this is not to say that structure determines everything to the exclusion of agency. The insight of rhetoric—and its important place in psychoanalysis—is to remind us that contingency matters and therefore the unique constellation that is Donald Trump is significant within the larger structure of which he is an appendage. The president of the United States has sole authority to use the country's nuclear arsenal. The balance between individual actors, contingent events, and the structural conditions of possibility is one reason why psychoanalysis and rhetoric should be understood as inextricably connected projects. The focus on what Trump does not know may come at the expense of examining the role of knowledge more generally in the nuclear weapons complex and the web of cultural significations that mold our approach to nuclear weapons and imbue them with significance beyond their sheer explosive power, just as the focus on broader context might understate the effect of the master's intervention in that web of signifiers.

What about Trump's use of Twitter? Surely, there is something uniquely dangerous about his choice of this medium to communicate American nuclear policy? Perhaps. Yet the great emphasis placed on Trump's use of this particular method of communication may also reveal larger cultural investments in the link between mediation and the Bomb. One central claim of this book is that *any* attempt to mediate nuclear war produces both horror and fascination by hinting toward the register of the "Real," an interruption that reminds us of the world beyond language and understanding. Media themselves become points of great affective attachment because they gesture beyond themselves to something that escapes mediation altogether. Because, as Jacques Derrida noted long ago, the kind of apocalyptic nuclear war that the Cold War threatened has never occurred; it exists only in language—it is "fabulously textual," and because such a war would destroy the material basis for any archive, it must always remain so.[12] We might amend Derrida's claim somewhat to say that nuclear war is *fabulously mediated*. It exists not only in words, but in images, sounds, film, and so forth, but despite its overwhelming power to capture the imagination, "the Big One" has no empirical reality. As the *hibakusha* and witnesses of aboveground nuclear testing age and die, nuclear explosions fade from lived memory, becoming more and more elements of myth.

The discourse of nuclear threat surrounding Trump's election demonstrates the mediated power of the Bomb in at least two ways. First, tweets have a catachrestic effect. Catachresis traditionally names the jarring effect of replacing one term with another that seems inappropriate. In this case, the discomfiture is between message and media. Critics recoil not just at the content of each tweet, but at the media form itself. After all, as Marshall McLuhan argued, the medium and message cannot be divorced so easily. The grave import of nuclear weapons seems diminished by 140-character messages on a social media platform. This view demonstrates that the Bomb still has great currency: Twitter seems like such an offensive platform because it is viewed as trivial in comparison to the unspoken (and unspeakable) gravity of nuclear weapons. This juxtaposition was prophesied some fifteen-hundred years ago by Pseudo-Dionysius the Areopagite, who wrote that all names for God are in some way profane relative to His ungraspable infinity, but the shock of their use reveals their limits.[13] Perhaps Trump's nuclear policy declarations are shocking because they are extreme examples of the general inability of *any* language to capture such a hideous vision as nuclear war. In this view, even Herman Kahn's famous *On Thermonuclear War* has great merit as a doorstop, but in all its detailed pages it does no better capturing the import of its subject. The president's rash statements are thus akin to the ancient Hebrew tetragrammaton, which demonstrated the same failure of language to grasp the infinite with 136 characters to spare.

This complicated relationship between media and nuclear war also sheds some light on Clinton's reworking of the Daisy Girl commercial. Luiz has no special qualification to discuss nuclear policy other than her childhood appearance in a well-known commercial (of a kind with Peter Bergman's line in a 1986 cough syrup commercial "I'm not a doctor, but I play one on TV"). Most superficially, Luiz's presence strengthens the basic intertextual link between the 2016 ad and its 1964 referent. The 1964 commercial was for another Democrat running against an unpredictable Republican cavalier about the use of nuclear weapons. Indeed, the infamous remark attributed to vice presidential candidate Curtis LeMay ("bomb [North Vietnam] back to the Stone Age") sounds much like Trump's more aggressive nuclear posturing. Stopping here leaves some important questions unanswered, however. If the commercial is meant to indict Trump's knowledge and expertise, why choose such an obscure figure alongside Blair, Obama, and other acknowledged experts?

One answer—developed in later chapters of this book—is that the mediation of nuclear violence and the destructive potential of the weapons themselves become conflated. There is a chain of rhetorical moves at work: Luiz's metonymic link between the 2016 commercial and the original Daisy Girl ad, the visual metonymy of the mushroom cloud for nuclear war, and the enthymematic threat of human extinction, woven together through the pathos of an innocent child. Luiz comes to represent something unrepresentable. To understand these moves we have to look beyond these rational connections to the Bomb's central paradox: at its limit, the Bomb exceeds language, but because it has no empirical existence on the scale to which it is imagined, it exists only in the Symbolic.[14] What makes Luiz a rational choice as an expert on the Bomb is the mere fact that there is nothing rational about the Bomb's symbolic power. Mediation has become too entangled with its imaginary objects to be disassociated from them, even when they are defined by the inability to mediate in the first place. Thus the cultural formations around nuclear weapons resemble Lacan's account of psychosis: the symbolic structure of the Bomb is primarily forged by metonymy, with Luiz standing in for the nuclear threat by virtue of her proximity to its images, not some more abstract metaphorical quality. The Bomb is more than a signifier for the sum total of nuclear weapons. It is a kind of contagion, a numinous agent that changes anything that comes to touch it even if it is never used in war.

Knowledge and Concealment

To understand the Bomb in terms of language and its limits situates it as a problem for the field of communication, especially for approaches centering on rhetoric and media. In communication studies, the peak of nuclear weapons scholarship occurred in the 1980s following Derrida's call for "nuclear criticism" and the psychological work of Robert Jay Lifton.[15] *Nukespeak* by Stephen Hilgartner, Richard C. Bell, and Rory O'Connor[16] helped to begin debates over nuclear language, and Carol Cohn's excellent work on the language of defense intellectuals further advanced this line of inquiry.[17] A number of rhetoricians participated in this debate by emphasizing their field's traditional concern for public deliberation, often in novel ways. David Cratis Williams attempted to combine Derrida's approach with the insights of Kenneth Burke.[18] Barry Brummett relied on Burke's language of perfection and motives to explain several nuclear debates current in the decade.[19] Today, Bryan C. Taylor[20] and Ned O'Gorman,[21] among others, continue to engage with these issues. These works have a diverse set of concerns. The earliest ones focused primarily on organization for political action with a clearly activist bent. Later ones often continue this theme but also analyze the formation of public attitudes, democratic oversight, or the content of specific metaphors, reflecting the longstanding preoccupation of rhetoric with political awareness and change based on language or symbolic action.

While much of this work is excellent, like academic work in the related fields of history and political science, it tends to focus on bombs, not the Bomb, the metaphorical condensation of the nuclear threat. As Gerard J. DeGroot says, "Before the Bomb there were simply bombs, lower case. . . . Bombs are as old as hatred itself. But only since 1945 have we spoken of *the* Bomb."[22] Weapons like the MX missile, SS-18, Fat Man, and so forth are the material artifacts of something that is more than the sum of their parts. The Bomb is an organizing metaphor, a symbol of human annihilation, a stand-in for the unspeakable void of extinction, a discursive construct that challenges the limits of communication itself. The Bomb is deployed as a figure imbued with its own agency, a vengeful God of our own making. It is a difficult target of analysis because it is ultimately defined by excess, especially for those spared direct exposure to the worst effects of the nuclear defense structure but fantasize about some connection to it. The study of specific Cold War legacies and their attendant texts is extremely important, but it misses something about the cultural force of atomic weapons and the gradual metastasis of the Bomb's influence to other postapocalyptic fantasies. Similarly, the scholarship cited above does important and valuable work, but it also leaves some remainder of awe, terror, affect, and compulsion. If not unique, the Bomb is at least first among the fallen angels of existential threats, figured by those most capable of actualizing its threats as something greater than the sum of its physical parts. Much of the language surrounding the Bomb would be understood as religious in another context.

Nuclear weapons scholarship evinces its own compulsion to repeat. A great deal of writing has been done on the subject, but the movements of *desire* are covered incompletely by scholarship primarily concerned with exposing nuclear dangers or developing an activist agenda. I am using "desire" in the Lacanian sense of attachment, of being drawn toward something: while very few people consciously wish for a nuclear war, the Bomb has effects that are hard to identify by focusing on its rational function. As I have already argued about the figure of Trump, focusing too narrowly on specific discourses and instrumental effects of language threatens to neglect the forest for the trees. The antinuclear peace movements of the 1980s were at best partial successes. Antinuclear discourse can achieve only limited goals so long as the subtle movements of desire that sustain the Bomb are not confronted directly. The material infrastructure of nuclear violence persists mostly unchanged and in some ways more dangerous than ever, despite extensive documentation about its effects. Nuclear waste continues to accumulate. The detritus of uranium mines blights the land of indigenous peoples. Thousands of weapons remain prepared for launch on a moment's notice, an endless profusion of war plans exist, and an official policy to secure peace through what amounts to a threat of genocide is stated policy. There is almost complete public ignorance about this rusting sword of Damocles, now suspended in its eighth decade. Since the high-water mark of nuclear concern in the 1980s, today ever fewer citizens even bother to check how much the rope is fraying.

This book should instill skepticism about the efficacy of current strategies meant to confront nuclear violence by challenging it discursively. A great deal of work about the Bomb has focused on the euphemistic character of nuclear language and deleterious effects of secrecy on public deliberation. Brummett, Daniel Zins, and Edward Schiappa have all published work in this vein. Schiappa criticizes terms like "Strategic Defense Initiative" and CORRTEX for "bureaucratizing" and "domesticating" nuclear issues. Through these verbal strategies, he argues, nuclear realities are "insulated from public inspection by acronyms or sanitized jargon."[23] Both Brummett and Charles Kauffman use the work of Burke to argue that naming practices constrain public knowledge and influence attitudes about nuclear weapons, either through perfecting "God terms"[24] or through references appealing to historical myths such as the American frontier.[25] Even Williams, who combines a Derridean perspective with the more familiar Burkean one, emphasizes that a chief goal of nuclear criticism is a "publicly accessible" language.[26]

The underlying theme of this work challenging the discourse of nuclear war is the *concealment thesis*. The basic assumption for proponents of this idea is that nuclear terminology conceals the reality of nuclear warfare and thus makes it palatable. The strategic thinking of RAND game theorists and others produced an arcane vocabulary for all aspects of nuclear conflict: "counterforce targeting," "throw-weight," "circular error probable," "post-attack state," "countervalue," "first strike," and many more. These terms mystify and enchant the public, just as they did public intellectuals during the Cold War, the fictional narrator of *End Zone*, and various aspiring policy wonks to this day. The theories of language used in the concealment thesis draw from different sources (e.g., Burke, Derrida, Aristotle, and George Orwell), but their least common denominator is a belief that a sanitized vocabulary upholds the complex of nuclear destruction by concealing the horror of nuclear war. The implication of this idea is that providing a new vocabulary for public debate, such as the "devil terms" Brummett suggests, would enable democratic deliberation and therefore constrain the nuclear state. As Schiappa puts it, a "negative nukespeak would consist of linguistic strategies to portray nuclear weapons and war as dangerous and immoral."[27] Such a strategy might "salvage" debate over nuclear weapons in the public sphere.[28] Nuclear critique of all kinds has dropped off considerably since the end of the Cold War such that the concealment thesis, although advanced most comprehensively in the 1980s, remains the chief contribution of communication studies to the politics of antinuclear activism.

This legacy should be revisited. The economy of nuclear discourse since the day of Trinity has been driven by the attempt to get closer to the Real, to have the Bomb as it "really is." Later, I will suggest that nuclear simulations were presented as more real and more rational than the doomsday imaginations of LeMay and the early Strategic Air Command. Schell's *The Fate of the Earth* was another effort to bring Americans face-to-face with the reality of nuclear war, as were the more explicitly fictional novels churned out over the last seventy years. Underlying these efforts is the fact that nuclear war remains "fabulously textual" in Derrida's terms.[29] There have been atrocities related to nuclear weapons and their production—indigenous peoples and downwinders subjected to nuclear testing, inner city populations confined and targeted in the name of the Bomb, US soldiers made to witness tests with inadequate protection, and nonhuman animals subjected to cruelty in the name of understanding just what a nuclear war might be like. But there has never been a nuclear war in the sense that strategists, novelists, and survivalists imagined. Superpower nuclear war exists only in writing, images, and film. To imagine the graphic details of a possible nuclear war does not reveal the truth but instead relies on the same dynamic that makes the Bomb so fascinating in the first place: a sense that the right symbols can access the Real. The supposedly sanitized official language of nuclear war does not always circumvent feeling or shut down thought. These terms can also elicit grim fascination by those not subject to their direct material effects. More than just a set of shibboleth words, the arcane terminology of nuclear warfare conveys power, threat, and control through litotes and catachresis. As Cohn has observed, these utterances can capture even those who set out to oppose nuclear violence.[30] Engaged scholarship requires that rhetorical criticism of the nuclear weapons complex includes a hard, perhaps uncomfortable look not only at the language of the Bomb, but the underlying ecology of desire that sustains it. That is the ultimate purpose of this book.

The 2016 election further supports the claim that knowledge does not automatically translate into resistance. Clinton's ads, Blair's letter, Obama's public statements, and many high-profile denunciations by national security experts demonstrated that Trump lacked even a cursory understanding of nuclear issues. Still, he was elected, as other populist right-wing leaders have been. Trump's virtue was not his knowledge, but quite the opposite: he openly rejected expert opinion and advice, and this only bolstered his antiestablishment credentials.

There is no reason to assume that exposing the quotidian violence of uranium mining on indigenous lands, the plight of dying downwinders, or the probabilities of nuclear war will change anything. Information about all of these topics is readily available alongside lurid postapocalyptic fantasies. As Lacan says in his seminar on Edgar Allan Poe's "The Purloined Letter,"[31] the message is in plain sight, but its contents are far less important than the relative positioning of the subjects around it. Today, information about all manners of oppression is available at the stroke of a key. Students read John Hersey's *Hiroshima* in school. Hundreds of documentaries examine nuclear issues in depth. The Doomsday Clock is trotted out on occasion. Excellent academic work exists about the ongoing consequences of Cold War defense structures for diverse groups around the world. It is not concealment that sustains the Bomb, but a web of imaginary investments and desires.

For this reason, I propose to examine the web of investments that sustain the Bomb within a particular discourse. My goal is not to document the violence suffered by those who are exposed to the material effects of nuclear infrastructure. While every entity on Earth is a potential sacrifice in the event of nuclear war, many suffer every day from the ongoing preparations for global nuclear violence. Their stories—and the similarities and differences contained within—are of vital importance because they illustrate the stakes of antinuclear scholarship. But to resist the depredations of the nuclear security state requires understanding what sustains it for those who inflict violence upon others. I am writing about, and primarily for, those who are largely insulated from the effects of this violence and, while not plotting impact points on maps or holding launch keys in their hands, are implicated to varying degrees in the vast complex of nuclearism through the taxes they pay, the media they consume, or the simple privilege of being able to ignore this violence in their daily lives. Like many academics, I am one of them. Even a critical perspective toward the Bomb often relies on security. Mary Manjikian writes that "*imagining* destruction may serve to launch the creative impulse involved in reimagining structures and society. However, when one is truly the subject of that destruction, the impulse is only to flee the building and to survive."[32] I have used "we" and "us" to mark this more privileged group and my complicity in it, rather than the more comfortable "they" and "them."

I am inspired in this focus by Lifton's studies on the perpetrators of genocide and the disavowals that allowed bureaucrats, soldiers, and civilians to understand themselves as good, ordinary people while committing the most extreme acts of violence,[33] alongside Cohn's beautiful cautionary work on the seductive power that nuclear language holds for both those in the national security infrastructure and their critics. As Masahide Kato has noted, "undeclared nuclear warfare" is occluded by the fantasy of a *global* nuclear exchange which by its scale and splendor disqualifies other forms of nuclear violence from consideration.[34]

This undefined, global fantasy is the dominant form of nuclear discourse for those minimally subjected to its violence, and it is their symbolic economies that most need critical engagement, because it is this relation of detached fascination which helps sustain nuclear violence and obfuscates its survival and metamorphosis. This economy is most powerfully distilled in the figure of the Bomb.[35]

The Bomb was often invoked during the Cold War as a singular entity. The first atomic tests shattered humankind's confidence in its own survival as a species. Trinity, Crossroads, and Ivy, not to mention Hiroshima and Nagasaki, seemed to beggar language itself. Nuclear weapons produced more than heat, light, and noise—they seemed to tear apart reality and offer a horrific view of what lies beyond. The language of the Bomb compensated somewhat for that ghastly vision by providing a general symbolic repository for the mix of terror and fascination that such phenomena evoke. Linguistic mastery of such a force is intoxicating. As Ira Chernus has written, "If there is a single Bomb of which all nuclear weapons are a part, then there is also a single nuclear holocaust, a single cosmic mushroom cloud, one big whoosh in which all reality is returned to its primal state, in which all limits are instantly transcended. Just as God works his will instantly, having no limits upon his power, so does the Bomb, and so do we as masters of the Bomb. In manifesting our infinite power we find the only solution to the problem of our infinite power. Once the button is pushed, there may be no future solutions to our problems, but neither will there be any problems to solve."[36] The Bomb may condense something complex and frightening, but it also promises simplicity, which is part of its appeal. The Bomb is problem and solution combined in one signifier.

Burke demonstrated a similar perceptiveness about the Bomb as a singular entity. The Bomb simplified not just by making reference to preexisting religious concepts or the purity of power. Unity itself is remarkable:

> If all the thermo-nuclear warheads
> Were one thermo-nuclear warhead
> What a great thermo-nuclear warhead that would be.
>
> If all the intercontinental ballistic missiles
> Were one intercontinental ballistic missile
> What a great intercontinental ballistic missile that would be.
>
> If all the military men
> Were one military man
> What a great military man he would be.
>
> And if all the land masses
> Were one land mass
> What a great land mass that would be.

And if the great military man
Took the great thermo-nuclear warhead
And put it into the great intercontinental ballistic missile
And dropped it on the great land mass,

What great PROGRESS that would be.[37]

Although the examples elaborated in this book, from the Trinity test to *Doomsday Preppers*, can be isolated and discussed separately, the present study is about the Bomb as a constellation of tropes that gestures ever outward at something that escapes signifying mediation itself. This book is about nuclear weapons in the same way that *Moby-Dick* is about the Nantucket whaling industry—concrete examples are important to the story, but they don't exhaust its mission. The central project of this book is to examine the Bomb as a figure of both horror and desire, not only for what it reveals about the persistent cultural echoes of the Atomic Age, but also to uncover its implications for language itself. My aim is to supplement more instrumental approaches to the nuclear issue in communication studies with an exploration of the fantasies and investments that animate the Bomb as a cultural force. The question I ask is not "how should we talk about nuclear war," but "what can the Bomb tell us about attempts to mediate what appears to exceed mediation itself?" There are two major concepts I will draw on to engage this question: the death drive in psychoanalysis and the tradition of the sublime in rhetoric.

The Death Drive

A sea of ink has been spilled since, but when the Trinity test lit the New Mexico skies on July 16, 1945, the first seconds of the Atomic Age were spent in silence. What followed for many was a search for words, an effort to assimilate a novel phenomenon. Many commentators have described the implications of nuclear war as unspeakable, and the concept itself as unthinkable. The awesome power of the Bomb reveals the fundamental inability of language to fully capture the universe beyond human reality, the precariousness of our existence, and the arbitrariness of our beliefs. The demonstrated possibility of destruction on this scale raised these existential questions even while it challenged older faiths and changed how human beings imagined doomsday. But the revelation of this monstrous force beyond our mediated reality also tempted many with the promise of unmediated truth. The Bomb expressed for some a purity both terrifying and alluring. Fascination with the Bomb exceeded the practical needs of nuclear policy. At times it was almost reverential. From the first moments of the blast, the godlike structural position of the Bomb was revealed in the halting words set down to describe it. Witnesses were often self-conscious about their inability to think about what they saw or say what they thought.

The loss for words in the presence of such an event does not suggest that communication always fails. For many tasks, language is entirely adequate. Through speech, symbols, and images—through mediation generally—we order and organize our world. We plan, classify, and describe. When this capacity fails, it is not because we are too small and our tools too weak. The universe is simply too big. By conjuring the possibility of our extinction, the confrontation with nuclear war is an example of something that forces us to consider the fact that the world we build for ourselves does not fully domesticate chance and chaos. The human order of the world represented in language always exhausts itself before mind-independent reality does.

This excess beyond mediation is Lacan's concept of the Real.[38] The Real is not just the world of nonhuman objects and forces that constitute reality independently of human beings. More significantly for our purposes, it is the eruption of that world into the mediated reality of human society constructed and maintained by our communication with one another. For Georges Bataille, there is continuity—the unmediated world without distinctions imposed by human classification, the world we seek in our pursuits of love and death.[39] For Martin Heidegger, what lurked in the shadow of human artifice was the "gigantic" (*das Risige*), an intimation of some incalculable greatness.[40] For Eugene Thacker, there is the world-for-itself, a frequent topic in the cosmic horror genre where the universe frightens due not to evil but to indifference and scale.[41] While this excess by definition exceeds language, it wells up nonetheless, distorting the landscape of what Lacan calls the Symbolic order, the structural register of language, the network of connections that is the underlying condition for the possibility of meaning.

The Bomb is an affectively powerful and capacious symbol capable of anchoring many competing fantasies simultaneously. Nuclear obliteration can be read as an offer to transcend the fallen world of mediation in which reality is never complete. To others, it is a threat to whatever makes human beings special and important, and thus signifies a denial of some intangible human spirit. In more concrete terms, it permits utopian visions of universal disarmament in the face of a common threat, or conversely, perpetual peace through the threat of mutually assured destruction. With such a contradictory set of attachments, it is hard to imagine that efforts to think about the Bomb can achieve their goals—while they might demonstrate their own consistent logic, the rationality of nuclear politics is warped by the intrusion of the Real. The Bomb's assimilation into religious frameworks can result in a desire to commune with it directly as a herald of transcendent power. It can therefore condense a desire for apocalyptic change amongst its adherents, secular or not. Evangelicals anticipating apocalyptic rebirth are not swayed by scientific reports on nuclear winter, and neither are those who put so much faith in war simulations that they are willing to gamble with the survival of vertebrate life on the planet. Socially conscious academics should therefore seek to account, however imperfectly, for the extra-rational appeal of this symbol. We have produced many cogent analyses of instances where language or other media worked very well indeed to persuade audiences, bind people together around texts, and change attitudes, but these accounts are incomplete without attention to the Real.

Even though the Real sometimes frustrates our ability to describe the world, the human impulse to signify cannot be suppressed. At the edges of the map, we insist on writing "here be dragons," a cryptic signifier of unknown dangers and exotic possibilities. To call the Bomb "unspeakable" is still to speak about it. The failure of words is simply met with more words in an effort to assimilate the excess of the Real into the Symbolic. This is the dynamic of *automaton* (order) scripted over *tuché* (contingency).[42] Having determined that nuclear war is unspeakable, we speak about it all the same, only to determine again that words have failed, leading to another attempt. In psychoanalytic terms, this is the repetition compulsion, in which the subject tries again and again to attain something that eludes its grasp. Telling stories about nuclear war—through video games, novels, films, and strategic simulations—allows us to regain some sense of control over the threat of catastrophe. We can fantasize about presence and absence on a grand scale—that of all human life—in alternation, even if no fantasy ever completely satisfies our desire for contact with the Real of the Bomb. There is jouissance in repetition not because speaking subjects necessarily enjoy the possibilities of destruction or rebirth in and of themselves, but because repetition itself gives a sense of mastery over the contingency of the world. Jouissance isn't happiness or joy. Rather, it is an investment in something, a kind of attachment that may very well be painful but is nonetheless compelling.

In *Beyond the Pleasure Principle*, Sigmund Freud illustrated this compulsion in his famous *fort-da* game. A child (Freud's grandson) makes an object disappear and reappear in succession, simulating the mother's coming and going and the possibility of her eventual disappearance, all the while exclaiming what Freud interprets as *fort* ("gone") and *da* ("here"). Enjoyment comes from the subject's seeming control over these states of presence and absence.[43] The child can't control the mother's presence, so rather than submit to a sense of helplessness, it simulates this power instead. What it enjoys is not so much one condition or another (here or gone), but rather the faculty of control over these states. Attempts to mediate nuclear war can be understood through this frame as efforts to impose some predictability over the chaotic intrusion of the Real. Imagining the ways that the war might happen and society might be destroyed and rebuilt returns a semblance of agency, allowing some to enjoy their own subjectivity again. This is the common thread between the cold-blooded excesses of Pentagon nuclear plans, the compulsion that leads survivalists to stockpile rooms full of MREs, and the appeal of apocalyptic video games for millions of players. In all of these pursuits, the world is made absent in the fantasy of destruction and present again in the myth of reconstruction, survival, and rebirth. Individual and collective preparations for doomsday are the practices that make up *fort-da* in the nuclear age.

This serial repetition is also called the death drive. Perhaps unfortunately named, the death drive is not literally an impulse toward self-annihilation—at least not always. As a condition of being discrete subjects separate from the world around us, we forgo a sense of unproblematic continuity with the world. This is the lack at the heart of every subject, and the cause of desire. The desire to revert to an (imagined) earlier state of harmony leads us to pursue things that might restore a sense of connection. Because what is missing is not any specific object but rather the hypothetical thing that would fill the lack (*petit objet a*); each target of desire is unsatisfying once attained, and something new comes to take its place. The displacement of desire is mediated by signification. The points of attachment for each subject are signifiers, but these signifiers stand in for or reference an entire network that is not available in its entirety. *Fort-da* is a performance of control, an act of evocation, substitution, and banishment that serves as something the subject can enjoy since the hypothetical object that would fill the lack is perpetually over the horizon, never finally accessible. This process is ultimately about the encounter between contingency and predictable order, mediated by signification, and thus squarely describes the field of rhetoric. As Lacan himself wrote, "*Fort-da* is already a rhetorical figure."[44]

The drive is not a result of biology, but rather the pursuit of the ever-elusive Real through the Symbolic. It is, therefore, squarely located in the realm of communication. Communication is not just symbolic interaction. In its most basic sense, communication retains an element of *communion*—a connection that exceeds language. John Durham Peters has persuasively argued that a key element in the development of communication technology has been the paradoxical goal of unmediated contact. As a "register of modern longings," Peters writes, communication, the term itself, "evokes a utopia where nothing is misunderstood, hearts are open, and expression is uninhibited."[45] This approach is consistent with Bataille's belief that individual subjectivity is maintained by the instrumental use of language to classify and manipulate a world seen as separated from the self, all the while desiring a return to continuity. For Lacan, the split subject forms with the ego, a token of Symbolic exchange permitting entry into language. The price paid by every subject is the lack—the hole from which desire springs. The objects pursued to fill that lack—and the logic of the signifier more generally—are linked through endless metaphorical and metonymic displacements. Language, in other words, is alienating, defining each of us in separation, but it is also the site for our cathectic attachments and fantasies.

Death drive is a fitting moniker after all because the subject's pursuit of continuity could only be fulfilled by its own dissolution. The workings of the drive, the operations of the signifier, and the formation of the subject are thus ultimately issues of communication. The traditional focus of American rhetoric on persuasion can be a helpful approach to the order-making aspects of signification. *Automaton* works by forging connections. It is rational, repeatable, and follows a logic of differentiation. This approach is not without remainder, however. How do we explain why some signifiers become objects of attraction standing in for a lost continuity, and others do not? Some trace of the Real persists as an anchor for cathexis, a whispered hint that our pursuit might find a truth more fundamental than language itself, represented nonetheless in its Symbolic order. The sublime, an ancient tradition in rhetoric, helps to explain this self-immolating tendency in language in which the speaking subject pursues the "beyond" of mediation through particularly affective powerful tropes.

The invocation of the Real in relation to nuclear weapons presents a seeming paradox for a book such as this one: how do we write about what exceeds mediation when all we have available for study are various attempts to mediate? The symbolically mediated world is our reality, but it is not the Real. We cannot expose the "reality" of the Bomb in writing, speeches, films, or any other media without implicitly insisting that language can accurately convey the excess of the Real. This book is not a study of the Real itself but rather the attempts to mediate it. Much scholarly work on nuclear warfare sidelines any attempt to understand the Bomb beyond representation, focusing instead on the techniques of organization and persuasion. This is understandable—the alternative is a sometimes frustrating project of speculation and abductive reasoning. However, because the Bomb is maintained as a symbolic force by cathectic investments, fantasy, and desire, to forgo a more speculative path comes at a cost. Doing so creates a linguistic framework in which these questions are written off as unwarranted mysticism, dismissed as unverifiable metaphysics, or at best appended as "useful embellishment," only "received into mainstream discourse when presented as appendages to currently debated political options."[46] That said, the approach of this book is to examine discourses surrounding the Bomb in an effort to provide as much evidence as possible for my conclusions. While the nature of my inquiry complicates things somewhat, I hope readers will agree that the issue is sufficiently important to proceed with imperfect information. After all, the need to make provisional judgments on the basis of imperfect information is precisely the traditional case for rhetoric.

The Sublime

The sublime has strayed from its rhetorical roots over the last few centuries to be understood largely as a matter of aesthetics. Edmund Burke's *A Philosophical Enquiry into the Origin of our Ideas of the Sublime and Beautiful*[47] and Immanuel Kant's *Critique of Judgment*[48] discuss the sublime as a reaction to overwhelming experience, broadening it beyond language, a move that is also evident in more recent treatments by Jean-François Lyotard and others.[49] But the theory originates in the work of the ancient rhetorician Longinus.[50] The sublime originally had to do with the power of language to overwhelm, to jar its audience out of comfortable subjectivity, to move them through splendor and revelation. In contrast to the (compulsively?) repeated Aristotelian association of rhetoric and persuasion, the sublime "does not persuade; it takes the reader out of himself [*sic*]."[51] I will argue in chapter 1 that sublime language is that in which a sense of the Real seems to shine through—not the unassimilable Real itself, but its outline, the enticement that it might be there even if we cannot capture it. It is the deployment of trope, but it evokes something more, leading us toward the edge of mediation and gesturing beyond. The sublime operates to conceal the artifice of language "by its very brilliance. Just as dimmer lights are lost in the surrounding sunshine, so pervading grandeur all around obscures the presence of the rhetorical devices."[52] Christian Lundberg echoes this concept in his discussion of repression, arguing that raising one "insular metonymic connection to the status of a metaphor conceals or renders latent the other metonymic connections that also inhere in the accreted history of a sign. But the condition of this concealment is the whole field of latent connections that are both accreted and expressed in the social use of signs."[53] Thus the sublime powerfully configures the unconscious,[54] concealing the underlying networks of meaning in metonymic connection by hyper-emphasizing particular links. I will argue that the condition for these powerful cathectic investments is a sense of the Real in sublime language, as is also evident in the Freudian uncanny. The sublime is the sense of excess in language—it is what beckons beyond our unreliable means of mediation to a Real we cannot translate perfectly, but that we nonetheless encounter as the limit of language. It should therefore be understood not as a *style* of language, as it is sometimes translated from Longinus, but as an *attribute* of communication, the degree to which it appears to gesture toward something beyond mediation.

Although the sublime was born as a rhetorical tradition, its import extends to communication more generally. Much of the work grouped under the contested name of speculative realism is consistent with this view. Timothy Morton's *Hyperobjects* is a kind of materialist sublime treating phenomena such as climate change and pollution.[55] Encounters with climate change, natural disasters, and other phenomena in which the external world frustrates human expectation should caution us against anthropocentrism, but nevertheless efforts to mediate them in language are still made. Material artifacts too can be attempts to mediate a world that exceeds individual subjects, an approach consistent with material accounts of communication. The persistence of radioactive waste over vast periods of time, the monumental architecture proposed for the Waste Isolation Pilot Plant, or the gorgeous, otherworldly devastation of a nuclear test crater all mean something sublime in the sense that they decenter humanity and disrupt the subject by revealing the vastness of the inhuman. Morton's work suggests that the sublime does not preclude attention to the material specificity of mediation and also that those objects play a signifying function that potentially decenters the human subject. This understanding is even consistent with Quentin Meillassoux's "arche-fossil": the encounter with the Real is what reminds us that the loop of "correlationism" is never fully closed, and objects that force this realization have a sublime function, although their recuperative function in the Symbolic casts doubt on our ability to think outside of the subject, or at least the efficacy of telling anyone that we have done so.[56]

Nuclear weapons themselves are a medium for communication. For some atomic witnesses, nuclear explosions roared of Doomsday and Almighty power, of Armageddon, the Fall, or sin. For others they signaled technological hubris, innate human destructiveness, or the indifference of the universe to human life. Nuclear explosions might promise eventual human obliteration or change their witnesses' lives forever. They might suggest perpetual peace through deterrence. Even unexploded, the Bomb is still a currency of meaning constantly in use. The Soviet footage of weapons on parade that transfixed me as a child was an effort to communicate resolve in defense of Soviet interests. The arcane incantations of nuclear deterrence understand the Bomb as a means of persuasion: the Bomb convinces another party not to take a political or military action that it might otherwise take through the enthymematic hint of slaughter and ruin. Persuasion might not be everything, but it is still important. Still, even nuclear planners recognize that the Bomb does more than persuade. Along with the more classical functions of nuclear arsenals, some defense intellectuals use language uncannily resonant with the sublime in stating that the Bomb's purpose is not simply to dissuade or deter, but to *overawe*, something that it might have a unique capacity to do.[57]

Structure of This Book

This book argues that the fascination and terror of nuclear destruction are essentially connected by their shared origin in the desire for contact with an unmediated Real. To square our existence as subjects marked off from the totality of the Real with our desire to experience it without mediation, we come to enjoy the illusion of control over the presence and absence of the world, as in Freud's *fort-da* game. In the nuclear context, we repetitively simulate destruction and salvation, worlds without us and ones made present for our resurgence. To acknowledge that the Real cannot be captured is not to say that efforts to do so are not productive. The elusiveness of the Real requires an account of the limits of communication and its efforts to overcome them. The links forged in the book between psychoanalysis, the sublime, and apocalyptic imagination are efforts to contribute to that account.

Because the subject of the Real makes unimpeachable conclusions elusive, this book is driven by examples. The case studies are not intended as ornamental vehicles for psychoanalytic theory, nor can they be definitive proof of the Real. My approach is inspired by a strange muse: the negative theology of Pseudo-Dionysius's *The Divine Names*. In this ancient meditation on the inability of words to capture the divine, Pseudo-Dionysius argued that the inexpressible force of God could only be approached by studying the proliferation of symbols that circle around what must necessarily be a "wise silence," for language itself is fallen.[58] One can only say what God is *not*. This approach has parallels in Zen Buddhism and the Hindu concept of *neti neti*. Although the Real exceeds mediation, the profusion of attempts to describe the Bomb allow us to trace its outline. Fantasies about the Bomb abound, as do efforts to fill its void with meaning. These artifacts reveal something in what they do not say, and how they position themselves in relation to what cannot be otherwise mediated. My hope is that a secular approach can benefit from these traditions.

This study will proceed in four parts. The chapters alternate between a relationship of *fort* ("gone") and *da* ("here") to contextualize the operation of the death drive. In chapter 1 I will establish the fundamental importance of the Real in human communication. By examining eyewitness recollections of nuclear testing, focused on Trinity, the Earth's first nuclear explosion, I will explore the failures of language that surrounded the Bomb and its extraordinary power. The central themes of this chapter are the silence, the Real, and the historical inception of the Bomb as a godlike signifier. I use the example of Project Plowshare, an initiative to use nuclear explosions for construction on a planetary scale, to demonstrate how the grand fantasies of nuclear weapons could oscillate between despair and hope.

Chapter 2 examines the attempt to incorporate the Bomb in the form of nuclear simulations. Defense intellectuals formulated complex theories for the conduct of nuclear war and tested them through a series of "war games," a cultural technology that was later adapted for an attempt at entertainment infused with antinuclear sentiment. Even when used for ostensibly antinuclear purposes, these games still require enjoyment to be meaningful and are thus examples of terror and fascination acting simultaneously to stitch together a durable cultural practice with contradictory effects. My primary example here is the video game *First Strike*, an expressly antinuclear game that still appeals to players through the guilty pleasures of simulated nuclear destruction.

Chapter 3 explores the notion of sacrifice and the imagination of space resulting from nuclear simulations and the efforts to calculate the infinite—another imagination of the world's absence. "Countervalue" targeting policies made urban centers rather than military installations desired targets for nuclear attack and theorized that the USA should want the Soviet Union to target American cities rather than military instillations for the sake of "stability." The material results of this strategy and the tropes surrounding it resonate closely with discourses of neoliberal economic dislocation, white flight, and urban destruction. The depiction of postindustrial "wastelands" today in cities like Detroit bears a structural similarity to postnuclear city spaces imagined ever since the development of the first atomic weapons. In the United States, these tropes are made manifest in culturally specific ways, concealing the sacrifice of disempowered groups under the banner of utilitarianism.

Chapter 4 is about survivalism, an insistence that the world will be made present again after catastrophic destruction. The low risk/high impact thinking of nuclear war planning helped produce the modern survivalist subject in opposition to the sacrificial populations slated to die in a hypothetical nuclear conflict. Beginning with civil defense initiatives in the early Cold War, the sign of survival came to organize a set of practices that would ostensibly reduce the uncertainty of the future. These gamelike practices consume a great deal of time and energy from their participants. They too are evidence of the copresence of fascination and terror: their participants, mostly fairly secure financially and socially, become obsessed with the end of the world because it promises a more "real" experience in which the abstractions of modern life are washed away and people can enjoy the hardships that technology and society take from them. Doomsday preparation is enjoyable as a simulation of the Real represented by a return to nature.

The conclusion takes stock of the ways that nuclear war organizes desire and seeks to identify lessons for communication scholarship and antinuclear politics. The uncanny allure of the Bomb calls for a continuation of the sublime tradition alongside the more traditional focus on persuasion in rhetoric. If our relationship to nuclear war is structured by the twinned forces of terror and fascination, it should change how we think about antinuclear efforts. A scholarly encounter with the politics of the Bomb might require that we first confront the truly unspeakable desires that keep us in its orbit. To this end, I propose a concept of rhetoric as *teratology*—a study of the monstrous convergence of desire and horror as made evident in the contingent eruptions of the Real into the Symbolic and our efforts to mediate them.

1
Fort
Trinity and the Real

The notion of extinction, utter extinction, is the most unbearable thought of all.
—Daniel Callahan, *The Tyranny of Survival*

With a wise silence we do honor the inexpressible. . . . And there we shall be, our minds away from passion and from earth, and we shall have a conceptual gift of light from him and, somehow, in a way we cannot know, we shall be united with him and, our understanding carried away, blessedly happy, we shall be struck by his blazing light.
—Pseudo-Dionysius, "The Divine Names"

Warned of Doomsday

Apocalypticism long predates the nuclear age. Around 600 BCE, Zoroastrianism predicted the imminent destruction of the world by fire, ushering in a period where good would triumph over evil. The repetition of this basic template—worldwide catastrophe and rebirth—would define Jewish and Christian apocalypticism for millennia, as it still does today.[1] A great number of apocalyptic predictions have been made over time. The year 1000 saw millennial panic that cropped up periodically throughout the Middle Ages as various seers, prophets, and even popes predicted the end of the world. Many European veterans of the First Crusade returned home at the turn of the twelfth century having experienced the hellish sieges of Antioch, Ma'arra, and Jerusalem. Some of them believed that they had witnessed miracles or even participated in Armageddon itself.[2] The Black Death (or "Great Mortality") of the fourteenth century again convinced many Europeans that the world would soon end. European apocalypticism also took root in the Americas. Followers of William Miller predicted that Jesus would return in 1844, resulting in the "Great Disappointment." Before European colonization, Aztec and Mayan prophesies included detailed visions of how the world might end. While apocalyptic belief faded and flared, it never entirely disappeared from history in the centuries before the Atomic Age. The exquisite English word *mundicidious*, "world-killing," had time to be coined, used, and fall out of favor before the first nuclear explosion, code-named Trinity by Robert Oppenheimer, ever took place. Even the advent of the atomic bomb had some precedent in fiction before 1945. H. G. Wells's novel *The World Set Free*, in which city-destroying atomic devices menace civilization, made early reference to the possibility of atomic warfare and may have inspired Leo Szilard himself. Similar destruction appears in Wells's novels *The War in the Air* and *The Shape of Things to Come*. Apocalypticism has a long history of influencing social orders throughout the world, and particularly in the western parts of Eurasia where American national identity drew its resources.

Although the Atomic Age was not the first time that human beings contemplated the end of the world, it was qualitatively different from previous apocalyptic eras. Nuclear energy is unique in some respects. First, it revealed a destructive capacity out of all proportion to previous instruments of warfare. While the firebombing of Tokyo killed more civilians than either atomic attack on Japan, nuclear weapons could compress a great deal of damage done over time at much effort and expense into a single bomb, instantly deployed. Even if this destructive power could be brought about by other means, the Bomb temporally compressed death in new ways. The destruction of cities and nations had long been possible, but the possible destruction of human civilization in an afternoon was novel.

Second, the Bomb was a unique combination of nature and artifice. The physical principles of nuclear fission and fusion are not human, but the intervention of advanced scientific knowledge is necessary to create nuclear explosions on Earth. Plutonium, named for the Greek/Roman god of the underworld, perhaps best exemplifies the uncanny principles of nuclear technology: while it is a product of natural laws, it is also a synthetic element not present in nature. Previous visions of doomsday tended to rely on extra-human agency, either natural (the collision of a rogue planet, as in the 1933 novel *When Worlds Collide*) or supernatural (e.g., Revelation). Nuclear energy made a deliberate, human-induced destruction of the planet feasible through the intervention of human artifice in the natural world. Fantasies of destruction became more plausible once these principles were demonstrated on Earth. They also created a new sense of control. It was now humanity, rather than God or nature, that could instigate destruction, a fact that makes nuclear fantasies particularly potent. While vast destruction had been imagined previously, the actual explosion of a nuclear device made the end of humanity more "real" and initially confounded previous fantasies. Atomic weapons seemed to erase the distance between fantasy and fact, which disrupted earlier apocalyptic discourses.

In this chapter I analyze the testimonies of Trinity and other nuclear tests to demonstrate that when excesses that don't "fit the script" of established discourses emerge, language initially ruptures. While this phenomenon signals chaos and horror, it also becomes an anchor for desire and fantasy. Faced with the revealed power of atomic destruction, Americans resorted to the language of religious experience as the only appropriate preexisting frame. Awestruck silence gave way to a torrent of words Secular philosophers, scientists, and politicians began speaking and writing in language reminiscent of Jonathan Edwards's *Sinners in the Hands of an Angry God*. The key to understanding nuclear discourse, and the rhetorical response to the limits of language more generally, is not in words or silence alone, but in the dynamic by which excess is mastered by language that seeks to gesture beyond itself and toward an "inexpressible" experience. To understand the awe and desire of encounters with this godlike power, I turn to religious scholar Rudolf Otto's concepts of the "numinous," "creature feeling," and "mysterium tremendum." To approach efforts to mediate these experiences, I employ Sigmund Freud's notion of *fort-da*, Georges Bataille's drive for continuity, and Jacques Lacan's pairing of *tuché* and *automaton*. I develop my claim advanced in the introduction that the defining characteristic of the sublime is the attempt to use language to invoke a feeling of direct encounter with the excess that language itself cannot capture, extending existing rhetorical investigations of apocalyptic discourse.[3] The ambivalence produced in this encounter is illustrated by the juxtaposition of nuclear weapons tests after Trinity and the "peaceful nuclear explosives" testing beginning with the Gnome test of Project Plowshare. In Plowshare, the Bomb's sense of despair was supplemented with an equally heady feeling that human beings could reshape the Earth however they desired. Both attitudes reflect a powerful attachment to the Bomb as a force that shattered traditional discursive frames, but never completely escaped them.

Trinity

There has been a great deal written about the Trinity test over the last seventy years. Accounts of the test mirror one another closely in both form and content. They form a miniature genre compelled to repeat the initial trauma of the Bomb. Nearly all of them begin with an exact date and time: five hours, twenty-nine minutes, and forty-five seconds after midnight, July 16, 1945. Minute-by-minute accounts of that day are common, referencing the weather-related delays, tension at the site, and usually the ominous place name Jornada del Muerto, part of the Alamogordo Bombing and Gunnery Range (now the White Sands Missile Range). There are usually descriptions of the procedures that witnesses were supposed to follow, including the use of dark welder's glass and feet-first positioning in trenches. Most accounts say something about the desert landscape of New Mexico—its nighttime cold its aridity despite the rain falling at the time of the test, and perhaps mention of the local wildlife. A few quotes are lifted from eyewitnesses to establish the tension of anticipation, the white-knuckled suspense of scientists, soldiers, and sundry credentialed indispensables waiting for the test.

Here the diligent Enrico Fermi, prepared to drop scraps of paper to estimate the bomb's force. There the cultured Oppenheimer, conflicted soul and brilliant scientist not yet dishonored by postwar allegations of Communist sympathies. Elsewhere, Edward Teller, who would later dream of digging canals with H-bombs and blasting the rim of the Moon to show resolve to the Soviets, but concerned on the dark morning of Trinity with the distribution of suntan lotion to protect against ultraviolet rays. And, of course, Leslie Groves, cast from the tough mold of the American wartime general, lacking the showmanship of Douglas MacArthur or the indifferent cruelty of Curtis LeMay, but blessed with their gruffness and organizational skills. These are four of the 425 personnel at Trinity. Sometimes one or two of these notables are omitted. Sometimes one or two more are added for a different emphasis—Klaus Fuchs, the Soviet spy who would accelerate Stalin's efforts to build an atom bomb; scientist George Kistiakowsky, the herald of doom who perhaps imagined the scale of the Bomb's potential destruction before anyone else; Vannevar Bush, the East Coast bureaucrat industrialist; James Conant, the elite university president. There were others sprawled in shallow trenches, perched on hilltops, even standing somewhat foolishly exposed. The War Department had helpfully advised that car windows be rolled down. Quotes from a common soldier or two usually make the cut in most accounts. The countdown (and radio interference playing the "Star-Spangled Banner") is included, all leading up to the implosion of the plutonium sphere and the false dawn of the first atomic detonation.

What follows the painstaking construction of this scene in every account is a *spectacular failure* of language. Writers trying to explain the test seem to compete with one another to find the most powerful descriptive phrases but never find the words. Solar metaphors are the most common. "The sun had been briefly recreated on earth," writes Gerard DeGroot. "A colony on Mars, had such a thing existed, could have seen the flash."[4] "The explosion created a brilliant flash," writes Ferenc Szasz. "It lit up the sky like the sun."[5] The "most awesome weapon" created "its first terrifying sunrise," writes Lansing Lamont.[6] Robert Jungk named his history of the Manhattan Project *Brighter than a Thousand Suns*, referencing a quote from the *Bhagavad Gita* supposedly remembered by Oppenheimer after Trinity, and Szasz called his book *The Day the Sun Rose Twice*. None of these descriptions capture the experience of watching the first nuclear test—the feel of rain, the taste of dust, the sight of unnatural colors, the reverberations caused by aftershocks. Experimental evidence from the test series confirms that witnesses cannot (or at least do not) convey their experiences perfectly in language. Heartbeat and blood pressure monitors suggested that soldiers were highly excited even when they reported not to be phased by nuclear tests.[7]

Nuclear test witnesses often reported silence immediately following a test. "The whole spectacle was so tremendous and one might almost say fantastic that the immediate reaction of the watchers was one of awe rather than excitement," remembered Edwin McMillan. "After some minutes of silence, a few people made remarks like, 'Well, it worked,' and then conversation and discussion became general."[8] Cyril Smith described an ebb in language, a gap before the symbols flooded back: "At the instant after the shot, my reactions were compounded of relief that 'it worked'; consciousness of extreme silence, and a momentary question as to whether we had done more than we intended. Practically none of the watchers made any vocal comment until after the shock wave had passed . . . elation of most observers seemed to increase for a period of 30 minutes afterwards, as they had a chance to absorb the significance of the achievement."[9] Ernest O. Lawrence concurred. "The grand, almost cataclysmic proportion of the explosion produced a kind of solemnity in everyone," he wrote. "There was restrained applause, but more a hushed murmuring bordering on reverence."[10]

Some observers claim to be overwhelmed, to have their identities temporarily suspended or reforged in the force of the Bomb. Melba Scott witnessed a later test as part of her civil defense activities in 1955. Forty years after, she said in an interview that "I don't remember. . . . What I remember is the silence, it was like—it was so awesome. [The atomic blast] was so much more than anybody could ever imagine, that you just weren't able—everybody kind of retreated into themselves. It was just so quiet."[11] Scott's language, long after the test, was still full of pauses, false starts, incomplete fragments. The interviewer pressed this exchange:

> Carol Ahlgren: I guess I should say, what were you feeling?
> Scott: I don't know. I don't know.
> Ahlgren: Overwhelmed?
> Scott: Yes. Mute. Which is really different for me [laughs]. And the quiet reigned. We had some responsibility to the state to speak. . . . And I remember some of us did that. . . .
>
> It's the same way I've survived as a widow. If I'd really ever let it all come in on me, I'd be immobilized.[12]

Scientist Bob Campbell watched thirty years of testing. At first glance, he seemed to refute any larger significance to the Bomb. Asked whether he had grander thoughts of what atomic explosions might do, he responded "No. Hell no." He described dramatic accounts as hindsight. "My experience . . . was that you really worry, think, concentrate on what you are doing, what your responsibilities are. . . . A lot of these folks, you know, have all sorts of thoughts later and all sorts of reasoning and all that sort of stuff. At the time it would be very, very rare."[13] On closer examination, Campbell's account could be taken to reveal something else.

In the moment of exposure to the nuclear event, one turns inwards. The first nuclear explosion *signified nothing* at the time, but was later subject to interpretation. There is first silence, then meaning: the Bomb.

Many accounts highlight the inadequacy of language in the first moments of the Atomic Age. Many witnesses used words like "indescribable."[14] Scientist Jeremy Bernstein wrote that "what I saw defies description."[15] The most striking account of Trinity was written by Brigadier General Thomas Farrell. It deserves to be quoted at length:

> The effects could well be called unprecedented, magnificent, beautiful, stupendous and terrifying. No man-made phenomenon of such tremendous power had ever occurred before. The lighting effects beggared description. The whole country was lighted by a searing light with the intensity many times that of the midday sun. It was golden, purple, violet, gray and blue. It lighted every peak, crevasse and ridge of the nearby mountain range with a clarity and beauty that cannot be described but must be seen to be imagined. It was that beauty the great poets dream about but describe most poorly and inadequately. Thirty seconds after the explosion came first, the air blast pressing hard against the people and things, to be followed almost immediately by the strong, sustained, awesome roar which warned of doomsday and made us feel that we puny things were blasphemous to dare tamper with the forces heretofore reserved to The Almighty. Words are inadequate tools for the job of acquainting those not present with the physical, mental and psychological effects. It had to be witnessed to be realized.[16]

Farrell's remarkable testimony acknowledges the limitations of language, claiming that the scene itself "cannot be described," and cannot be imagined or "realized" by any who do not witness the event itself. The break he identifies in language is not merely a negative observation (that words have limits) but a positive one—that there is some excess beyond signification. This account was not written immediately, of course, although it was written soon after Farrell witnessed the Trinity test. By the time he put it into words, Farrell had fit his overwhelming experience roughly into the language of Christian apocalypticism.

When Farrell, Bernstein, and other witnesses report silence or the inability of words to capture the experience of nuclear testing, they reveal more that an absence. Silence is not just the failure of words. As Max Picard argued, it is an affirmative presence. Silence is the world asserting itself against the human, reminding us that although a world without language can be imagined, a world of *only* language is impossible. It thus conjures up the totality of nonhuman nature and reduces the human perspective to its tiny, partial corner of a vast universe beyond our control. This is echoed in Farrell's feeling of being "puny" and Scott "retreating" into herself. "Simply not to be talking," Picard writes, "is not the same as to be silent. Silence must be present within a man [*sic*] as a primary reality in its own right, not merely as the opposite of speech. . . . It points him beyond the life that is in the word to a life beyond the word, and it points him beyond himself."[17] For the test witnesses, silence combined with light, heat, physical pressure, a visual display on a massive scale, and sounds that "warned of doomsday." This is clear in historian Richard Miller's description of the Hiroshima explosion: "[T]here appeared to be no sound. The chaos . . . was somehow *beyond* the meaning of the word."[18] The reality of a human-constructed world, that we usually experience as an ordered, predictable system full of meaningful symbols, is briefly torn apart by experiences like nuclear explosions. Language returns to stitch the gap, but what reveals itself for a moment isn't simply an absence but a world of full existence in-and-for-itself, indifferent to the human standpoint. Order and predictability, captured and mediated to form a human reality, sometimes give way to something that resists meaning and thus seems "more real." This is what Lacan designated as the Real, using the capital letter to distinguish it from the "reality" of the Symbolic register. It is here that language (and the world of human artifice more generally) finds a limit.

The Subject and the Real

Trinity is a metonym for other nuclear explosions, and by extension, the nuclear age more generally. The "entire basis" for a people's existence was "fundamentally altered" by it, according to historian Paul Boyer.[19] As a momentary disruption of meaning, the silence at Trinity unsettled the linguistic order and struck witnesses thoughtless. While it is possible to see films of nuclear explosions, read testimony, or read about them, many observers would follow Farrell's insistence that the awesome display of a nuclear explosion could not be grasped by any who did not witness it directly. Jonathan Schell, for example, insisted that nuclear war is not just unthought, but in some way "unthinkable."[20] This theme is echoed in a number of book titles on nuclear war: *Thinking the Unthinkable*, *Where No Man Thought*, *Fathering the Unthinkable*, and others. Clearly, silence did not persist. The Bomb is a product of the Symbolic order, capable of connecting many discrete signifiers, but its persistent force stems partly from this connection to an unthinkable, unspeakable power of the order of the Real. The intensity of the horror and fascination the Bomb produced shows the intersection between these two orders of experience.

Lacan's notion of the Real is notoriously difficult to define. In his book on the subject, Tom Eyers calls it the "most elusive" of Lacan's concepts, but also one that is "central" and "determining" for psychoanalysis.[21] Slavoj Žižek defines the Real in a number of different ways concerned with its overlap with the other (Imaginary and Symbolic) registers advanced by Lacan.[22] The ambiguity of the Real extends to rhetorical scholarship as well. Kevin Johnson and Jennifer Asenas, for example, attempt to develop the critical potential of the concept through a number of discrete definitions.[23] These include the Real as recalcitrance, the Real as a return, the Real as enjoyment, and so on. For others, the Real is an underlying but inaccessible logic, or simply the impossible.

There are common elements of the various definitions. First, an agreement that both the economy of tropes that allows the conditions for meaning to emerge (the Symbolic) and the meanings and values invested in these tropes, including the subject itself (the Imaginary), do not and cannot perfectly capture all of existence or experience. Something is left over. The Real, in this sense, is less the order of mind-independent reality and more the subject's confrontation with that order. It is the excess that escapes signification and meaning. Second, this remainder structures the Symbolic and Imaginary, just as they structure each other, and thus all three registers are knitted together as demonstrated in Lacan's famous Borromean knot. The eruption of the Real is traumatic in the sense that it reveals the limitations of subjectivity and language. The ensuing symbolic engagements with this trauma are not by definition the Real, but they take shape in reaction to its effects on reality.

This traumatic experience leaves its mark on every speaking subject in the form of the lack, which Lacan understands as the price of entry into language. At first, individual human beings do not have a strong sense of differentiation between self and world. Boundaries are porous. Hungry babies cry, and food is provided. They do not understand the breast (or bottle) as belonging to the caregiver as a wholly different entity. Rather, it is a transitional object, merging self with world. Both psyche and body are disorganized and indistinct because the infant does not have a strong sense of corporeal identity. This experience is perhaps not always pleasurable, but it does bring with it a sense of continuity that is necessarily lost when individuals come to understand themselves as discrete entities as a result of identification with a signifier that forms the ego.

The subject, as opposed to individual, gains coherence in the mirror stage when it moves from a fragmented entity to the "finally donned armor of an alienating identity that will mark his [*sic*] entire mental development with its rigid structure."[24] In Lacan's account, the baby sees a reflection in the mirror. When it wills movement, the reflection moves, and the baby comes to identify the reflection as itself. We identify the ego or specular image as the self. This is an important distinction because the ego in this account is not a unified inner being that is simply represented by an image, but a product of identification with an external signifier. This process of investing meaning in a symbol is the basis for the Imaginary register, but the mirror stage also describes our entry into the

Symbolic. The baby turns to its caregiver for affirmation that the specular image is indeed the self. The caregiver's nod of assent represents the "big Other" fixing the subject's identity.[25] The image of the mirror phase becomes a kind of currency through which we enter the economy of language, reduced to an identity (a signifier) capable of being linked together with others and identified by other subjects. While the Imaginary is the order of meaning invested in specific symbols, the Symbolic governs the differentiation and connection between them through metaphor, metonymy, and other mechanisms of transfer. It is therefore an inherently rhetorical phenomenon—an "economy of trope" as Christian Lundberg calls it.[26]

This "social *I*"[27] comes at a cost. The subject is only possible through an act of alienation because what makes it a subject is differentiation from the world. The lost sense of connection to the world is what Romain Rolland called the "oceanic feeling." Bataille described it as "continuity." The Symbolic categorizes, orders, and structures experience so that communication is possible, but the nagging sense of incompletion never goes away. The same cut that creates the subject also creates the lack, a vacuum left by our identification with a limited subject. It is also the engine of desire: the reason why we continue to seek things in excess of our biological needs is this sense of incompletion combined with our inability to recognize it in ourselves. We cathect to various objects believing that they will satisfy us. Perhaps they do, for a time, but they can never completely fill the lack. Each object stands in for something else, an endless signifying chain that has at its bottom "*objet petit a*," so-called because it is a structural position rather than an actual thing. *Objet petit a* is the missing piece that completes the subject. Any tangible thing cannot fulfill it because it is by its nature impossible to find. What the subject desires is a continuity with the world that would undermine the very conditions for the subject to exist. In this sense, all drives are the death drive: even the loss of self in unity with another that we might call love is a will to dissolve the subject. As such, each subject's desire remains perpetually unfulfilled, and to the extent that we socially determine the objects to which we cathect, our societies lack something, too.

This argument has important implications for rhetoric. First, it illustrates the significance of the Real. More than just the failures of the Symbolic economy, the Real is the excess that seems to exist beyond mediation. It is the momentary experience of continuity. This is not to say that the "oceanic feeling" is always pleasant when it suddenly returns to a differentiated subject. The experience of the Real may overwhelm the subject, making it feel like a "puny thing" in the face of something greater. Still, desire stemming from the Real both fascinates and terrifies. Lundberg has argued that the traditional focus of rhetoric on meaning elevates the Imaginary at the expense of the Symbolic.[28] Rhetoricians should therefore attend to the Symbolic economy that creates the necessary conditions for meaning, not just the content of individual signifiers or the local contexts of speech. The intrusion of the Real, however, suggests that we also attend to its function in shaping the Symbolic, as Johnson and Asenas argued. The Symbolic contains the tropological moves through which signifiers order our human reality and is thus the condition of the Imaginary, but the Real represents the impossible, always-in-excess sense of something greater, which in turn is the condition for the Symbolic.

Second, effects of the Real on language suggest that the long tradition in rhetoric focused on persuasion, symbolic action, and public deliberation be supplemented, not only with an account of the Symbolic as the tropological network which makes meaning possible, as per Lundberg, but also silence, interruption, awe, and terror, which influence both meaning in the Imaginary and the conditions by which Symbolic connections become durable. Language is not only the mechanism for subjects to persuade each other toward a common end, or the inaugural mechanism through which subjects are formed in the first place; it is also a paradoxical medium through which we try to communicate experiences that we consider incommunicable. Faced with encounters that defy our understanding, we often respond to the failure of language by crafting new discourses and attempting to assimilate new experiences into old ones. It may be impossible to communicate the Real, but there is no shortage of attempts. The rhetorical tradition of the sublime provides some insight here—metaphors like those Longinus analyzed in *On Great Writing* were explicitly differentiated from persuasion. Instead, they attempted to overwhelm audiences and use words to convey some sense of what words themselves could not capture. The sublime is a mechanism for how speaking subjects gesture toward the Real; psychoanalysis adds an explanation of why they do so and what effects these attempts have.

Finally, describing the lack in terms of the Real situates the death drive in its relationship to rhetoric. The death drive is the link between the Real and rhetoric in two ways. The institution of various specific objects supposed to fill the lack, and the condensations and displacements between them, can be understood rhetorically, but the effort to compensate for the failure of language can be understood this way as well. The desire for a "return" to continuity with the world is directed toward specific objects, or more properly, signs. These signs are linked through the operations of trope, which is how the meaning we attach to them always eludes us. These attachments are rhetorical ones—nothing essential connects our various objects of desire other than that they serve to fill the lack. The death drive turns the lack outward toward a series of objects but to explain how one object stands in for another and how it is made meaningful, the tools of rhetoric are necessary. Lacan repeatedly emphasized the importance of rhetoric in developing what he called "erotology," a theory of linkage between desiring subject, affect, objects of desire, and the Real.[29] The theory of the death drive helps explain why fascination and terror are spoken together so frequently. All drives are the death drive in the sense that they seek the Real and thus the dissolution of the subject, which can be both frightening and exhilarating. These efforts are doomed to fail in some sense because the subject cannot access the condition of its own nonexistence through language, but fleeting glimpses of the Real compel us to repeat the effort anyway.

Although all aspects of the drive can be characterized at least in part as the death drive, it should not be understood as a desire for the actual biological death of the subject's body, or even the desire to inflict death on others. This interpretation is an easy one to apply to nuclear weapons—what else accounts for the "madness" of collective suicide? Still, death itself is only one means of encountering continuity. The self-destruction of the death drive is a desire to break the limits of the self as the alienating armor of the subject by experiencing unmediated contact with the Real. The last portion of Lacan's "The Function and Field of Speech and Language in Psychoanalysis" explains the metaphorical centrality of death as the center of a torus formed by incessant symbolization. Death in this sense is the dissolution of the subject, the hard kernel that escapes language, which is not a biological end so much as the limit of the subject as a *speaking* entity. The *fort-da* game, which Freud uses to describe the death drive as repetition compulsion, is most significant not because it shows that the child wishes to destroy its mother or even inoculate itself against that possibility, but because it assimilates the child into the Symbolic order through the repetition of the signifiers *fort* and *da*, which stand in for presence and absence. Death is central to language because the symbol itself invokes the absence and loss of nonexistence since its function is to stand in for something that is gone. Language swirls around this absent center of death, a primordial absence encased in the inner ring of the torus, while the outer surfaces of language hold all else that cannot be symbolized at bay on the outside.[30]

Death and the Real are therefore not identical, but are closely linked. Death is an aspect of the dissolution of the subject that is glimpsed when it experiences the Real. The most important characteristic of the Real is not just that it suggests existence beyond language, but that this world-for-itself intrudes on human reality and reveals it to be incomplete. Encompassing Picard's concept of silence, the Real is not the absence of human reality so much as the traumatic revelation that that reality was *always* incomplete, always feigned in the face of existence so much more than human mediation has already covered. Lundberg uses Lacan's distinction between reality and the Real to develop his own distinction between *failed unicity* and *feigned unicity*. The Symbolic operates as an economy of interconnected and mutually referential tropes weaving a kind of fabric that is the precondition for meaning, an environment in which social relationships can be understood in context. When the unified illusion of the social fails, we are compelled to stitch the tears in that fabric to maintain the world that gives us meaning.[31] This idea of feigned unicity helps to make sense of witness accounts of nuclear testing and the discourses that derived from them. Following that initial silence, witnesses attempted to make sense of what they had experienced, first by fitting it into the closest available discourse—that of religion—and then by adapting new patterns to compensate for the trauma of the Real without losing the sense of awe that it inspired.

The Horror and Allure of the Real

The silence following nuclear tests is one example of the eruption of the Real, but witness testimony demonstrates a larger process of traumatic breakdown followed by attempts to compensate for the failure of language. Bill Laurence, a Pentagon favorite with a long career covering nuclear testing, was also the only journalist allowed to witness the Trinity test. While "not a sound could be heard" for the period after the flash and before the thunder, Laurence claims to have seen civilization itself collapse in an instant: "The big boom came about one hundred seconds after the great flash—the first cry of a newborn world. It brought the silent, motionless silhouettes to life, gave them a voice. A loud cry filled the air. The little groups that had hitherto stood rooted to the earth like desert plants broke into a dance—the rhythm of primitive man dancing at one of his fire festivals at the coming of spring. They clapped their hands as they leaped from the ground. . . . The dance of the primitive man lasted but a few seconds, during which an evolutionary period of about 10,000 years telescoped. Primitive man was metamorphosed into modern man—shaking hands, slapping his fellow on the back, all laughing like happy children."[32] Once the actual explosion took place, the predictable order of the human social world seemed to cease. The horror of the Bomb is its sudden demonstration of physical forces that, although unleashed by human beings, are products of an obscenely powerful universe indifferent to humanity and capable of destroying it. Conant, president of Harvard, thought of human extinction: "My first impression remains the most vivid, a cosmic phenomena [*sic*] like an eclipse. The whole sky suddenly full of white light like the end of the world. Perhaps my impression was only premature on a time scale of years!"[33] Kistiakowsky said the spectacle was "the nearest thing to doomsday that one could possibly imagine. I am sure that at the end of the world—in the last millisecond of the earth's existence—the last man [*sic*] will see what we have just seen."[34] The Bomb differed from much religious apocalypticism in that its threat of extinction was not tied to any greater cosmic plan for humanity.

The Bomb brought to mind the insignificance of human beings and the possibility of a world without them. Although speculative fiction writers had already contemplated human extinction, the possibility was no longer hypothetical. Suddenly, human beings were faced with the possibility of auto-annihilation, and therefore made to contemplate, like Kistiakowsky, a world where Homo sapiens had been eradicated. Witnessing a nuclear explosion changed everything for some observers. Scott was both made aware of the failure of mediation and gripped with a new determination:

> Ahlgren: I remember reading, some observer, a general, maybe it was during the Trinity test, that when the bomb was exploded they said that they looked into the mouth of Hell.
> Scott: They did. I said that at the talk, remember? I said, "You just can't look into the bowels of Hell and not be changed." And you can't . . . any more than you could believe what it looked like. It's hard to visualize it, and certainly after seeing it, you'd be a fool not to let it [affect you]. You've got to build on something and that was building on the most potentially dangerous thing mankind has ever faced. . . .
>
> You do the best you can with what you've got. That's what it boils down to, every day of your life. That was a big challenge. I have to admit that there were people, maybe even some people that worked in civil defense, that did not have the intensity that I had. I don't know if it was the test. It isn't really anything you can transfer to another person—your understanding of whatever something is. I can't transfer that knowledge or feeling to you.[35]

Here Scott asserts the impossibility of communicating ("transferring") her encounter with something beyond words—the Real—and claims that this experience gave her a new "intensity" in civil defense work. Postapocalyptic survival was not the Second Coming of Jesus or a rebirth in the afterlife. If human beings meant to survive their own apocalypse, they would have to do it themselves with no guarantees.

Fission and fusion may be human-instigated in the case of the Bomb, but they are also forces that stem from the "natural" world that precedes, and will follow, human life. In his book *In the Dust of this Planet*, Eugene Thacker distinguishes between the human social world (the world-for-us), a world that functions independently of humanity and sometimes "bites back," reminding us that we are not completely in charge (the world-in-itself), and finally, a speculative world sometimes hinted at in these bites, where we no longer exist (the world-without-us).[36] The experience of nuclear detonation and the ensuing fantasies unite these three dimensions—the collision of the first two eventually gives rise to the third. We might fear the natural disasters brought upon by the world's dangerous contingency, but *horror* is a result of the paradoxical thinking of the unthinkable—not just our complete annihilation, but the meaninglessness of such an event. Todd

Gitlin recalled primary school duck-and-cover drills as a part of life for the "first American generation compelled from infancy to fear not only war but the end of days."[37] One could never be sure that humanity would endure at all. "Under the desks and crouched in the hallways," he wrote, "terrors were ignited, existentialists were made."[38] Like the cosmic horror of H. P. Lovecraft, the Bomb questions the significance of life itself by compelling us to imagine its destruction.

The Bomb reveals the "puniness" of humanity as something that occupies a world not of its own making and thus does not determine the value of all of nature. If all that we hold dear is arbitrary, a vain conceit by an irrelevant species, we must confront a void that dissolves any meaning and value that we assign to ourselves. Why live? Why bother? The universe is full of horror, and our lives mean nothing. Before the Bomb brought these existential questions to the fore, Lovecraft wrote to Frank Belknap Long that there is "a kind of hideous irony in the assumption of the human point of view at all—in the exaltation, celebration, or even detailed notice of the contemptible organic processes of the filthy louse called man. I could not take humanity seriously if I wanted to, and it rather sickens me to see a poet's vision hound up in the trivial sensations and affairs of this crawling insect-species. . . . When Kleiner showed me the sky-line of New-York I told him that man is like the coral insect—designed to build vast, beautiful, mineral things for the moon to delight in after he is dead."[39]

Lovecraft imagined "winged fiends" for whom "the name of man [*sic*]—and even the name of organic life—is unknown."[40] In this imagination of a world-without-us, human consciousness is no longer central. Lovecraft's "cosmic" horror is distinguished from other varieties by its basic premise that other powers in the universe are not hostile to humanity, but rather indifferent to it. There is little in Lovecraft's work that is strictly supernatural. The "gods" worshipped by atavistic cults are beings so alien that human beings cannot fathom them. The "horror" of this situation is simply the realization that in the vastness of space and time, human concerns are insignificant.

Thomas Ligotti, a more contemporary philosopher and horror author, takes this insight to its logical extreme: the sole purpose of human consciousness, he argues, is a "long con" designed to conceal the truth that humanity is "malignantly useless," tricked into continuing by the same attribute that also guarantees its misery by making it aware of its own inevitable death.[41] Ligotti's nonfiction book *Conspiracy against the Human Race* extends a long tradition of philosophical pessimism, revived in popular culture by the widely acclaimed first season of HBO's *True Detective*. His insight is close to Bataille's argument about the role of language in discontinuity and death. Death becomes meaningful only because the human subject considers itself separate from nature through consciousness, but then must endure the constant threat that it will be dissolved. The power to categorize, name, and create a human world of utility both enables the subject and forces it to confront the inevitability of death and corruption.[42] The advent of the Bomb made this fear operate at the level of the entire species. The thoroughly human accomplishment of atomic fission introduced the possibility of extinction, and the contemplation of this collective death raised questions about the ultimate purpose of life—or lack thereof. This encounter began at the very minute of the first nuclear explosion if Kistiakowsky's report is accurate.

What Ligotti and other misanthropes ironically fail to explain is the appeal of their own imagination: we can also enjoy what inspires horror. As Ira Chernus writes, the "lure of nothingness—the possibility of extinction—has always fascinated human beings and enticed them into situations of lethal risk. There is an intensity about such situations, where we encounter the 'bottom line' of life and death, that cannot be matched elsewhere."[43] By definition, we cannot affix our desire to the Real, as it is what exceeds mediation and understanding. The Real is pure contingency, and the mechanism of desire scripts regularity, but as we attempt to mediate the Real we find symbols to which desire can attach. What we desire is not the Real, but our (at least partially) symbolized and circulated memories of encounters with its excess. After the period of stricken silence at Trinity ended, witnesses fit the experience into a comprehensible order. Confronted with the inability of quotidian frames of reference to contain what they witnessed, the stricken scientists and military personnel started to weave together the means to feign unicity in the face of its failure. The Bomb produced its few moments of speechless encounter, but it did not occur in a vacuum, and soon elements of the Symbolic began to stitch over the gap.

The language of religion was a natural choice. It is designed to put transcendent, superhuman power into the base words of mortals. Scientific revelations about the natural world gradually whittle away at the Real in some ways by providing a means to understand novel experiences, even if this advance is destined to be asymptotic by the inherent limitations of language. At the same time, science introduces new and unexpected phenomena of its own. As Lacan argues, humanity quickly struggles to fit these experiences into a preexisting framework. In *The Triumph of Religion* he writes, "If science works at it, the real will expand and religion will thereby have still more reasons to soothe people's hearts. Science is new and it will introduce all kinds of distressing things into each person's life. Religion, above all the true religion, is resourceful in ways we cannot even begin to suspect. . . . Religion is going to give meaning to the oddest experiments, the very ones that scientists themselves are just beginning to become anxious about."[44]

Science and religion are not mutually exclusive forces, at least on the symbolic level (think here, too, of the God Particle). Science is not just a set of explanations. It is also a method of inquiry, and especially in physics, its questions sometimes coincide with the domain of religion. As David Noble has argued, the more ambitious and radical scientific discoveries are often deeply intertwined with religious language, motivations, an even faithful conviction.[45] Nor was the Bomb the first military technology that had evinced such a response—the tank was greeted in similar terms on a more limited scale.[46] Some people feel awe at its accomplishments that more closely resemble religious rapture than the impassive reaction of a neutral observer whether or not they think of themselves as exclusively secular.

Observers at Trinity followed a similar pattern. From his interviews with Manhattan Project scientists, Jungk gathered that "they all, even those—who constituted the majority—ordinarily without religious faith or even any inclination thereto, recounted their experiences in words derived from the linguistic fields of myth and theology."[47] Even before the explosion, many Trinity witnesses acted as if they anticipated a specifically divine power. At least one had a nervous breakdown hours before the test and had to be escorted away, while another—a Nobel Prize winner—muttered in his trench "I'm scared witless, absolutely witless."[48] Farrell, writing about the moments before the test, said that the "feeling of many could be expressed by 'Lord, I believe; help Thou mine unbelief.' We were reaching into the unknown and we did not know what might come of it. It can be safely said that most of those present—Christian, Jew and atheist—were praying and praying harder than they had ever prayed before."[49]

These sentences describe the scientists priming themselves in the moments before the test—a test that Oppenheimer had supposedly named "Trinity" after this John Dunne poem:

> Batter my heart, three-person'd God; for you
> As yet but knock, breathe, shine, and seek to mend;
> That I may rise, and stand, o'erthrow me, and bend
> Your force to break, blow, burn, and make me new.
> I, like an usurp'd town, to another due,
> Labour to admit you, but Oh, to no end;
> Reason, your viceroy in me, me should defend,
> But is captiv'd, and proves weak or untrue.
> Yet dearly I love you, and would be lov'd fain,
> But am betroth'd unto your enemy;
> Divorce me, untie, or break that knot again,
> Take me to you, imprison me, for I,
> Except you enthrall me, never shall be free,
> Nor ever chast, except you ravish me.

Like the child playing *fort-da*, witnesses prepared themselves for the coming of something both present and absent, something catastrophic, and yet were still overwhelmed after it made itself apparent. Not all of these references were Christian, as Oppenheimer's famous reference to the *Bhagavad Gita* shows. For Bernstein, who witnessed a later test, the burning Joshua trees in the desert were like "some obscene pagan rite."[50]

These powerful reactions mirror those long noted by scholars of religion. Otto saw the *numinous*—that transcendent quality of God that cannot be rationally understood or completely communicated in language—as the unique element of religious experience.[51] God's power exists outside and beyond us in such a way that to experience it is to be reduced to "creature feeling," like Abraham's claim to be "dust and ashes" before the Lord when negotiating over the fate of Sodom. This feeling of nothingness "cannot be expressed verbally, and can only be suggested indirectly through the tone and content of a man's [*sic*] feeling-response to it."[52] The experience of the numinous shatters the artifice of both self and social reality, according to Otto. "[A]s soon as speculative thought has come to . . . analyse this 'majesty'—we . . . come upon the ideas, first, of the annihilation of self, and then, as its complement, of the transcendent as the sole and entire reality . . . the personal 'I' as something not perfectly or essentially real . . . in rejecting the delusion of selfhood, and so makes for the annihilation of the self."[53]

God's power is awesome and terrible. But with the *tremens* of terror before the Lord, Otto also identified *fascinans*—our capacity to be transfixed by divine power. What is on the one hand terrifying is also fascinating, and for the same reason: these overwhelming experiences reveal simultaneously the limitations of our own world and the existence of something more, and unaccountable excess. The annihilated subject may even seek some kind of contact with this tremendous force. As Otto writes, "These two qualities, the daunting and the fascinating, now combine in a strange harmony of contrasts, and the resultant dual character of the numinous consciousness . . . is at once the strangest and most noteworthy phenomenon in the whole history of religion. The daemonic-divine object may appear to the mind an object of horror and dread, but at the same time it is no less something that allures with a potent charm, and the creature, who trembles before it, utterly cowed and cast down, has always at the same time the impulse to turn to it, nay even to make it somehow his [*sic*] own."[54]

When the Lord threatens Sodom with destruction or describes the unimaginable beast Leviathan, God's hapless auditors imagine that they have already been destroyed and must come to grips with their ephemerality. At the same time, Abraham and Job both respond with devotion. God's sheer power to destroy fixates them and inspires worship, even love. These Old Testament stories are essentially cosmic horror fiction in the sense that their effect relies on gesturing toward something that exceeds the human world and reduces individual human subjects to tiny, irrelevant husks. Where the Old Testament moves beyond Lovecraft and Ligotti is God's attention to humanity. Lovecraft's godlike beings simply appear indifferent—any agenda they have toward humanity is inscrutable. They also have relatively fewer worshippers. The Old Testament God is vengeful and often destructive, but it demands adherence and receives it. This God, with all of its terrible power, is more palatable. The transition is evident in the comparison between Otto's notion of "daemonic dread" and holiness. The first describes our initial reaction to the awesome power of the unknown, while (for Otto) the second represents a more mature relationship to the divine.[55] The Old Testament God is familiar and understandable in human terms, at least to some extent, and thus a remedy for the cosmic horror that might result from the realization that our "dust and ashes" have no greater significance. Even occasional malevolence is an affective response of the Other that fits within the realm of human reference. As Lacan writes, anxiety revolves around the *uncertainty* expressed in the question "What does the Other want with me?"[56] The structure of a religious system compensates for this initial anxiety by attempting to incorporate the pure contingency of the Real into the more predictable order of the signifier.

When footage of nuclear explosions, postapocalyptic films, and all manner of cultural ephemera spread out from Los Alamos like evangelist texts they captured the impersonal power of "daemonic dread," but also fit easily within a framework that was structurally, if not strictly, religious. The godlike qualities of the Bomb even include transcendence of time itself. The Bomb's reign over the future is most evident in Schell's *The Fate of the Earth*, which argued that the threat to future generations made nuclear weapons of literally infinite importance (the implications of this argument will be discussed more fully in chapter 2). Despite the official dawning of the Atomic Age in 1945, the Bomb has even adopted a mythic historical role in the wilder hinterlands of speculation. Internet prophecy and conspiracy websites have espoused the ancient nuclear war theory, naming Atlantis (sometimes A-Tlan-Tis in the Great Lakes region of modern North America), the lost continent of Mu, Sodom and Gomorrah, or the Indus Valley as supposed targets of nuclear warfare, sometimes citing Oppenheimer as an advocate. This theory has exploded on the Internet with the help of David Hatcher Childress's 2000 book *Technology of the Gods: The Incredible Sciences of the Ancients* and Erich von Däniken's *Chariot of the Gods*. The History Channel (a masterwork of euphemistic naming) has given a platform to these ideas, which also appear in the explicitly fictional *Battlestar Galactica*. In *Ancient Atom Bombs: Fact, Fraud, and the Myth of Prehistoric Nuclear Warfare*, Jason Colavito argues that this theory is a response to modern anxieties about extinction from the atom bomb, providing both a morality tale and a promise that this horrific technology can be survived;[57] in other words, domesticating and assimilating this history-threatening power. John Brandenburg, a physicist who argues that nuclear war might have eliminated past life on Mars, moves the Bomb from before recorded history to before humanity itself.[58] Here the Bomb becomes akin to Quentin Meillassoux's *arche-fossil*, a reminder of ancient time that dislocates humanity from the center of the universe.[59] Unlike the *arche-fossil*, atomic explosions are a natural force, but they differ from earthquakes, volcanoes, and so forth in their relationship to human artifice since they are direct products of our own agency.

Much has been written of the apocalyptic fervor for the end times and the desire to hasten their coming in the form of nuclear war.[60] Noble argues that this attitude toward the Bomb is contiguous with a larger metaphysics of technology that sees progress on Earth as a product of divine guidance. Technology is a means of transcending this Earthly life, and thus some desire even for nuclear war fits the pattern of techno-theology.[61] The Bomb made a world-ending Armageddon a literal possibility, and thus made possible beliefs like those of Claire Schaus, who declared the coming of a new "Atomic God" with the Bomb as its "Hand," exceeding humankind and demanding reverence.[62] Theologian Wilbur Smith, one of the first to write systematically about religion and nuclear weapons, noted that "writers seemed forced" to turn to Biblical language to describe the atomic test in New Mexico and the world it gave rise to.[63] Smith's declaration that "the next D-Day will be doomsday, unless men turn to God"[64] was perhaps the first in a long line of statements tying the Bomb to Biblical prophecy, the most notable being Hal Lindsey's *The Late Great Planet Earth* and Billy Graham's various proclamations on the topic. There is a certain smugness in Smith's book directed toward all of those who dismissed the literal truth of the Revelation of John: finally, they will be forced to see the light, as it were, and pay for their obstinance. Air Force ethics training for launch officers relied until quite recently on explicitly apocalyptic Christian themes and Biblical interpretation, including a training session called the "Jesus loves nukes speech" by its participants.[65] Freeman Dyson described the "glitter of nuclear weapons."[66] In the words of one Los Alamos worker who regretted never witnessing an atmospheric test, "I want to feel the heat. This is the most there is; this is the closest you get to playing God."[67]

The need to fit novel experiences into familiar understandings of the world may account for the religious language of nuclear war, but what accounts for these specifically salvific notions of the Bomb or the desire to be close to it? The aspect of religious language dealing with terror in the face of inhuman power may lend itself naturally to the Bomb, but why do so many also embrace the desiring, even worshipful, side of this discourse? Perhaps to answer these questions we should understand the Bomb not just as a historically specific constellation of discourses and technologies, but as an example of the more general dynamic of intersections between the Real and Symbolic orders. Desiring subjects are forged in this intersection, but desire is never simple. To *enjoy* the Bomb in a Lacanian sense is to attach to it, to ascribe it great importance relative to the subject, not necessarily to derive pleasure from the attachment. The paradox of desire is that we seek what we literally cannot have: a return to a state of wholeness that exceeds symbolization, but is itself only imagined and pursued through signifiers that displace endlessly upon one another. The web of signifiers in which we live is both the obstacle to desire and the only medium for it. As a result, we attach to symbols, but we do so because they signify something for us beyond the mundane of the Symbolic order itself. This is the fundamental process of the death drive.

What the experience of twinned horror and desire in the nuclear imagination suggests is that we attach ourselves to signifiers in which the Real "shines through," signifiers that promise a connection to something "really real." Hence the desire to "feel the heat," or to experience the "glitter" of nuclear weapons by some participants in the nuclear weapons complex. The possible futures of human destruction and the attendant jarring realization of humanity's precarity exist in the present in the form of fantasy. The exact set of signifiers that produce us as subjects is mediated by culture, life experience, and a host of other factors. I am not suggesting that there is a general theory of desire that explains the wants, hopes, and disposition of every individual subject. Context and a host of contingent individual factors, from life experience to genetics to dumb luck, still affect behavior, and the precise discourses that emerge in response to the Real create very different subjects and subjectivities, not a universal and neutral "human." What I am suggesting is that this sense of the Real is the attribute of signifiers that creates an attachment point for subjects to cathect and thus is an important factor in the interplay of structure and contingency, which should be of interest to rhetoricians. The tradition of the sublime is most helpful in this regard as it attends to the paradoxical qualities of powerful signifiers that test the limits of language itself. The death drive suggests a new way to understand the sublime, not as a *style* of grandeur nor as an *aesthetic* of overwhelming phenomena, but as the *aspect of signifier that indicates the Real.* This sense of the Real is the *uncanny* aspect of language.

Uncanny Metaphors of the Real

In a short essay, Freud developed the uncanny as an affect of discomfort in response to the perception of some repressed, generally frightening thing in the guise of something more familiar. The concept is based in signification—it is a repressed signifier that bleeds through a more familiar one, although Freud notes that there is a reversibility to the uncanny as well. Familiar things appear alien, and alien things appear familiar. The phenomenon occurs with confusion of symbol and reality. As Freud writes, "[A]n uncanny effect is often and easily produced when the distinction between imagination and reality is effaced, as when . . . a symbol takes over the full functions of the thing it symbolizes."[68] This conflation of symbol and reality is an attribute of all language to some extent, as all signifiers are catachrestic in that a word stands in for an absent thing. For language to work it cannot function with perfect efficiency—the premise of rhetoric as a field is that lexical meaning is not the whole story, so to speak. Although language operates on a generally unexamined connection between signifier and signified, discomfort arises when that connection is "too real." When the *heimlich* world woven by language seems worn down and something else emerges, the reaction is anxiety.

Lacan argues against a common division between fear and anxiety based on the presence of a specific object in the former. It is not the case that anxiety lacks an object altogether. Rather, it is "not without an object." Subjects can typically enjoy their objects through the *fort-da* game, which permits them a sense of mastery over the conditions of presence and absence in this object. Anxiety arises when the *fort-da* game is disrupted by the sudden, uncanny presence of the Other's desire—when the object representing it to the subject becomes too close for fantasy and the sense of control is lost. As an "exercise in mastery," *fort-da* requires that "a certain void is always to be preserved, which has nothing to do with the content, neither positive nor negative, of the demand. The disruption wherein anxiety is evinced arises when this void is totally filled in."[69] Anxiety is "the failing of the support that lack provides." He continues, "Don't you know that it's not longing for the maternal breast that provokes anxiety, but its imminence? What provokes anxiety is everything that announces to us, that lets us glimpse, that we're going to be taken back onto the lap. It is not, contrary to what is said, the rhythm of the mother's alternating presence and absence. The proof of this is that the infant revels in repeating [*fort-da*]. The security of presence is the possibility of absence. The most anguishing thing for the infant is precisely the moment when the relationship upon which he's established himself, of the lack that turns him into desire, is disrupted . . . when there's no possibility of lack."[70] In other words, when the subject, imagining itself as the fulfillment of the Other's desire, perhaps even the center of its world, must confront the immediacy of that desire, no space remains in which to harbor fantasy because suddenly something—"anything whatsoever"[71]—appears that represents the Other's desire in a form inconsistent with that fantasy. The "possibility of absence" is necessary to the "security of presence."[72] In Žižek's terms, the gap that separates an object of desire from one of disgust is "the very gap that separates reality from the Real: what constitutes reality is the minimum of idealization the subject needs in order to be able to sustain the horror of the Real."[73] This reaction is consistent with Otto's "creature feeling" of dread before the Divine. Suddenly, an imagined part of the subject's order is supplanted by a revelation that decenters the subject, reducing it to "dust and ashes." Witnesses at Trinity were intellectually aware of the possible effects of fission energy, but actually experiencing it reduced many of them to awestruck silence or even terror. Anxiety does not deceive, but rather signals that we are already deceived by our Symbolic order which conceals *something, anything*, in excess of itself.

Anxious subjects do not simply fall silent for the rest of time, however. Anxiety still results in speech, as the Trinity witnesses demonstrate. The overwhelming experience of the Bomb, like more quotidian intrusions of the Real, is followed by attempts to mediate that experience through the familiar paths of language. The ensuing statements are not just a return of normality, however. As the overtly religious language of nuclear war shows, these familiar words attempt to convey something unfamiliar, and in fact, impossible—the Real. In this sense, language may be uncanny. Although expressed in ways that are easily recognized and understood, the artifice of language (symbol) is contrasted with something other (Real), and because there no signified that can contain the experience of something by definition beyond signification, the words themselves become akin to the reality they represent, covering a lack that nonetheless remains unfilled. The uncanny language of the Bomb may therefore compensate somewhat for anxiety by returning some of the signifier's distance, averting a direct confrontation with the limits of the subject, but this effect is incomplete. The sense of the (uncanny) Real that persists maintains its power to inspire both horror and fascination, as Otto proposed. This is the crucial aspect of nuclear rhetoric: it is not merely an issue of persuading or organizing an audience, or even producing subjects. It is a way of hinting at their absolute unmaking as well, insinuating the limits of language, and inspiring anxiety that must be dealt with somehow for the subject to continue enjoying its sense of control over its world.

As mentioned in the introduction, the sublime is an ancient rhetorical tradition centered on the dislocating function of language. Around two thousand years ago, Longinus wrote of the overpowering potential of figurative language, likening it to the grandeur of natural phenomena. The sublime is not only an aesthetic concept—which is how it has largely been taken up in contemporary scholarship outside of rhetoric—but an aspect of language that did not persuade an audience so much as discomfit them by revealing "like a thunderbolt" an excess beyond words.[74] For Longinus, sublime language is most effectively conveyed in metaphors which serve to overwhelm the audience so thoroughly that artifice is accepted as if it were natural. If "the best use of a figure is when the very fact that it is a figure goes unnoticed," then an orator uses sublime metaphor to conceal artifice "by its very brilliance. Just as dimmer lights are lost in the surrounding sunshine, so pervading grandeur all around obscures the presence of the rhetorical devices."[75] Longinus thus conceives of the sublime as artifice, but it operates on its audience as if it was something more, seeming "natural" in the inhuman sense and concealing the signifying networks that make language meaningful by overwhelming auditors. This aspect of the sublime is not simply about aesthetic qualities—as rhetoricians have sometimes overlooked, the sublime is also about the formation and discomfiture of identity.[76] It is a mode of language suited for anxiety: the sublime hints toward something *awful* in that word's double sense while still functioning as a mode of speech rather than silence. It reminds an audience that language is not omnipotent, but it does so through the very power of that medium. The network of signifiers concealed by the sublime do not go away, however. Individual identities, social concepts, and various modes of being are partially determined by culture and history through the medium of language. The sublime merely represses those elements into an unconscious web by focusing attention on what they might not capture. Julia Kristeva argues that the sublime has no particular object, but is "nothing other than the possibility of naming" what precedes the names, and therefore precedes the specificity of objects. It is a means of keeping powerful encounters that threaten the subject "under control" through speech.[77]

For Lacan, ostensibly following Quintilian rather than Roman Jakobson, the two basic tropes are metonymy and metaphor. Metonymy relies on connections that seem to be of substance or proximity rather than abstract qualities—"blood" is a metonym for the family; "hands" stand in for the sailors to which they are attached, and "thrones" indicate the people who sit on them. Metonymy proliferates meaning because these choices of substance are largely accidental in the sense that other connections could be chosen—nothing but decency stops us from speaking of family as "mucous," sailors as "spleens," and monarchs as "chamber pots." Metaphor, however, condenses meaning. To substitute one thing for another in metaphor focuses the audience on the essential trait that links the signifier and its referent. Thus Achilles is a lion because both are brave and ferocious in battle, a linkage of defining yet abstract traits rather than contiguity. For Lundberg, the difference between metonymy and metaphor is affective rather than formal. The connections that animate a metaphor represent some accreted affective investment that makes signifier and referent powerfully associated such that to replace one with the other elides the centrifugal work of metonymy. The elevation of one metonymic connection to the status of metaphor therefore conceals both the labor that produces it and the persistence of other metonymic connections.[78]

Lacan's concept of the unconscious is based on the capacity for some connections of trope to overshadow others. The unconscious is not a hidden, interior set of motivations for a subject, but rather the elements of transpersonal discourse that shape the subject without its direct attention. These signifiers are "repressed" because they are neglected in favor of other, more obvious pathways for meaning. Discussing Lacan's take on Freudian repression, Lundberg explains that raising one "insular metonymic connection to the status of a metaphor conceals or renders latent the other metonymic connections that also inhere in the accreted history of a sign. But the condition of this concealment is the whole field of latent connections that are both accreted and expressed in the social use of signs."[79]

All symbolic connections require some degree of labor if we reject the idea of natural signifiers, but metaphor is particularly demanding. Denis Donoghue finds that little distinguishes metaphor and simile in a formal sense, but the former requires an audience or reader to divine the connection themselves, making it a kind of enthymematic trope.[80] That metaphor is not thought of as a revolutionary, disruptive act of imagination is, for Donoghue, because the "understanding of metaphor has been inordinately governed by a few sentences that Aristotle jotted down," instead of the "wilder" philosophers or the "flamboyant" sublime of Longinus.[81] Trope is not mere ornamentation. It describes the topography of the Symbolic, the pathways through which meaning can move, and the process of subject formation. Indeed, a rhetoric focused only on persuasion, motivation toward concrete political goals, identification, or incipient action may miss the forces of language identified in the tradition of the sublime, looking straight into the light of the sun of the figure rather than the dimmer lights it may conceal.

What makes a trope "shine" is, in Lundberg's language, the affective labor that links signifier and signified—what I will generally call "cathexis."[82] The Symbolic can be understood as an economy of affect where repeated investments give symbols value as the currency of meaning and exchange. This economic metaphor, also used by Lacan, is employed with sophistication by Lundberg to argue that rhetoric could be understood as a science if more attention were given to the Symbolic context currently diminished by excessive attention to the Imaginary. To understand how some symbols become objects of cathexis, we might introduce an allied scientific discipline as a metaphorical resource: not the *oikos* and *nomos* of economics, but the *oikos* and *logos* of ecology. While energy transfer, trophic levels, and equilibria could all be adapted to the Symbolic, nuclear weapons testing gave us a perfect metaphor for the uncanny in radioecology. Much of modern environmental science evolved from ecology with the help of radionuclides, which allowed cybernetic-systems theorists to track ecological relationships.[83] Radioactive contamination is now almost universal due to open-air nuclear testing, not to mention Chernobyl, Fukushima, Three Mile Island, Lake Chagan, and other disasters great and small. But it was the early detection of fallout particles and their effects on human beings that inspired fear—the downwinders movement, Civil Defense, the various test ban treaties—and fascination—Project Sunshine, a host of science fiction stories, and so forth.

Radioactive isotopes are alien particles incorporated by an organism. They are not organic, and their radiation causes bodily trauma. Often the first sign is not the particles themselves, but the cancerous growths that result as the contaminants warp surrounding cells. Quickly, the body will expend great energy trying to incorporate them into the preexisting scheme of the organism—thus strontium-90, similar to calcium, is knitted into bones, and cesium-137, similar to potassium, ends up in soft tissues.[84] It is possible to speak of an ecology of the Real, where the grains of radioactive dust represent these unassimilable interventions that are assimilated anyway by a body determined to put them where they belong, although their assimilation comes at the cost of permanently distorting the (genetic, Symbolic) plan that orders the phenotypical body. Perhaps the renowned linguist Thomas Sebeok saw a hint of this parallel when he suggested that human DNA might be reworked deliberately to encode the locations of nuclear waste sites.[85] This information would assist an "atomic priesthood" to watch over the abject refuse of the nuclear age for millennia to come.[86] The presence or absence of byproducts from Trinity are now used to prove that old wine is authentic, that ivory is legitimate, and that sediments are a certain age.

This metaphor is not perfect, of course. It is only meant to highlight one process: the means by which the Symbolic attempts to incorporate the Real, and the deformations that result. What makes strontium-90 so dangerous is that it provides sites for other atoms to form bonds that mirror calcium. This is how it is absorbed into the body—it is close to the components that should fit into a larger design, but still foreign. It is this sense of authenticity that lets the new disruptive element bind with the old ones as if it belonged—all the while warping the tissue into which it is woven. Strontium is not calcium, but it is assimilated as if it were, changing the body's code to reflect its new presence gradually through radiation. It is a similar trait that makes nuclear tropes in language so powerful. The Real cannot be a site of cathexis, but a sense of it is precisely what makes these tropes attractive. The sense of the Real in a trope—in other words, the uncanny—is what creates the conditions for strong bonds to form.

Here we could add a third trope to the metaphor and metonymy Lacan developed in his seminar on psychosis. The trope of the sublime is catachresis, a wrenching metaphor that draws attention to the failure of a connection between two things. Catachresis works precisely because it never covers the inadequacy of language completely, just as the mutant cells caused by radioactive exposure do not seamlessly restore the body to its prior state. For Paul de Man, catachresis is the figure of "mixed modes," "capable of inventing the most fantastic entities by dint of the positional power inherent in language. They can dismember the texture of reality and reassemble it in the most capricious of ways. . . . Something monstrous lurks in the most innocent of catachresis: when one speaks of the legs of the table or the face of the mountain, catachresis is already turning into prosopopoeia, and one begins to perceive a world of potential ghosts and monsters."[87] Just as Lundberg argues that metaphor and metonymy should be distinguished by degrees of affective charge rather than formal differences, catachresis is distinct from metaphor primarily in the way it effects subjects. Metonymy links things together through proximity and consubstantiality. Metaphor links them together through abstract principle. Catachresis dwells on the uncanny aspects of language to decenter subjects by gesturing toward the limits of mediation. It is the trope most appropriate to an understanding of language as the *fort-da* game because it responds to the anxiety of the proximate Real by preserving some distance while still letting a sense of excess bleed through our speech, playing a game with presence and absence while obscuring the larger set of Symbolic relationships in which our identities emerge.

Swords and Plowshares

I have argued that the sublime aspects of discourse about the Bomb located it in a position akin to God. From the first moments of silence at Trinity, the Bomb signaled something beyond the limits of language. A key feature of the sublime as a mediated discourse of the Real is the ambiguity of this excess: sublime language both terrifies and fascinates. We should expect that the Bomb would do both. As it took on the connotations of God through this explicit language, one would expect other godlike associations—salvation, omnipotence, paradise—to remain in the unconscious too, simply repressed by the oversaturated link between atomic destruction and God's vengeful aspects. The Bomb would not just herald the end of the world as Kistiakowsky and Farrell reported, but also activate these other connections. To demonstrate how this was so, this section will examine Project Plowshare, a Cold War scheme to use the power of the atom to literally remake the surface of the Earth for human satisfaction.

Nuclear energy had a powerful effect on military thinking, starting with fantasies of total destruction and leading eventually to more refined, if equally grandiose, ideas of rationality and control treated in chapter 2. Nuclear strategy in the 1940s and early 1950s did not go far beyond what LeMay termed the "Sunday punch," an unrestrained and potentially world-ending nuclear conflagration. A huge array of weapons was created in the first decades of the Cold War, from impractically enormous Soviet Tsar Bomba to the impractically small "nuclear bazooka" called the Davy Crockett.[88] Atomic power seemed capable of fulfilling every wish. In one proposed scheme called Project A119, the United States would detonate a nuclear explosive on the moon, ostensibly for scientific purposes.[89] Another plan reported by *Popular Science* would have had US troops equipped with "Atomic Six-Shooters" police the Cold War frontier using firearms loaded with californium bullets.[90] These plans for destruction were coupled with fantasies for world redemption—not just the peaceful use of nuclear energy in electricity generation or propulsion, but the potential of nuclear explosions to be used for civilian purposes as well.

Project Plowshare was the peak of these salvific fever dreams. Plowshare was the brainchild of Trinity scientist Edward Teller, hardline anti-Communist and inventor of the hydrogen bomb. The program was intended to prove the feasibility of nuclear earthmoving, using hydrogen bombs to "change the earth's surface to suit us," in Teller's words.[91] The possibilities of "peaceful nuclear explosions" were first discussed following the Suez Crisis in 1956, when engineers contemplated excavating a second Suez Canal through Israeli territory. Later, schemes for another Panama Canal received congressional funding.[92] Serious efforts were made to study the feasibility of creating a new deepwater port in Alaska, and a few nuclear tests were done in the Southwest. Teller co-authored a textbook about the opportunities for PNEs that ranged from space exploration, reservoir construction, and highway clearing to oil and natural gas development, meteorological studies, chemical production and mining.[93]

Plowshare was justified as a project for the creation and accumulation of mineral and commercial wealth, a way to unlock the earth's resources and facilitate global trade to overcome scarcity. The program's name itself is presumably drawn from Isaiah 2:4, which in the King James Bible reads, "And he shall judge among the nations, and shall rebuke many people: and they shall beat their swords into plowshares, and their spears into pruninghooks: nation shall not lift up sword against nation, neither shall they learn war any more." One chairman of the Atomic Energy Commission argued that God himself willed that humanity unlock the peaceful potential of the atom, and in fact our destruction was impossible due to divine providence.[94] Teller's own promise to "change the earth's surface to suit us" evokes a similar power which again allows the Bomb to work in geological timescales rather than human ones to change the Earth forever. Even Nobel Prize winner Willard Libby embraced this vision, hoping to "move mountains," and guarantee prosperity for all humankind.[95] All of these statements fit well with the concept of a world in excess of humanity and forces beyond our control. Plowshare marked a turning point after Trinity in which the awesome power of the Bomb could be dreamt of as a force amenable to human manipulation.

Although these promises appear to have been earnestly believed by at least some Plowshare supporters, the program was also a cover for "clean" weapons development.[96] Plowshare was supposed to allow nuclear testing as an exception to test ban treaties, and with it the development of low-fallout bombs for use against the Soviet Union. "Cleaner" bombs reduce the barriers to nuclear use and allow territory to be safely occupied with greater speed.[97] "Peaceful" and destructive nuclear explosions share a common theme. Both permit human beings to do things to each other and the Earth that were reserved for God in older worldviews. The range of nuclear dreams and nightmares are compatible with one another because these fantasies all derive from an initial encounter with the Real. The sublime language surrounding nuclear weapons has an almost apolitical ring to it—in Ned O'Gorman's words, "Nothing inheres in the sublime that is political, as the sublime can only breathe power and force, not words, bodies, or beings, let alone the judgements, actions, and associations necessary to politics."[98] The practical utility of the Bomb is almost an afterthought; there is space enough for all fantasies to coexist. Even the program's title contains a hint, for the Bible contains another reference to plowshares in addition to Isaiah, this one in Joel 3:10: "Beat your plowshares into swords and your pruninghooks into spears: let the weak say, I am strong."

Although the Soviets balked at Project Plowshare and fallout concerns undermined it, the idea of "civilian" nuclear explosions did not stop. The USSR itself eventually blasted out Lake Chagan with a nuclear bomb. Schemes to use the Bomb for good persist in the twenty-first century. When the Deepwater Horizon oil spill in the Gulf of Mexico caught world attention in 2010, Russian newspaper *Komsomolskaya Pravda* suggested that a nuclear detonation could solve the problem as it apparently had several times in the Soviet Union.[99] The National Oceanic and Atmospheric Administration's Hurricane Research Division felt compelled to explain why nuclear detonations are not simple solutions to hurricane formation—apparently a frequently asked question.[100] The National Aeronautics and Space Administration has been surprisingly sanguine about the Bomb as a means of saving humanity from asteroids. NASA found that it would be the "most effective alternative" to deal with a "threatening object" in the "likely range of threats over million-year timescales."[101] A messianic discourse of "infinite energy" surrounds fusion power and was sometimes used by the National Ignition Facility, even though that program too (and inertial confinement fusion more generally) is probably a cover for weapons development.[102]

If the Bomb induces horror and a sense of meaninglessness, how does one account for Plowshare and other utopian visions of nuclear power? At first, these things may seem inconsistent. The Plowshare dream is essentially an embrace of artifice in the grandest way—human designs would reshape nature itself to bring it into conformity with the demands of the social. The "world-without-us" would be transformed into a "world-for-us," that even long after our extinction (made far less likely by these changes, so the proponents claim) would continue operating according to the codes we had put in place. This is accumulation for the propagation of the social order, but it is done with a weapon that heralds death, decay, poison, even human extinction. In this light, the seeming contradictions of Teller and Plowshare dissolve: the H-Bomb and Plowshare are linked by the taboo uniting continuity and discontinuity and the transgressive Bomb that allows passage between the two. The Treaty on the Non-Proliferation of Nuclear Weapons (NPT), the primary legal embodiment of the taboo against nuclear weapon use, asserted an "inalienable right" to peaceful nuclear explosives, even outlawing price gouging on future projects.[103] Nuclear states could thus enjoy the numinous power of the Bomb free of guilt, justifying it as an accumulative technology rather than a disintegrating weapon. Nuclear weapons tests following Trinity and Plowshare tests following Gnome were officially conducted for different purposes, but in both cases, they allowed the illusion of control over the vast destructive forces that we still struggle to fit into language. As such, they commanded both terror and fascination, giving rise to a discourse closer to Otto's thoughts on God than the hard scientific language associated with many other technologies. Plowshare fits into the broader discourse of the Bomb after the trauma of the first nuclear explosions because the Bomb as a signifier stands first and foremost for inhuman power. The valence of it is less important than its location in the structural place of God.

Contingency

This chapter demonstrates that the discourse surrounding nuclear weapons testing, including Trinity and Plowshare, calls for an expanded understanding of the sublime. Rhetoric has traditionally attended to artifice in various forms, such as persuasion, collective action, and identity formation. The revelation of the Real decenters the subject by revealing the artifice of our reality and the inability of its order-scripting functions to overcome completely the contingency of the world-without-us. We live day-to-day in a reality that we have constructed for ourselves in concert with others, passed between us by various forms of mediation. Trinity suggests that our account will be incomplete without an engagement with the excesses that seem to escape mediation. Most of the time, reality "works" so efficiently that we do not have to be aware of it. We can treat artifice as nature and misrecognize the Symbolic as the Real. Events like Trinity burst the seams of this reality and force us to confront the fact that it is ultimately artificial. This can inspire a sense of vertigo, even terror, as we are suddenly confronted with the presence of a world that exceeds our ability to capture it entirely and translate it amongst ourselves in language. Language does not just fail. Silence intrudes as an affirmative force. Our concerns seem small indeed when compared to the unimaginable vastness and energy of the cosmos as revealed in the Bomb, but just as Otto sought the words to describe an unfathomable God, we seek out ways to safeguard the fragile ship of language when the sea starts rushing in.

For all the overwhelming terror of the Real, it would be a mistake to underestimate the resilience of language. Confronting the Real certainly produces a crop of true nihilists, but for the most part, words help to smooth over the cracks. Symbolic communication works because we agree that certain signifiers are linked to certain signifieds and not others. The network of metaphor and metonymy keeps the whole scheme running. In fact, it sometimes works too well—language has something of the Golem in it, an artificial thing that comes to act on its own. Some tropes serve as more powerful links in this network than others, and the sense of the Real in language helps to explain why. This is the uncanny aspect of language that allows specific tropes to serve as sites of cathexis. Some things seem more portentous, more significant, than others, and even the words we use for them exercise a certain influence due to our investments. The Bomb is a powerful locus because it stands in for something beyond language, even beyond our ability to imagine. This sense cannot be imparted directly, because by its nature, it is in excess of our ability to mediate, but language can act as currency until it reaches that final limit where it is exposed as inadequate.[104] The sublime character of language is its uncanny capacity to be misrecognized as the Real. The Bomb as a symbol, sometimes with its own agency ascribed to it, makes the Real palatable by integrating it into language. In a sense, the Real is nothing but contingency, and the Bomb symbol imposes some order.

The contingency of the Real is an important intersection for rhetoric and psychoanalysis. Lacanian psychoanalysis has been criticized by those who argue that it reasserts an unjustifiable division between representation and reality, ultimately rigging the game by positing a deep structure inaccessible to us that determines social organization, whether it be the Real or the unconscious. To posit such a thing also insulates one from criticism since the Real cannot be discussed directly, what Andrew Robinson calls (after Judith Butler) a "theological" project.[105] Robinson is in line with Derrida's critiques of psychoanalysis in *Archive Fever*: the critic always finds what they are looking for because the whole system is designed to produce such a result.[106]

Robinson's argument should caution us against a reading of the Real as the "deep structure" of reality that determines it in its entirety. This is where sublime rhetoric can be an important remedy. Rhetoric's traditional concern with contingency extends to this understanding of the Real. If the Real is the contingent eruption of nonhuman reality into a Symbolic order, then it is not deep structure with a set of laws that determine society—or, if indeed it does have a set of laws, they cannot be determined by us. The Real is what is inaccessible. It does impact our world, but it does so through distortion and disruption, not determination. The interplay of the Symbolic and the Real is essentially one of structure versus contingency. The ceaseless work of *automaton* scripting order over *tuché*, mentioned in the introduction and explained further in the next chapter, creates a set of rules that might provide predictable order, but they only appear to be inevitable and natural. Rhetoric is the study of this interplay of contingency and structure, and although we might seek to describe the influence of the Real on language, it is the latter which remains our object of study. Psychoanalysis in this rhetorical mode is not an effort to interpret hidden truths that are accessible only to an initiate class elevated above the hoi polloi. It is an effort to understand how the contingencies that escape us *all* leave their impressions in language. As Lacan wrote, "To be a psychoanalyst is simply to open your eyes to the evident fact that nothing malfunctions more than human reality . . . nothing is more stupid than human destiny, that is, that one is always being fooled. Even when one does do something successfully, it is precisely not what one wanted to do."[107]

The desire to experience the Real is therefore bound to be frustrated. The final advent of the Bomb always seems imminent but is never realized, so obliteration is endlessly deferred.[108] The desire for the Real described in this chapter is thus a source of inevitable failure and frustration. But it is only one part of the death drive. We are dislocated and decentered by the Bomb, but we do not accept our being as dust and ashes. Unable to commune with something that is defined only in opposition to our powers of comprehension, we enjoy the fantasy of control instead. We can imagine various things that stand in for the Real, both fascinating and horrifying, and also imagine that we control their presence and absence. This is the dynamic of Freud's *fort-da* game, and its medium is language. In the context of nuclear war, it manifests itself in the compulsion to repetitively simulate nuclear destruction. Atmospheric nuclear testing ended for the US in 1963. Ultimately only a relatively small number of people witnessed nuclear explosions anywhere in the world, so awareness and imagination of the Bomb's overwhelming presence could only spread through other media. War games as rituals helped to sustain a nuclear priesthood in its (necessarily incomplete) access to the revealed truth of the Bomb after the original "desert fathers" left the scene.[109] The Bomb, first perceived as a wild force beyond human ken, was transformed into a target for endlessly complex techno-theological debates as the tools of rationality were brought to bear on its mysteries. Simulations, video games, and ostensibly anti-war representations, would democratize access to the Bomb's numinous power, this time with the veneer of rational control. The explicitly unpredictable was slowly managed into something else: risk.

2

Da

War Games

> [W]ar and business are conflicts resembling games, and as such, they may be formalized as to constitute games with definite rules. Indeed, I have no reason to suppose that such formalized versions of them are not already being established as models to determine the policies for pressing the Great Push Button and burning the earth clean for a new and less humanly undependable order of things. —Norbert Wiener, *God & Golem, Inc.*

> I'd be the last one to use the nuclear weapons, because that's sort of like the end of the ball game. —Donald Trump

Ipsos Custodes

In his "Seminar on the 'The Purloined Letter,'" Jacques Lacan wrote that "it is the symbolic order which is constitutive for the subject," and that the subject receives "major determination" from "the itinerary of a signifier."[1] One is "possessed" by the signifier, a thrall to its agency: "the signifier's displacement determines subjects' acts, destiny, refusals, blindnesses, success, and fate . . . everything pertaining to the psychological pregiven follows willy-nilly the signifier's train, like weapons and baggage."[2] Human agency does not operate without restriction, but constitutes a negotiation of rules that prescribe and channel our behaviors, even if they do not fully determine them. In the itinerary of an individual life, one can see the influence of accreted structures that give it form and the interplay between the structure of the Symbolic which creates the conditions for action and the contingency of individual choices and behaviors.

The little-known case of Vice Admiral Tim Giardina is an excellent example. Giardina was the former deputy head of the United States Strategic Command (STRATCOM) at Offutt Air Force Base in Nebraska, the primary command responsible for US strategic nuclear weapons (and the successor to the Strategic Air Command parodied in *Dr. Strangelove*). In June 2013, Giardina was caught using counterfeit poker chips at a local casino. It was revealed in the ensuing investigation that Giardina had spent almost 1,100 hours gambling in an eighteen-month period. He was such a common sight that other casino regulars remembered him as "Navy Tim," and recalled comments he had made about the polygraph requirements for US nuclear forces (he was quoted as saying that the purpose is really to find out if one is "having sex with animals or something really crazy"). Giardina was banned from several casinos but continued to play even after being caught with counterfeit chips.[3] Following an investigation by the Naval Criminal Investigative Service, he was removed from his post, demoted to Rear Admiral, and reassigned to Washington.[4]

It is not illegal for Navy officers to gamble. Giardina's poker games did not seem to have any effect on his official duties. His problems arose when he sought to lie about the forgery and was caught through surveillance footage and DNA evidence. Criminal behavior is of course not unheard of in the American military, even among officers, but Giardina's case is interesting for its structural parallels to his official duties at STRATCOM. His actions were not out of line with the ethos of the Strategic Command, but might be read as an eruption of the disavowed foundation of US nuclear weapons policy, a kind of return of the repressed. Giardina enjoyed gambling on poker, but in forging fake chips, he seemed to enjoy gambling on gambling: his was a kind of "meta-gambling," taking risks on the rules that regulate risks. In doing so, Giardina exposed what Slavoj Žižek calls the "obscene supplement" of nuclear strategy. Ideological fantasies are maintained by disavowing their central, obscene foundation, a gesture necessary to the function of the fantasy but impossible to acknowledge, for the lack of distance would collapse the whole edifice.[5] Around the time of Giardina's dismissal, Admiral Cecil Haney, commander of STRATCOM, said that the core mission of the organization remains to deter attack on the United States. This means minimizing pervasive uncertainty and risk. In Admiral Haney's words, "America's nuclear deterrent force provides enduring value to the nation. It has been a constant thread in the geopolitical fabric of an uncertain world, providing a moderating influence on generations of world leaders."[6] More directly, it is necessary to identify "where we are taking risk and where we cannot accept further risk."[7] "Risk" and "uncertainty" appear constantly in Haney's statement, which is focused on developing "contingency plans" to control the consequences of unforeseen events.

The Real, as explained in the previous chapter, can be understood as the eruption of contingency into the order of the Symbolic. It is the failure of prediction and routine, in the most mundane—or the most catastrophic—ways. At Trinity, the Real of the Bomb was followed by efforts to repair the Symbolic order and to make novel events fit into the script of language. Lacan describes this dynamic of contingency and order as the interplay of *tuché* and *automaton*:

> Where do we meet this real? For what we have in the discovery of psychoanalysis is an encounter, an essential encounter—and appointment to which we are always called with a real that eludes us . . .
>
> First, the *tuché*, which we have borrowed . . . from Aristotle, who uses it in his search for cause. We have translated it as *the encounter with the real*. The real is beyond the *automaton*, the return, the coming-back, the insistence of the signs, by which we see ourselves governed by the pleasure principle. The real is that which always lies behind the automaton. . . . [I]t is this that is the object of [Sigmund Freud's] concern.[8]

This is the central element of the repetition compulsion. Driven to make our encounter with the Real, we are perpetually disappointed, but the Symbolic world of reality abhors a vacuum. *Automaton* describes the endless attempts to reach the Real, which are doomed to failure but cannot be surrendered, so are repeated again and again. These repetitive behaviors thus develop an aspect of order, and are, paradoxically, orderly attempts to reach the chaos of contingency. They are also linked by Lacan to gambling, death, and signification.[9]

Nuclear deterrence can be read in this frame as an attempt to secure the world against the contingency of the Real of nuclear war, something that can be planned, debated, and modeled, but not encountered beforehand in its empirical reality. Deterrence is the STRATCOM *automaton*'s answer to the chaos of the Bomb's *tuché*. Chance can never be totally eradicated, however, nor can every eventuality be predicted beforehand. In a history of nuclear defense intellectuals, Fred Kaplan described them in the 1980s at the height of their power having come with the mission "to impose order," but lacking any means to control the wild abandon of the Bomb in a hypothetical war for which there was no precedent, "in the end, chaos still prevailed."[10] Nuclear planners desire contact with the Real in particular ways. The awestruck witnesses of nuclear tests sometimes claimed that they saw unique events that had to be experienced to be understood. Some, as the last chapter argued, desired such experiences. Nuclear planners, on the other hand, sought contact with the Real as a means of mastery to control contingency and read it back into order. Nuclear war as an abstract possibility still served as a site of enjoyment. While they may not desire war, they are nonetheless drawn to the uncanny imagination of it, always failing to grasp it entirely, but compelled to repeat the effort to encounter it somehow.

Desire is the motive force, and the fact that what we desire cannot be attained is what requires repetition. In our everyday lives, the object of desire is something that stands in for the lack created by the entry into language. Attaining one thing may provide pleasure, but it doesn't extinguish the existential conditions of desire. In the context of nuclear planning, what is desired is the Real of nuclear war, which is by definition impossible to attain. Planners can never fully access the chaos of war, but they repeatedly attempt to do that through language and imagination, the only tools available to them. When the chaos of *tuché* continues to emerge despite these attempts to render the world predictable, *automaton* does not surrender. Repetition becomes an end in itself and a fixture for enjoyment. In repeatedly simulating nuclear war, defense intellectuals who could not experience the Real of nuclear violence could enjoy the illusion of mastery over the terror and fascination inspired by the Real by appearing to simulate the conditions of presence and absence—in this case, the presence of the world-for-us and its absence in the Bomb's inferno.

Langdon Winner distinguishes between *risk* (a term prevalent in both nuclear war and poker) and *threat* or *hazard* on these grounds: risk always has an implied benefit to it, an element of desire and an opportunity for control.[11] There is little empirical basis for nuclear war simulations and the calculations of probability they rely on—as Derrida cogently observed, there has never been a full-scale nuclear war—so war plans always require a good deal of faith, and thus to adopt them is a *risk*—a calculation of both hazard and reward.[12] Available evidence suggests that their parameters are set somewhat arbitrarily by the personnel who design them. In other words, they are games of chance in which we also manipulate the rules. This is the obscene supplement of nuclear deterrence that Giardina could not be allowed to reveal: we don't just repeat nuclear simulations again and again because we think that they will someday be perfect. War planners must acknowledge that the mere existence of nuclear weapons makes some risk of nuclear war inevitable. War games are sites of investment, and we don't always care about the rules. Poker, after all, was rumored to be the genesis of game theory at the RAND Corporation, prominent modelers of nuclear war, and was a favorite pastime of the defense intellectuals who sought to tame the world with human reason.[13]

This chapter explores continuing efforts to simulate nuclear war, starting from the perspective of Lacan's *tuché/automaton* and Freud's *fort-da*. Chapter 1 detailed the disruptive advent of nuclear force as an element of the Real, followed by early attempts to incorporate it into the Symbolic through religious frames. Simulations extend this work by further normalizing the Bomb, creating a narrative of management in place of excess and awe. As the Cold War continued, the narrative of the Bomb as godlike subject was gradually supplemented with discourses stressing predictability and control. Desire for the missed encounter with the Real of the Bomb is gradually channeled into the simulations themselves, permitting subjects to enjoy the sense of mastery, always supplemented by risk. Supposedly rational imaginations of future scenarios retained an element of the uncanny, but the shift to new kinds of enjoyment created its own enduring cultural legacy. I begin with an exploration of war games as sites of cathexis, tracing a thread from RAND Corporation military simulations through contemporary consumer games. John von Neumann's game theory and Kenneth Arrow's resulting rational choice theory, both elaborated at RAND, attempted to quantify human conduct to explain the world. Video games like *First Strike* (first released in 2014) demonstrate the persistence of enjoyment even among those who ostensibly resist the nuclear status quo. The second part of this chapter will deal with a problem that arises from attempts to make decisions based on nuclear war predictions. Because the Bomb as a herald of the Real occupies a place beyond rational calculation, the mathematical language of nuclear war attempts to calculate the incalculable. The result is a theological impasse that provides argumentative resources equally to activists and their enemies, suggesting that the "rational" discourse of nuclear war has not altogether banished its irrational underpinnings.

War Games

Herman Kahn and Bernard Brodie, perhaps the most prominent American strategists of the early Cold War, tried to make nuclear war "thinkable" in the sense that they tried to explain how such a war might start and what options would exist for national leaders. At the same time, both acknowledged that the outcome of a full-scale nuclear war was indescribable. In Brodie's words, to "make an intellectual prediction of the likelihood of war is one thing, to project oneself imaginatively and seriously into an expected war situation is quite another."[14] The unwillingness or inability to think "seriously" about a nuclear war—in other words, to understand it instrumentally rather than through dislocating language of the sublime—was met by organizations like the RAND Corporation with an attempt to systematize nuclear strategy and develop the intellectual and technical means to actually fight and control a nuclear war. Among the Strategic Air Command's earliest plans for nuclear war was the "Sunday punch," an all-out nuclear attack on the USSR, Eastern Europe, and the People's Republic of China eventually enshrined in SIOP-62 (Single Integrated Operational Plan, 1962). It might have killed 285 million people in the initial attack.[15] Despite its intricate planning and detailed execution strategies, SIOP was immensely inflexible, essentially just a codification of massive nuclear attack with a detailed list of targets. Asked whether the US had any options to attack the Soviet Union without striking China, which might not even be a combatant in the war, General Thomas Power replied, "Well yeh [*sic*], we *could* do that, but I hope nobody thinks of it because it would really screw up the plan."[16]

Starting in the 1960s, a set of war games of various complexity was developed to test a broader range of nuclear theories and attack options at RAND and elsewhere.[17] Games like them continue to be used for strategic military planning today.[18] Most of these games—or at least their results—are classified, as they became the basis for US nuclear plans. In politico-military games, military officers, civilians, and generally mid- to low-ranking government officials would play various roles as US and/or foreign decision makers. Another group, "control," would feed them information about the actions of countries or groups not played by the participants or about world events that might influence the context of their actions. In more limited military simulations, extant or proposed war plans would be evaluated by computer or human players to identify possible flaws and improvements.

The games themselves never had a guarantee of accuracy and were sometimes quite obviously flawed. In one Navy game, American aircraft carriers were declared to be unsinkable. In others, the Soviet Union was assumed to have no effective airpower. Because factors like air pressure, prevailing winds, defense effectiveness, early warning, and missile failure rate were largely random or incalculable, a fudge factor simply declared estimated success. Even their designers sometimes admitted that the games were inaccurate, unprovable, or simply wishful thinking.[19] Especially in the case of nuclear war, these games cannot possibly be understood as accurate simulations of a real-world system, because there is no empirical data on the compound effects of many near-simultaneous nuclear explosions and no data on what factors cause states to cross the nuclear threshold against other similarly armed states, a fact that bedevils nuclear planning in general (and always has).[20] By the admission of many of those who create and play them, they are "social science fiction" with no tangible effect other than that they are entertaining.[21]

Others have suggested that warfare is a stochastic system that we could never identify laws for, no matter how diligent we might be, because its initial conditions are simply too complex to model and they do not conform to linear causality.[22] Indeed, military planners tended to be far less willing to predict the conduct and outcome of a conventional war—despite an enormous data set spanning thousands of years—than a nuclear war fought between two superpowers, an event that has never occurred in recorded history. Fred Iklé, a former RAND strategist who was at times head of the Arms Control and Disarmament Agency and Undersecretary of Defense for Policy, criticized these semi-mathematical abstractions in harsh terms that deserve to be quoted at length:

> The prominence of the calculations continues because we know how to make them. . . . [W]e have tailored the problem to our capability to calculate. The seemingly rigorous models of nuclear deterrence are built on the rule: "What cannot be calculated, leave out." . . . Such thoughts, especially those focusing on deterrence, lack real empirical referents or bases. No other field

> of human endeavor demands—absolutely compels—one to work out successful solutions without obtaining directly relevant experience, without experimenting. There can be no trial and error here, no real learning.
>
> Curiously, we are far more skeptical in accepting the calculations of traditional conventional military campaigns than the calculations of nuclear warfare. In fact, the more battle experience and information military analysts have, the more modest they become in predicting the course of conventional war. Such modesty is missing for nuclear war, where pretentious analyses and simplistic abstractions dominate and blot out the discrepancies existing between abstractions and possible reality—a reality that for so many reasons is hard even to imagine.[23]

Iklé is drawing attention to two unique aspects of nuclear war planning: first, that no empirical data (or at least very little) can be gathered for the species of war that planners concerned themselves with, and second, that unlike other military problems where little data exists, defense intellectuals were willing to display great confidence in untested (and untestable) theories. Despite this lack of empirical grounding, nuclear war simulations were repeated again and again over the decades while nuclear doctrine remained fundamentally the same.[24]

There has been some dispute in military circles about whether these exercises should be called simulations or games, with "simulations" becoming more popular by the 1980s.[25] To call politico-military exercises "roleplaying games" conjures images of adolescents rolling dice and weaving fantasies about orcs and dragons. To call battle simulations "war games" might associate them with video games produced for entertainment. Still, even military officers responsible for the creation of these artifacts had trouble distinguishing between *game, model,* and *simulation* and used them interchangeably. In his comprehensive history of US war gaming, Thomas Allen writes that the three words "hover over imaginary battlefields like a *mysterious, ever-shifting concept of the Trinity*."[26] Edward Berger, Harvey Boulay, and Betty Zisk, writing in the journal *Simulation & Gaming*, acknowledge that "[d]efinitions of simulation are legion," but center on representations of a system that allow users to model behavior.[27] Garry Brewer Martin and Shubik define games as a subset of simulation and simulation as a subset of modeling, the key defining feature of a game being the inclusion of human beings playing roles. Still, their extended attempt to define these terms results in the acronym MSG, grouping them all together.[28]

The difficulty in Brewer and Shubik's definition is that *all* models and simulations require that human beings make decisions at least indirectly, at a minimum defining the variables and parameters of the exercise. As a result, they all create some possibility for investment in the outcome. In common usage, the difference between simulations and models on the one hand and games on the other appears to be a ludic dimension. Games are for play, with an agent making decisions within a set of prescribed rules to change the outcome, while simulations and models may simply represent the rules of a system. Still, in all cases, a set of rules is deliberately created to make some process possible with the goal of producing certain variable outcomes within constraints. Calling such an endeavor "gaming" makes its ludic dimension obvious; calling it by another name provides a veneer of objectivity, but in both cases, games are channels fundamentally rhetorical paths of desire.

The least common denominator between games, simulations, and models is that one artificial rules-bound system—the game—stands in for another—for some aspect of the world. These processes therefore have a metaphorical quality to them.[29] Games persuade players that a particular outcome may occur, but their very design must first convince prospective users that the simulation does stand in for the world. In his work on video games, Ian Bogost identifies what he calls procedural rhetoric as "the practice of persuading through processes in general and computational processes in particular . . . a technique for making arguments with computational systems and for unpacking computational arguments others have created."[30] Whereas oral rhetoric attempts to persuade an audience to adopt a particular viewpoint through speech and written rhetoric does the same through writing, procedural rhetoric has its own unique goals and characteristics suited to the medium of games. Video games create a digital process that simulates a real-world process, allowing the player to model something extant in the world of flesh, blood, steel, and glass that exists outside of the game. Procedural rhetoric refers to this persuasive aspect of simulation. Bogost's argument might be adapted to the metaphorical aspects of games as well. The replacement of the tenor (the thing represented) with the vehicle (the signifier standing in for it) makes an enthymematic argument that draws the audience to do the work of cathexis in connecting the two based on the shared principle that allows the substitution.

This does not suggest that we read games as texts. Games require their players to invest in a specific way because they are called on to make choices that alter the outcome. Players identify with their characters: what is shared is not just a set of traits, but decisions over time that, to maintain the interest that keeps players playing, require at least some minimal attachment. Most written texts do not follow this mold. One can identify deeply with Sauron, but no reading of *Lord of the Rings* can make him finally subjugate his haughty human and elven foes, let alone order the Scourging of the Shire and its bourgeois hobbits when he still has a chance to succeed.[31] This is the key element of Bogost's theory: it is the procedure that links the system with its representation in the game, and the sense of control that binds us, something that differentiates this medium from others. One doesn't have to decide that play matters and narrative doesn't—

it is the interaction between the two that channels the player's investment in a game. Games are particularly powerful media because they foster a sense of control. The outcome is dependent on the player's actions, is a key feature that distinguishes games (and, in principle, other simulations) from traditional linear texts in which the reader's more limited choice minimizes exposure to "risk."[32] This is a challenge for work that understands gaming simply as a metaphor where one term replaces and conceals another, as Barry Brummett argues, without acknowledging that gaming is both a linguistic choice and a material *practice* of substitution and connection.[33]

In war games, attachments are formed even when a computerized Sam fights a computerized Ivan to test the SIOP and RSIOP.[34] Allen's book is full of examples of war game players becoming emotionally tied to their games, sometimes in perverse ways. Failing in a game that he was allowed to play, Allen himself described his team reacting with "shock, *real* shock, not just a reaction to a bad break in a game. We were really feeling upset about what was happening in our imaginary world. 'What is happening to our institutions?' someone indignantly asked, as if real institutions were really going through what the situation paper had described. I had an unreasonable feeling of helplessness and failure. Some of us spoke softly to each other about having failed."[35] The prevalence of this reaction is confirmed in more recent scholarship by Paul Bracken, himself a war game participant. Bracken puts the case simply: "People get emotionally involved in games."[36]

This identification with the social image—the character, nation, or faction one directs in a game—describes a process in Lacan's Imaginary register. Recall that in his famous essay on the mirror stage, Lacan argued that one comes to identify with an image and adopt it as the self so that the subject is not a product of discovering the "real you" but identifying with an signifier capable of commerce in the economy of the Symbolic. Lacan writes that the "core principle" of the "general theory of the symbol" is a twofold movement in the subject. One makes one's action into an object, but only to return it to its foundational place. More simply, one acts *as* an identity, then associates other elements of that identity with the self. He gives the example of a worker forming his identity: "in phase one, a man who works at the level of production in our society considers himself to belong to the ranks of the proletariat; in phase two, in the name of belonging to it, he joins in a general strike."[37] This same dynamic is evident in war games. One player, made to represent the Soviet Union, did more than just adopt its strategy. He found himself wanting to punish his subordinates, to treat them cruelly as he imagined the Soviets would. Another player adopted the Red perspective so thoroughly that an Army general demanded to have his security clearances checked.[38] A terrorism expert played a game as the terrorists he studied and decided at one point to kill hostages. "I thought I wouldn't be able to identify with terrorists. But after two hours I think that I was one of the hard-liners on our team, and I must confess that I really enjoyed killing those two people."[39]

War game players often enjoyed their roles in starting nuclear war. While military players were famously reticent about escalating to the nuclear level, civilian weapons scientists were notoriously bloodthirsty. Steve Pieczenik, a crisis management specialist in the State Department, said that in Pentagon games it is "usually the wishy-washy liberal or the political appointee who comes in and feels very desperate and resorts to force. The ones who do frighten me are the scientists. God almighty! Those nuclear boys, you know, the ones from the labs. They're *deadly*. They love to think in megatons."[40] The so-called "nuclear boys" would be the generation after Trinity, the one that still wanted to "feel the heat." The perverse enjoyment of destruction was no secret, although Bracken claimed that a game called Proud Prophet (!) so frightened President Ronald Reagan that he no longer contemplated war with the Soviet Union.[41]

Just as metaphors are made meaningful by the repeated investments that tie signifier to signified, war games are made meaningful by the investments that tie them to nuclear war. The simulations are enjoyable because of their link to the power of the Bomb. Lacan explains the enjoyment of subjectivity in the Symbolic by analogizing it to the Freudian *fort-da* game mentioned in the introduction. Freud's grandson had a wooden reel attached to a string that he would throw over his curtained cot, making it "gone" (*fort*). Then he would pull the spool back into view, rejoicing that it was "there" (*da*). He would repeat these actions again and again. The game can be read as the child inuring himself against the potential absence of his mother, but a more productive reading would locate enjoyment not in the conditions of "gone" or "here" but in the exercise of control over the conditions of presence and absence, essentially a simulation that permits agency over a situation in which the child must be passive.[42]

Norbert Wiener speculated that games would be used to "determine the policies for pressing the Great Push Button and burning the earth clean for a new and less humanly undependable order of things."[43] Noting that there is not enough experience to establish criteria for nuclear war games, Wiener emphasized the importance of accuracy: "The chief criterion as to whether a line of human effort can be embodied in a game is whether there is some objectively recognizable criterion of the merit of the performance of this effort. Otherwise the game assumes the formlessness of the croquet game in *Alice in Wonderland*, where . . . the Queen of Hearts . . . kept changing the rules and sending the players to the Headsman to be beheaded. Under these circumstances, to win has no meaning, and a successful policy cannot be learned, because there is no criterion of success."[44]

This argument may well be correct, but it misses the most important trait that sustains nuclear war games: they are enjoyable even when they aren't accurate. They serve as a site for cathectic attachment and solidify the subject's sense of itself. Nuclear deterrence resembles gambling, just like the poker games favored by Giardina. In the exchange for one set of risks for another, nothing is produced—counters are merely moved around, made meaningful by their assigned values, but ultimately traded and expended by the players with no real increase in value during the process, a useless exchange that serves the subject's enjoyment by creating a space for play separate from work and art.[45] Fudging the numbers in a nuclear simulation, just like forging fake poker chips, is a kind of cheating, but not a threat to the game itself—breaking the rules maintains a certain fidelity to them, recognizing them as existing constraints to be manipulated, and reinforcing the logic of the game even if the cheater is dishonorable. The "cheat" only sustains the game. The only threat comes from one willing to say that the game is arbitrary and therefore completely worthless, to "break the spell."[46] That critics of war games continued to play them demonstrates that some element of games other than their outcomes can moor attachments. Nuclear war simulations are particularly strong examples of imaginary attachment because the point isn't just to test how some strategy conforms to the "rules" of nuclear war, but to figure out the rules themselves since no such war has yet been fought.

More important than the games themselves therefore is their role in organizing the subject vis-à-vis the "reality" of the Symbolic order. Christian Lundberg describes this relationship as one of "useless subjectivity":

> Enjoyment is useless in a very specific sense: although the effect of the habitual capture of affect in the form of enjoyment purchases a sense of unity for the subject, enjoyment is useless in regard to the specific site of its exercise. When a subject enjoys a relationship to an object, or a specific habituated practice, it is tempting to read the subject's investment in the object or practice as a validation of the fact that the subject values the thing in and of itself. But, if Lacan's account of enjoyment is correct, enjoyment in an object or practice is less about the dignity of the thing invested in than the ways that the object or practice serves the subject in negotiating a relationship to the general economy of exchange. Thus, the exercise of enjoyment is often somewhat counterfactual: the subject invests in objects or practices for the sake of something that is beyond the object or practice and for the sake of accommodating to failed unicity.[47]

The subject, permanently frustrated by the condition of the lack, enjoys its own *capacity to enjoy* rather than reaching fulfillment through any particular object. Thus the death drive works in two stages in response to the eruption of the Real. First, there is a desire to experience the Real itself, manifested through uncanny signifiers that the subject understands as touchpoints for uncanny, excessive power, like images of nuclear tests. Next, because the fundamental alienation of language prevents access to the Real even through these symbols, subjects instead come to enjoy the only thing to which they have direct access, which is serial repetition itself—the capacity to enjoy.

In the context of nuclear war games, players could enjoy not just the sense of control, but also what Lundberg calls "habituated practices" which in the context of nuclear war resemble religious rituals. Thus computerized nuclear models "take on quasi-religious overtones. Offerings are put into the black box by acolytes who are never sure what is going to come out; those who come to worship are often not sure what has happened either. . . . With large simulations, unfortunately, unlike large cathedrals . . . the whole structure may collapse or become meaningless without anyone's realizing it."[48] In some sense, the outcome hardly matters. Nuclear war simulations create a hypertrophied sense of control over presence and absence: the simulated stakes are usually the presence and absence of human civilization and perhaps all life on Earth, and risk makes games exciting.

The high stakes of planetary destruction magnify the gratification that comes from fantasies of control, as Lacan noted,

> [Scientists] have begun to get the idea that they could create bacteria that would be resistant to everything, that would be unstoppable. That would clear the surface of the globe of all the shitty things, human in particular, that inhabit it. And then they suddenly felt overcome with pangs of responsibility. . . . What a sublime relief it would be nonetheless if we suddenly had to deal with a true blight. . . . That would be a true triumph. It would mean that humanity would truly have achieved something—its own destruction. It would be a true sign of the superiority of one being over all the others. Not only its own destruction, but the destruction of the entire living world. That would truly be the sign that man [*sic*] is capable of something.[49]

It is possible Freud's grandson enjoyed *fort-da* primarily because it allowed him to inure himself against his mother's loss, but also because it gave him a sense of control over an essentially uncontrollable condition—his mother's presence or absence. Nuclear war games did the same. The possible conditions of a nuclear war involved a great deal of chance. Some of these were known questions (How would the war start? How would the Soviet Union act? What would weather conditions be like?). But in the complex system of warfare, any number of small variables could radically affect the outcome in ways that couldn't be accurately predicted. Would missile launch officers disobey orders? Do the Russians have secret defensive technologies? How many of the bombs would fail? A breakdown in logic is perhaps a necessary condition for nuclear war in the first place, since its risks far outweigh potential rewards. The possibility of extinction could make this predictive exercise a source of despair. War games, at least in part, domesticate this risk, just as *fort-da* prepared the child for his mother's absence. But some surplus enjoyment remains beyond that goal in the form of the game's ludic elements and sense of control. For this aspect of enjoyment, the high stakes and low certainty of nuclear war only make the sense of mastery more intoxicating. Human beings become masters of their own fate, "capable of something."

This image of war-mongering generals callously ignoring the human cost of their plans is a very familiar one. But nuclear war games have also made their way into civilian culture, sometimes explicitly for the purpose of inspiring horror. Just as rhetoricians in the Cold War era hoped to inspire opposition to the Bomb by showing the horror behind its sanitized language, game designers sometimes claim to be opposing nuclear violence by making its twisted logic and bloody consequences clear on computer screens for all to see. A number of ostensibly anti-war games have been developed in this mold. *Balance of Power* was described by its creator Chris Crawford in the early 1980s as "a grand, idealistic, make-my-contribution-for-peace crusade," intended to show the irrationality and danger of nuclear war.[50] Players who started a nuclear war were shown only a black screen admonishing them, refusing to display images of nuclear war, and stating "we don't reward failure." The Natural Resources Defense Council (NRDC) created its own simulation of nuclear targeting after the Cold War. Despite the demise of the Soviet Union, SIOP remains a closely guarded secret. NRDC hoped to create a rough picture of current US nuclear war plans based on the theory that exposing the "grotesque results" of nuclear war would turn the public against it.[51] Lack of access to the tools of simulation undermines democratic debate, the argument ran, which the NRDC simulation set out to change.[52] The assumption shared by both Crawford and the NRDC is that nuclear war plans survive only due to secrecy and therefore exposing the way things "really are" is an effective project for antinuclear politics. The factor of enjoyment presents a paradox for these antinuclear tools, however. Antinuclear games do not reveal the horrors of nuclear war any more than Pentagon simulations provide scientifically accurate strategic plans, but to reach a large audience, they must above all be *fun*, not just educational. Whereas military simulations grant a sense of control to professionals forced to deal with nuclear threats, civilians can refuse to think much about nuclear war, much less play video games about it. These games require another element: they must be *fun*. To examine this argument and further illustrate the common processes of enjoyment anti-war games share with official war planning, the next section will analyze the popular 2014 nuclear war simulator *First Strike*, an ostensibly antinuclear video game developed by the Swiss Blindflug Studios, which combines these elements of moral instruction and ludic play.

First Strike

First Strike is a game first developed for handheld devices such as the iPad and iPhone, expanded in subsequent editions to home computers. The first version of the game was deceptively simple. Players are given control over one or several territories on a pristine, simplified globe, where they can research, build weapons, defend, or attack, but may only take one action at a time. There are no limitations on the player's choices regarding money, personnel, or raw materials—only time. Gameplay involves research, defense, and offensive nuclear attacks, and only these, despite some early mistaken accounts.[53] The player wins when all enemies are completely destroyed. To accomplish this goal, billions must die.

According to its developers, *First Strike* was intended to have a political message. Game designer Moritz Gerber claimed that this antinuclear sentiment was present "[f]rom the beginning." His argument for the video game mirrored those made in defense of previous antinuclear simulations and games:

> We're definitely of the opinion that the video game is a very strong medium for [antinuclear politics]. Blindflug wants to combine the big issues of the world with gaming, so people can participate in, and not just talk about, nuclear war.
>
> Games let you see what happens if you launch a nuclear missile, or what happens when you hit London, for example. And that should bring people closer to these issues.[54]

Executive producer Moritz Zumbühl made a similar argument, claiming that Barack Obama and Vladimir Putin "should play more games [like] *First Strike*," repeating his belief that games are "powerful tools" to oppose nuclear proliferation.[55] The game's release in March 2014 provides additional cues for its interpretation, coinciding with Cold War–like tensions between the United States and Russia over the latter's involvement in Ukraine. *First Strike*'s official blog intersperses advertising materials, some of which mentioned this context, with informative clips on various real Cold War nuclear incidents, media representations of nuclear war, disarmament advocacy statements, and nuclear tests (including Trinity).[56] These elements comprise what Matthew Thomas Payne calls a "paratextual vanguard" for the game, priming players to interpret its diegetic elements in a particular way, as does the political situation in which the game is released.[57] In the case of *First Strike*, in-game text reinforces the disarmament message. Successful players are rewarded with "You Win?" and a stark estimate of casualties, often in the billions. Repeated play unlocks a message from the NORAD supercomputer Joshua in the 1983 movie *War Games*: "A strange game. The only winning move is not to play."[58] Game site IGN notes that a portion of the game's profits go to nonproliferation efforts and claims that *First Strike* "just may save the world," reinforcing the player's sense that *First Strike* is not "merely" a game but an example of political action in and of itself.

The narrative elements of *First Strike* and its political paratext thus contain a consistently antinuclear message. The game is clearly designed to support the idea that nuclear war plans, if implemented, would be catastrophic and out of proportion with their stated aims of security. *First Strike*'s procedures, however, are enjoyable despite the grim message. Because nuclear powers are the only ones with agency in the game, it is a good example of Lacan's thoughts on global catastrophe and the fantasy of control. The player has more than a powerful character—they can choose any nuclear nation and develop special powerful "superweapons." Non-nuclear territories are simply empty space for the player or nuclear enemies to capture and control. Imperialism pays: not only are more territories available for the game's core actions, but conquests of some places by some countries (e.g., annexation of Africa by the European Union) yield special rewards. Although the victory screen contains a question mark ("You win?"), success and failure are clearly different states and winning is rewarded. There is no human extinction or nuclear winter in *First Strike*, and despite the game's enthymematic arguments, victory is possible.

The procedures of the game thus carry a different message about the value of speed, aggression, and ruthless decision-making as keys for success in a nuclear war. The game's creators clearly researched nuclear war planning and the history of the arms race, but ultimately, they designed a set of rules for players to enjoy. This ambiguity has been noted by reviewer Carter Dotson, who wrote that "most of the social commentary [in *First Strike*] seems to come from the way that players interpret the situation, rather than any conscious message that the game gives. There's no reward for not striking first, or any punishment for being the aggressor." The (para-)textual message of the game runs somewhat counter to the methods by which players will actually engage in its process. Advertisements for the 2017 upgrade of the game even contradict this message textually: "You are in control of the world's fate. . . . Be the one to ignite our world."[59]

Developers frequently said that this game about nuclear war had to be "fun," and this is reflected in its gameplay and aesthetics.[60] The game's crisp, *Tron*-like graphical model of the Earth is reminiscent of (but richer than) the similar Introversion game *DEFCON*. The aesthetic of the game is almost clinical. Although casualty numbers are sometimes displayed, these transmissions are matter-of-fact, even soothing when they reflect a successful attack by the player. In the background, calm, ethereal music conveys a certain nostalgia for 1980's synth. It is possible to argue that this sanitization is intended to produce an uncomfortable cognitive dissonance, akin to what Bogost calls "simulation fever," the "the nervous discomfort caused by the interaction of the game's unit-operational representations of a segment of the real world and the player's subjective understanding of that representation."[61] Some of this discomfort is apparent in player reviews, but it seems subdued, the minor embarrassment of a guilty pleasure. One reviewer called it "worryingly fun."[62] Another reviewer acknowledged the game's stated message while recognizing the thrill of simulating destruction:

> There's a maudlin, desperate undercurrent to *First Strike*. It tells a tale of the inevitability of destruction. Rockets miss their targets, cities are laid waste, and millions fall under the push of a finger on the screen.
>
> A percentage of each sale goes to anti-nuclear proliferation charities, and while you're always disconnected from the barbarity of your actions, by ticking numbers and less-than-real graphics, there's a constant reminder that you're doing something wrong, and a bit silly.
>
> The fact that that message is wrapped around a fantastic strategy game makes it even stronger.
>
> First Strike has worthy and important things to say, but while it's saying them, you get to blow up Greenland.[63]

The procedures themselves capture players even when the horror they represent is acknowledged. Two image captions read, "Radial menus make mass murder a breeze" and "The sun never sets on my empire of corpses." Another ("Suck it, Greenland," with echoes of Cohn's critique of the hypermasculinity of nuclear discourse) shares a sentiment expressed by General Thomas White who described the likelihood that noncombatant nations would be destroyed in a nuclear war as an unintended consequence in a meeting with Robert McNamara. "Well, Mr. Secretary," White is reported to have said, "I hope you don't have any friends or relations in Albania, because we're just going to have to wipe it out."[64]

First Strike therefore exhibits some dissonance between its explicitly antinuclear message and the fun of world destruction. In Owen Faraday's comparison of the game to *Call of Duty* he wrote:

> First Strike is doing its utmost to both eat and have that particular cake. The game aspires to be a stern lecturer, opening and closing with dark admonitions about mankind's suicidally large stockpiles of horrific nuclear weapons. And we need to be reminded, especially now that the Cold War is remote, unlived history to an entire generation of adults.
>
> But First Strike the game—the thing you're actually playing in-between those dire bookended warnings—*loves* nuclear war. It makes the prospect of ICBMs hurtling through space to targets on the far side of the globe look downright lovely. First Strike is a reasonably clever (though flawed) game—but as pure spectacle it's second to nothing on mobile.[65]

The "fun" of *First Strike*'s procedural gameplay thus seems to contradict its paratextual context and on-screen text about the futility of nuclear war. That the game can be "worryingly fun" suggests that simulation fever does not repel players. Instead, they find enjoyment—jouissance—in simulation itself. Reviews suggest that players invest not in one side or the other of the nuclear fascination/horror discrepancy, but in the aporetic encounter of the discrepancy itself. Of course, *First Strike* is "just a game," but that it is a game that allows players to direct a nuclear war makes it more than fun. It also gives a sense of minor transgression. Players don't enjoy killing people necessarily, but they seem to enjoy the guilt of enjoyment, the fact that they attach to the game in the first place despite its premise. Players of *First Strike* can thus enjoy the capacity to enjoy, even when it causes some discomfort, just as the child enjoys *fort-da* even though it stands in for the loss of the mother. The game is an exercise in subject creation, where the sense of agency intersects with the pleasure of an act prohibited by the big Other, all in the guise of a progressive political message.

In *First Strike*, players are compelled to repeat by the incentive structure of the game. But even without this procedural reward, the game encourages repetition. It is almost impossible to play a "perfect" game, and the outcome could always be changed somewhat, and as no two sessions are identical, repetition is always repetition with a difference. "The replay value is through the roof," reviewer Lory Gil wrote, "since every experience is different. Even without multiplayer, you will come back over and over again."[66] The same reviewer who reveled in the destruction of Greenland wrote that the game is a "replayable single-player strategy game that I kept coming back to long after I had enough material for my review."[67] The game is restricted by a short window of time, making it a perfect ten-minute break from other activities. *First Strike*'s repetition allows players to enjoy useless subjectivity, or the capacity for choice primarily rather than the results of specific choices, much as military war games allowed their participants to enjoy killing hostages, defeating enemies, and fighting campaigns on behalf of the "enemy" with the alibi of simulation. It demonstrates a core principle of the drive: subjects are compelled to repeat because they don't attain what they strive for, but instead earn a compensatory pleasure from the process of repetition itself.

Christopher Goetz describes the "tether" fantasy in video games as a means of enjoying risk from the distance of simulation. Players enjoy repeatedly exposing themselves to "danger," expanding out into the world of the game, and then withdrawing into a safer space. Being caught in a vulnerable state can be a "playful act" even when this play is "repetitious of an originally horrifying event."[68] The "worrying" fun of *First Strike* is understandable as the uncanny effect of repetition. Freud's understanding of the uncanny, discussed in the previous chapter, includes the notion that "an uncanny effect is often and easily produced when the distinction between imagination and reality is effaced, as when . . . a symbol takes over the full functions of the thing it symbolizes."[69] Players of *First Strike* are made uncomfortable by the juxtaposition of fun and war, but the illusion of control, the ability to exit the game and continue their lives, creates a tether like that attached to the child's reel, permitting them to control the conditions by which the simulated world is made present and absent. Players enter and leave at any time, and if they don't like how things are shaping up, they can always simply quit and start again.

Discomfort is a core dynamic of the game. The metaphorical connections maintained by gameplay overshadow more abstract connections, such as the horror of radiation injuries and death that players can imagine or extrapolate from information they already have. These elided connections persist in the unconscious as described in the previous chapter—in other words, they remain live connections that structure the experience without being an explicit part of the "text," or in this case, game. This can be seen in Jason Ruddy's *First Strike* review. He calls the game "wickedly fun," although its "hope" is "not quite enough to shake off the uneasiness you'll feel every time you read the stats at the end of a game." His discomfort is palpable near the end of his review. "I had a lot of fun playing it," he wrote, "and feel as though the only negative bits in my experience were tied to . . . the bad taste it left in my mouth after each game was complete. Every 10 minutes met with the same result, billions dead and a 'You Win?' stats screen. If that sort of thing won't stop you from having a good time, then I recommend giving this one a go."[70] Here is enjoyment, unease, an acknowledgment of the game's contradictions, transgression, and a decision to play this program "meant to be played . . . repeatedly" because it allows players to practice and improve their decisions.[71] Players like Ruddy might be put off by the game, but they may continue nonetheless because enjoyment of the procedural metaphors (radial menus standing in for target selection, screen touches for nuclear research, and so on) overwhelm other associations about what a "real" nuclear war would mean. *First Strike* is structurally similar to the US Office of Naval Research MMOWGLI (Massive Multiplayer Online Wargame Leveraging the Internet), a collaborative online simulator that relies on the fun of playing to crowdsource defense policy ideas. Players of MMOWGLI don't have to confront the results of their play because their investment is captured by its procedures themselves.

This interpretation of *First Strike* relying on game procedure could be criticized for an overreliance on structure at the cost of attention to contingency. Bogost argues against structural determinism on these grounds. What he calls "system operations" are "totalizing structures that seek to explicate a phenomenon, behavior, or state in its entirety. Unlike complex networks, which thrive between order and chaos, systems seek to explain all things via an unalienable order."[72] Bogost argues that psychoanalysis tends too much in this direction at the expense of smaller-scale "unit operations."[73] This roughly equates to a reading of Lacan as "structural poetics" in which individual subjects are epiphenomenal to the agency of the signifier.[74] On the other hand, it is possible to give too much weight to the immediate context of speech or action rather than the larger economy of the Symbolic, a charge sometimes leveled against the American tradition of rhetorical scholarship which Lundberg describes as "radical contextualism at the expense of any governing formal relation."[75]

An overly structural reading would occlude the differences between nuclear simulations, while a hyper-contingent one would overemphasize them, missing the common threads of enjoyment that tie *First Strike* to RAND Corporation military models. However, this impasse between structural psychoanalysis and contextual rhetoric is not a necessary one. Rhetorical expression is contingent on subject, audience, and so forth, but repetition and enjoyment explains how habitual connections between different tropes create durable alliances in the unconscious of language. We don't need to believe in a hidden deep structure to acknowledge that there are ingrained connections between signifiers that channel meaning in particular directions.[76] The intrusion of the Real (*tuché*) is by definition contingent and unpredictable, but efforts to script over it and retain the illusion of coherence (*automaton*) are predictable in that the Symbolic requires such an illusion to operate.[77] The intersection of psychoanalysis and rhetoric is much like the concept of play as contingent agency within a structural set of procedural constraints. Repeated actions may even change the rules eventually, although it takes time and investment to do so.

This intersection of psychoanalysis and rhetoric helps explain both the appeal of *First Strike* as a specific instantiation of nuclear simulation and the appeal of nuclear war gaming more generally. Almost all of these games—*First Strike* included—are zero-sum, just as game theory models dictate they should be. Conflict is inevitable, and any gain by the opponent is a loss for the player. In the "prisoner's dilemma," a classic of RAND Corporation strategic modeling, one party must choose to betray or cooperate with the other without knowing what their competitor/accomplice will choose. The attempt to predict what the "other side" would do was of capital importance during the Cold War, and simulations like this one were meant to reveal underlying principles of decision-making. The prisoner's dilemma let one determine what *they* would do, then map this logic onto an opponent. Strategic planners stressed "objective" elements: states and their leaders act "rationally" in response to a set of interests and values, and therefore their behavior could be predicted. To play a game and "win" meant applying predictable, logical rules deftly, overcoming the will of the enemy with superior logic in a specific scenario, with the attendant satisfaction of one's own agency ("a true sign of . . . superiority of one being over all the others") and the mastery of something so threatening to life ("the sign that man [*sic*] is capable of something").

In the traditional liberal critique of the arms race, this process is "mirroring": one assumes certain hostility in the other, and therefore, one has to adopt that same hostility. The belief that the agents involved will be rational and that the "rules" in which they work give rise to objectively superior decisions leads the two sides to converge over time. Lacan's discussion of repetition provides a different perspective. In Lacanian language, mirroring is an Imaginary dynamic that plays out within the constraints of the Symbolic. One's intentions are defined by the perceived intentions of the adversary, and one comes to identify with them. But in a competitive, zero-sum game, the player must assume that the enemy will know that the player is guessing its intention, and therefore adopt a different strategy. But perhaps the enemy also knows that the player knows that it will make this assumption, and so forth. The imaginary modeling of opponent behavior with limited options is thus potentially intractable. "Hence each player," writes Lacan, "if he [*sic*] reasons, can only resort to something beyond the dyadic relationship—in other words, to some law which presides over the succession of the rounds of the game."[78] In a discontinuous world of imperfect communication and information where the other cannot be perfectly known, players reach for some transcendent order to retain the coherence of choice. The objective rationality that is supposed to structure the game isn't about identification with the other except to the extent that both self and other are recognized as effects of the Symbolic order, the set of rules that constrain choice in this case. The depiction of nuclear enemies as inherently aggressive due to objective principles of international order can thus be understood not (just) as a failure of imaginary identification, but as a necessary solution to the game within apparently inflexible rules. When confronted with the contingent choice of a specific other (*tuché*), nuclear planners appealed to the transcendent logic of the Other instead, attempting to structure chaos with order (*automaton*). Thus the religious language of dislocating terror at the advent of the Bomb gradually found a locus for faith: this time, in reason rather than the numinous. But reason and the attendant language of risk could not be total solutions because the variables they were meant to manipulate could not be defined objectively. I turn to this problem next.

Pascal's Wager

John von Neumann, a famous mathematician who worked on the hydrogen bomb, is rumored to have formulated an early precursor to game theory playing poker.[79] RAND analysts played the game regularly, many with some passion (although there is no evidence that they relied on counterfeit chips). These players apparently thought of the game mathematically rather than an exercise in psychology, since RAND was "stumped" by human behavior. As RAND president Frank Collbohm said about an Air Force–ordered pilot reaction study, the one "machine" that remained a mystery "is called a 'pilot.'"[80] The basic assumption in reducing war games to mathematical simulations was that the universe could be rendered in such a language, that "numbers could save the world" because life was ultimately a game of risk, calculable and controllable.[81]

Later, diagnosed with terminal cancer, von Neumann supposedly converted to Catholicism on his deathbed, convinced by another, long dead mathematician, Blaise Pascal.[82] Pascal's wager, that one should believe in God even if its existence is unlikely because the consequences of eternal damnation are infinite,[83] has metastasized to other areas of apocalyptic fantasy predictions, starting with nuclear war. If the destruction of a nuclear war is infinite then even a tiny risk of it should be avoided, so the logic goes. This argument demonstrates the limits of rational calculation as a persuasive device, however, because it has been used to seemingly equal effect by advocates of nuclear weapons as well as detractors. This fact is not due to manipulation of logic, but as I will argue here, it results from the limits of rational argument itself in recuperating the predictability of the Symbolic after the Bomb's revelation of the Real. The excess of *tuché* frustrates *automaton*, and this secular version of Pascal's wager is the broken machinery it leaves behind.

Jonathan Schell's *The Fate of the Earth* was a major inspiration for the disarmament movement and one of the best-selling books ever written about nuclear war. It is an attempt to make nuclear war seem real through the unabashed use of sublime language and vivid imagination. The first of its three parts is full of beautiful passages about the destruction that a nuclear war might produce before ending in a "republic of insects and grass." Relying heavily on the assumption that a nuclear winter would follow a war between the USA and USSR and that such an event would cause humanity to go extinct,[84] Schell contemplates what the end of the human species might mean and what its possibility suggests for defense policy. Schell, like George Kistiakowsky at the Trinity test, thought of nuclear war as the end of humanity. He wrote that all value was human value, so a nuclear war would destroy everything meaningful in the known universe. Nuclear war must, therefore, be avoided at all costs:

> [T]he mere risk of extinction has a significance that is categorically different from, and immeasurably greater than, that of any other risk, and as we make our decisions we have to take that significance into account. . . . It represents not the defeat of some purpose, but an abyss in which all human purposes would be drowned for all time. We have no right to place the possibility of this limitless, eternal defeat on the same footing as risks that we run in the ordinary conduct of our affairs in our particular transient moment of human history. . . . [A]lthough the risk of extinction may

> be fractional, the stake is . . . infinite, and a fraction of infinity is still infinity. . . . [M]orally they are the same, and we have no choice but to address the issue of nuclear weapons as though we knew for a certainty that their use would put an end to our species.[85]

This passage comes at the end of the first part of *The Fate of the Earth*. The next section, "The Second Death," is about future generations. Schell's argument is a version of Pascal's wager where "infinite" value replaces the punishments and rewards of God. "Infinity" as a concept reduces something that by definition cannot be resolved in language or understood by human beings in its entirety into a single word, a placeholder to represent with finite bounds something that can never be represented. It is the ultimate license in metonymy since all associations are included within it; no proliferation of meaning is prohibited, because it is the one whole that ostensibly contains every part. Its symbolic function can be compared to the various names of God in negative theology, all of which stand in for something that is acknowledged to be inexpressible.[86] Some version of Schell's infinite risk argument was used by antinuclear activists in public rallies,[87] and occasionally shows up in other discussions of existential risk. Even representatives of the Vatican have used a milder form of this argument, signing on to a statement reading in part "as long as nuclear weapons exist, there remains the possibility of a nuclear explosion. Even if the probability is small, given the catastrophic consequences of a nuclear weapon detonating, the risk is unacceptable."[88]

Even when the hazard is expressed as "catastrophic," or quantified with some suitably huge number, it is effectively infinite. As Eliezer Yudkowsky argues, human beings calculate scale poorly, and a sufficiently large number is not rationally understood. "Human emotions take place within an analog brain," writes Yudkowsky. "The human brain cannot release enough neurotransmitters to feel emotion a thousand times as strong as the grief of one funeral. A prospective risk going from 10,000,000 deaths to 100,000,000 deaths does not multiply by ten the strength of our determination to stop it. It adds one more zero on paper for our eyes to glaze over, an effect so small that one must usually jump several orders of magnitude to detect the difference experimentally."[89] In the more parsimonious formulation attributed to Joseph Stalin, one death is a tragedy; one million deaths is just a statistic. Like the rabbits of *Watership Down*, numbers over a certain threshold are simply *hrair*: "a great many; an uncountable number; any number over four."[90] Any very large number serves the same structural function of expressing loss beyond practical measure by imposing a placeholder that we know we cannot truly comprehend—hence the difficulty in mentally visualizing a billion of anything next to a trillion of the same thing. Thus, although the Global Challenges Foundation argues that "infinite risk" is not meant in a mathematical sense and that calculations are possible, they are in effect meaningless: the investments of "infinity" exceed our ability to calculate, as indeed the report acknowledges when it argues for a categorically different treatment of these risks.[91]

The limits of imagination display the failure of the Symbolic to coincide entirely with the world. Words like "infinity" are signifiers with functions and effects. Unlike ideographic terms like "justice," "freedom," and "pride," these are words intended to capture a mind-independent material reality—and that reality is indeed mind-independent in the sense that no one mind can fathom it. A shadow always remains in the quantification of infinity and the attempt to master it, a remainder that haunts the edges of supposedly perfect reason. This is Martin Heidegger's previously mentioned concept of the gigantic, something much like the sense of the Real that shines through in the sublime: "The gigantic is rather that through which the quantitative becomes a special quality and thus a remarkable kind of greatness . . . as soon as the gigantic in planning and calculating and adjusting and making secure shifts over out of the quantitative and becomes a special quality, then what is gigantic, and what can seemingly always be calculated completely, becomes, precisely through this, incalculable. This incalculable remains the invisible shadow that is cast around all things everywhere when man [*sic*] has been transformed into *subiectum* and the world into picture."[92] Through this shadow the modern world extends itself into "a space withdrawn from representation" and gestures toward something which we are denied to know.[93]

For Schell, the losses possible in a nuclear war are infinite because they threaten future generations beyond count. Preventing the birth of future individuals is immoral, by this logic, which has some (apparently unintended) echoes in the Catholic view on abortion.[94] As no future individuals are cotemporal with those assigning them worth, the value of future generations is symbolic, not unique to the individuals actually "prevented."[95] The reason we must not immolate ourselves in nuclear fire, then, is that we must continue to reproduce—the value of each individual lies in that person's ability to create more individuals. There is no discussion of anything else that we are obligated to do for the future.[96]

For Schell, responsibility seems to be a finite obligation to an infinite number of people. This infinite future is frequently represented by the metaphor of the child. In Lyndon B. Johnson's infamous Daisy Girl campaign ad, a child pulls petals off a daisy, accompanied by a mechanical countdown and interrupted by the familiar mushroom cloud of the Bomb. "These are the stakes," a man's voice intones. "To make a world in which all of God's children can live, or go into the dark. We must either love each other, or we must die."[97] Lee Edelman's description of the Child as a figure for "compulsory investment in the misrecognition of figure" could have been about the Johnson ad. "And lo and behold," he writes, "as viewed through the prism of the tears that it always calls forth, the figure of this Child seems to shimmer with the iridescent promise of Noah's rainbow, serving like the rainbow as the pledge of a covenant that shields us against the persistent threat of apocalypse now—or later."[98]

Unfortunately for disarmament activists, nuclear strategists have children too, and some, like Jim Lipp, express the value of their own work in the same terms—as a matter of caring for "grandchildren's grandchildren" through nuclear deterrence.[99] The "fraction of infinity" argument has also been used by those defending an aggressive defense posture beyond deterrence. The George W. Bush administration invaded Iraq citing that country's possible future development of weapons of mass destruction as the primary casus belli. By the logic of Schell's wager, there was no time to waste—every second that the decision for war is delayed increases the chance that a rogue regime could develop nuclear weapons. Any nonzero risk is equivalent to an infinite one.

Vice President Dick Cheney went one further, however, establishing the "Cheney doctrine" in response to nuclear terrorism. Told at a briefing with CIA director George Tenet that Pakistani scientists could potentially be assisting Al Qaeda in the development of nuclear weapons, Cheney responded that if "there's a one percent chance . . . we have to treat it as a certainty in terms of our response." The response must be immediate, regardless of proof. "It's not about our analysis," he said, "or finding a preponderance of evidence. It's about our response."[100] Members of the security community often assert that nuclear terrorism is an "existential risk," a threat to American "civilization" or even the entire species despite the complete lack of evidence to this effect.[101]

There is no mathematical way to distinguish between infinite risks. If any fraction of infinity is infinity, then every fractional risk is infinite—Heidegger's unquantifiable "gigantic" casts its shadow over attempts to calculate. While the last part of Schell's book is a passionate case for disarmament, the opposite is equally plausible: if there is any chance greater than zero that disarmament opponents are right and American nuclear weapons are deterring a nuclear war (and uncertainty in calculation alone ensures that there *must* be), then the risk is infinite. The future is compressed entirely into the present, since any action we take now could determine whether that future exists at all and what character it might have. We are enjoined to do *everything, right now, as fast as we can*, because any delay might cost trillions of deaths—an argument Nick Bostrom has made about space colonization using the same structure of Pascal's wager used by Schell.[102]

At the same time, we must be in (literally) perfect stasis and do nothing at all, for any change might be the one that cascades into nuclear war. If we extend this infinite value to human extinction more generally, it might even be imperative that we *deliberately cause* a nuclear war as soon as possible to destroy industrial civilization and thus prevent the collapse of global ecosystems on which all life depends.[103] The logic of infinite loss results in aporia. It is simultaneously true that no risk is worth taking and that every risk must be taken. Each decision we make now is of limitless import, and thus we can enjoy the imagination of destroying future generations because it invests us with the power over existence and nonexistence on a cosmic scale.

Play Again?

The quasi-secular iteration of Pascal's wager and nuclear war games are connected. Both attempt to make rational calculations about nuclear war by quantifying variables that cannot be quantified. Both are attempts to master the Bomb through a set of rationally derived rules. The Symbolic order can be analogized to a set of operations, like an equation, that provides the conditions of possibility for meaning, while the Imaginary describes the value of specific variables in that equation. If the value of the Bomb is infinite, then the rest of an operation is overshadowed: no probability assigned to another variable fundamentally changes the result. Like the sun outshining dimmer lights in Longinus's treatment of metaphor, the threat of human extinction as an unquantifiable evil outshines the issues attached to it (preemption or pacifism, counterforce or countervalue, disarmament or militarism, and so forth) such that many paths lead audiences to the same result: the poorly healed scar in the Symbolic that results from *automaton*'s sutures over the wound of *tuché*, in this case, the failure to reconcile our understanding of the human world with the power of nuclear weapons.

The "infinite risk" of Schell's argument relies on guesswork, just like nuclear war games that incorporate limited testing and conventional war data. Both operations are sustained by enjoyment. As Cheney said, it's not about our analysis—it's about our response. In the case of war games, simulations allow players to enjoy their ability to enjoy—to attach to subjectivity itself. The appeal to infinite destruction is remarkably similar; only those who use it can enjoy the capacity to make the world present and absent in speech. Imagining the apocalypse is fun; doubly so if apparently sophisticated simulations allow us to alter the models of its occurrence.

While this kind of scenario planning and simulation had its most important early developments in Cold War nuclear games, the cultural technology has become deeply ingrained and proliferated in a number of different discourses and practices. A cottage industry in extinction prediction has blossomed in the last few decades, concerned with everything from asteroid collisions and ice ages to magnetic pole shifts and whether the universe is a simulation that might be switched off. The 2014 outbreaks of the Ebola virus in Africa are a recent example. Modelers quickly produced simulations of the spread of this disease. A survivalist article on the conspiracy theory website Infowars discusses the most extreme of these disease models, asking if "you really want to wait until *after* infections have been identified in the United States to make your preparations?"[104] An embedded YouTube link leads to a video entitled "Mathematical Model Shows How Ebola Will Spread: 'Worse Case Scenario . . . An Extinction Event'" posted by TheDailySheeple.

The graphical presentation of this video closely resembles the gameplay of *Pandemic 2*, a game with millions of online plays, which was popular long before the outbreak. In *Pandemic 2*, the player controls the disease and the object is to kill everyone in the world.[105] The notorious difficulty of infecting Madagascar in the game has spawned its own Internet meme where players express frustration in sympathy with their fictional pandemic (interestingly, the aforementioned Ebola video leaves Madagascar untouched). The website for Northeastern University's Laboratory for the Modeling of Biological and Socio-Technical Systems (MOBS Lab) shows efforts to model the spread of Ebola using graphical icons that also closely resemble *Pandemic 2*, right down to aircraft flight paths and a similar color-coding system for the incidence of infection.[106] It is no wonder that many people might share the feelings of journalist Abraham Riesman who recently wrote a self-reflective piece on his "amoral twinge of excitement" on reading Ebola news and imagining the end of the world.[107]

The powerful imprint of apocalyptic threats mediated through news reports, academic work, games, and official policy persists. The promise of dissolution also animates a powerful resistance. The material, emotional, and cultural labor of postapocalyptic survival is an expression of enjoyment organizing life in response to the threat of death, creating communities bound by the notion of survival. We might imagine many apparently credible threats to the existence of human beings on Earth; the ways that the world might end seem nearly endless. While RAND tried to calculate how a nuclear war might begin and how it should be fought, Schell argued that probability hardly mattered. Alongside nuclear war there are many other low risk/high impact events that introduce the possibility of extinction and thus represent metonymic expansions of the Bomb's grand place as the monarch of American terror since the 1940s. As a result, there are subjects marked by the sign of general survival. Perseverance becomes a duty: despite attempts to calculate risk, the specter of societal annihilation motivates them to refuse extinction, to live so that a new, even better society can be built. If they cannot predict, they must instead prepare, for the specter of apocalypse enjoins us to *survive at all costs*. After all, if the end of the species is an infinite evil, then sacrifice at any price is a good bargain. But for the fantasy of postapocalyptic survival to be fulfilled, the world must end, and thus destruction and renewal are twinned aspects of the same sign, one that has exerted its powerful influence from Cold War civil defense to contemporary zombie narratives. Survivalists are not irrational fringe elements circulating their own disharmonious language in an otherwise orderly society. The sign of survival speaks through them, organizing communities of those who are willing to undergo—and enjoy—hardships, real or imagined, in order to increase their odds of survival in the end times. These commitments have material effects on social organization. The next chapter examines the logic of sacrifice motivated by apocalyptic imagination, the first half of another *fort-da* dynamic completed in chapter 4.

3
Fort
Desired Ground Zeroes

> I really wonder if our interest is so much in survival as in the fascinating possibility we might be legitimately able to get rid of our neighbors. If we really want to be safe, we'd better start shooting our neighbors now, to be sure we get them all.
>
> —Frederick E. Jessett, letter to *Christian Century*

As we have seen in previous chapters, Jacques Lacan considered the subject to be a product of the Symbolic order. Some signifiers, habitually invested with meaning by the society into which the subject enters, have powerful ordering effects on our identities, providing the resources (and bounding the choices) by which we make meaning. Scholars have long recognized that the *city* as an organized constellation of anxieties, fears, and aspirations is one such anchor for affective investments. The city is a complex and ancient signifier bridging many different strands of desire. Therefore, a wide variety of critical tools must be brought to bear. As Roland Barthes wrote, "anyone who wants to sketch a semiotics of the city must be at once a semiologist (a specialist in signs), a geographer, a historian, an urbanist, an architect, and probably a psychoanalyst."[1] Keeping with the central commitments of this book, I will stress the latter of these specialties while proposing that scholarship in communication includes elements of many of them. Indeed, a broad interpretation of communication in its material and linguistic senses (if even this division should be permitted) encompasses much of the Barthes list. The city is "built" for an expansive discipline, although other perspectives might add in precisely what we lose in such expansiveness.

In one operation, the city stands in as a site of chaos, danger, and difference, to form the identity of (white) suburbanites as good Americans, ordered and pure, opposing the corruption and disorder of the urban center which threatens the comfortable, predictable operation of the Symbolic. This opposition of the city as a racialized place of abjection opposed to an innocent (generally white) "real America" is easily discernible in the contemporary right-wing discourse on violence in Ferguson, Baltimore, and Detroit. These names have become pathologized as metonymies for blight and fear. This discourse is not new, however. This chapter examines an earlier incarnation in the apocalyptic climate of the Cold

War. While the Cold War discourse itself was an outgrowth of earlier investments, it marked the first time in recorded history where rational city planning and the possibility of massive, near-instant destruction of urban spaces coincided. Urban populations have been targets of violence from the razing of Carthage to the Fourth Crusade to the destruction of the Warsaw Ghetto, but the Bomb introduced a new sacrificial logic and discourse of survival. Recovering this older "structure of feeling"[2] can help to reveal how the signifier of the city maintains durable (although hopefully not inevitable) attachments that show continuity with contemporary constructions of urban spaces as potential zones of sacrifice.

The imagination of apocalypse had an effect on the spatial order of American cities. While scholars have long renounced dualism, some specter of it still remains to be banished. It is tempting to discuss language and materiality as separate things, despite the protestations in material rhetoric, media studies, and psychoanalysis, but the two are indivisible. Not only do words have material presence (sounds, movements in pronunciation, electrical signals in the brain), but signifiers as paths of meaning create material orders in the world and leave their marks on human bodies. This understanding of the Symbolic should help to reveal how the web of language stitched over the threatening incursions of the Real is perceptible in the physical order of objects arranged in space. Thus the depiction of cities as zones of chaos helps to make them so, as resources are channeled elsewhere, spaces are segregated, and repression is meted out through physical violence.

The Cold War signifier of the city as a "wasteland," a place of potential destruction and sacrifice, is one example. The prospect of destruction in the wasteland trope was not solely responsible for violence, but it provided cover for white flight and industrial relocation, demonstrating the capacity for one powerful trope to conceal other logics—racism and neoliberalism in this case. The populations imagined "gone" in the *fort-da* game of catastrophe and postattack survival were not arbitrarily chosen but instead reflected the preexisting racial and class anxieties of Cold War America. Under the guise of rational tradeoffs, poor and minority populations would bear a disproportionate risk from Soviet attack. The wasteland trope became a self-fulfilling prophecy as people and industry fled city centers and left them to decay, in a sense diminishing their value as targets by destroying them in advance. This is significant because it demonstrates the material effects of cathectic investment in the signifier. The nuclear-survival impetus of this investment cannot explain all of its particularity, however. The decay and further economic divestment from postindustrial cities seems natural once they have been sacrificed already in the imagination of nuclear war, just as the contamination of desert spaces with nuclear waste seems almost natural since these places resemble imagined postapocalyptic landscapes already.

This chapter explores the structures of desire that framed urban areas as nuclear targets—bombed cities-to-come—and the parallels between nuclear defense logic and neoliberalism. Both are structures in the register of the Symbolic—the ordered, largely predictable, set of scripts composed of mutually referencing tropes sustained by affective investment. Because the order of the Symbolic can never perfectly capture the material world or the contingent events that defy human mediation, there are dislocating eruptions—the order of the Real—that reveal our socially constructed world to be a product of artifice, something that we may know but usually ignore. Neoliberalism and nuclear strategy both claim a privileged access to the Real: they present themselves as inevitable structures derived from "the way things are," rather than contingent, normative formations sustained by a network of constant affective and ideological investments. The first two chapters of this book demonstrate one *fort-da* dynamic, between the "gone" of the Real manifested at Trinity and the "here" of nuclear simulations, which seek to restore order to the Symbolic with predictable rules. This chapter concerns the urban wasteland trope as one half of another *fort-da* dynamic, the "gone" that is complemented by the "here" of survivalism, examined in the next chapter. The elevation of rationality in nuclear simulations reaches its logical endpoint in neoliberalism and nuclear targeting: populations are exposed to the threat of death based on the supposedly inflexible rules of deterrence and the market. The purpose of this analysis is twofold: to demonstrate that the Symbolic networks of language and belief are not divorced from the material realities of the built and natural world, and to demonstrate how contingent cultural formations influence the social even as they are covered over with a discourse of inevitability.

To illustrate this point, I will begin with a discussion of Cold War nuclear targeting. Recent scholarship has emphasized the link between space and sacrifice, but a psychoanalytic approach might help to illuminate how those connections are forged and what physical structure they manifest. Next, I turn to civil defense programs, including shelters, highways, and dispersal, to expose the racial and class biases that underpin supposedly neutral, utilitarian policies. These policies destroyed the cities they were meant to save by imagining them as doomed places, sacrifices to the "inevitable" logics of deterrence and neoliberalism, as a discussion of Detroit shows. Detroit is the prototypical urban wasteland due to its racial history, economic segregation, and the morbid media fascination with its physical decay. Finally, I will tie these disparate threads together in an effort to describe links between the signifier and built structures.

Nuclear Targeting

Critical work on nuclear targeting has tended to focus on the ways in which it maps foreign targets for destruction. Following from Martin Heidegger's essay "The Age of the World Picture," Rey Chow argues that we are now in the "Age of the World Target," in which enemy territories are known and mapped in order to be attacked.[3] Chow implicates Western "theory" broadly, but argues that area studies in particular serve as a vehicle to know the world and thus prime it for destruction. Although Chow does mention some domestic implications of this policy,[4] her focus is primarily on how the United States imagines enemies outside its own territory and how xenophobia results in violence against them. Historian Matthew Jones has a similar focus, extending the work of John Dower to argue that the decision to bomb Hiroshima reflected a fundamental devaluation of the Japanese. Jones applies this insight to American nuclear policy in Asia throughout the early Cold War, arguing that racial discrimination repeatedly characterized American nuclear policy.[5] Other work examines enemy construction, stereotyping, and racism more generally, treating the devaluation of the Japanese during World War II and the demonization of Soviets during the Cold War as examples of a deeper psychological process of enemy construction in the "world as target."[6] Nick Turse confirms this link between spaces of death and devalued foreign populations in his study of American atrocities in Vietnam including "Free Fire Zones" and attitudes of racial hatred and superiority amongst rank-and-file US troops.[7] All of these authors recognized that the value of life was not universal to American policymakers, and most also argued for a connection between spatial imaginaries and violence.

The argument that strategic nuclear planning in particular was linked to race was advanced by Dean MacCannell in the same issue of *Diacritics* in which Jacques Derrida's more famous call for nuclear criticism was published. Focusing primarily on the works of James Conant, a president of Harvard who witnessed the Trinity test, MacCannell argued that there is an unconscious connection between urban planning and nuclear warfare. Relying on Conant's transition from defense intellectual to advocate of "ghetto" education, MacCannell argues that the deterrent balance has been undermined because "macrosocial changes" in the form of white flight and minority concentration in cities "can be interpreted as making the use of nuclear weapons, not on an enemy, but on our own society, the realization of a collective unconscious desire."[8] The warrant for this argument relies on a particular understanding of the Lacanian unconscious as a "subjectivity which has the power of consciousness, but a consciousness which has lost its ability to speak." The unconscious bears a relationship to "macrosocial arrangements" beyond analogy for MacCannell. Both are agents that cannot be identified except through their effects, but structure the world and organize symmetries such as minority urban confinement and the imagination of cities destroyed in nuclear war.[9] MacCannell is also careful to insulate himself from criticism by arguing that a defining trait of efforts to describe the unconscious structure of society or the structure of the unconscious itself will be met with criticism and denial.[10]

MacCannell's pioneering work might be further refined through a more explicit distinction between the Lacanian orders of the Symbolic and the Real.

For MacCannell, macrosocial arrangements are located explicitly in the Symbolic as evidence of both its "fragility" and its tendency to connect apparently distant concepts. The agency he ascribes to these forces, however, and especially their inability to "speak," seems to risk conflation of the Symbolic and the Real. The unconscious here seems to be a hidden underpinning for social signification, rather than the set of signifiers that are overshadowed by more affectively charged tropes. Whatever we choose to call macrosocial arrangements, fundamental antagonisms, or the unconscious, to the extent that we can describe their operations and material effects, these things must be located in the Symbolic rather than the Real because they are products of human artifice. To think otherwise is to give in to their central obfuscating move: the confusion of inevitable, unchangeable structures and durable, but fundamentally contingent social ones. This conflation is a fundamental mechanism of what Lundberg calls "feigned unicity" in that it makes the highly durable signifying networks of the Symbolic appear to be natural and immutable, rather than the products of sustained and repeated affective investments. As Andrew Robinson argues, the conflation of Real and Symbolic in this sense makes a political response impossible because the basic determinants of political life are presented as beyond our capability to influence. This is precisely the danger that Robinson identifies in Lacanian psychoanalysis. By claiming privileged access to an unconscious order (here conflated with the Real), psychoanalysts can immunize themselves from criticism with the appeal to deeper, hidden meanings.

As developed in previous chapters, the Real is what distorts the Symbolic through disrupting the social fabric built within it. The ameliorative responses of *automaton* repair these fissures, but never exactly, because the distorting shape of the lack persists. It is more productive to see social arrangements as things that do in fact "speak" in the sense that the sign speaks through the subject and not vice-versa, reserving the Real as a concept for silence and contingency, both of which shape these relations but do not directly structure them. MacCannell's conception of the Real paints it as the deep structure for which the social is epiphenomenal and is also not falsifiable, the core of Robinson's objection to these concepts as politically meaningful.

If the Lacanian unconscious should be understood as the sublimated but present tropes concealed by metaphors of unusual cathectic purchase, then the best starting point for an investigation of the connection between targeting policy and macrosocial (spatial) arrangements is the set of tropes that serve to conceal these connections through the intensity of affect invested in them.[11] The social world is not ordered by preexisting signs speaking through their subjects. While Lacan argues that the signifier "speaks through" the subject, he also acknowledged the diachronic changes that occur from individually contingent expressions and the influence of changing cultures. The sign is necessarily mutable, and its work is done largely by concealing metonymic connections that are overshadowed by powerful metaphorical ones. Even if one accepts that some form of exclusion and violence is inevitable, the history of debates over nuclear targeting is necessary to identify how and why this particular order of violence emerged.

The Allied tradition of area bombing began against Germany in World War II. If one believes the official statements, its goals included all manner of destruction other than killing civilian human beings. It was war waged against an *economy* expressed in *areas* rather than a *population* expressed in *lives*. Historian Richard Overy, for example, describes the targets of area bombing as "factories, transport facilities, supporting services and workers' housing," aimed at "the destruction of Germany's industrial areas" with some acceptable "collateral damage" in lost lives.[12] Nuclear plans further advanced this thinking. The Cold War differed from the Second World War in that throughout most of it both sides were susceptible to massive attacks against their cities, which was not the case in the latter conflict after the Battle of Britain in 1940 until the end of the war in 1945. Mutually Assured Destruction (MAD) embraced this vulnerability as a condition for stability.

All Cold War nuclear targeting schemes relied to some extent on the threat of massive retaliation against cities full of civilians, but strategists distinguished between "counterforce" targeting, in which nuclear weapons would target other nuclear weapons and their supporting infrastructure, and "countervalue" targeting, in which nuclear forces would be employed against civilian populations.[13] Despite the insistence on counterforce targeting at various times during and after the Cold War, American nuclear policy ultimately relies on the countervalue threat against cities. Even a hypothetical counterforce attack aimed only at nuclear weapons infrastructure still required an implicit threat against enemy cities to deter wanton retaliation.[14] The characteristics of nuclear weapons are such that they are always capable of genocidal massacre of civilians. As a result, "city swapping" is a potential outcome if deterrence fails.[15] Even a counterforce attack with no deliberate civilian targets would certainly have killed tens of millions of civilians during the Cold War due to the yield of nuclear warheads and the proximity of military assets to major population centers, so although the adherents of countervalue and counterforce targeting each argued that their chosen policies better maintained peace by making a superpower nuclear attack less appealing, both advocated preparations that would amount to unprecedented destruction of "enemy" people,[16] and US nuclear weapons technology and deployment was consistent with a countervalue strategy.[17]

Robert McNamara, originally horrified by the excesses of a Strategic Air Command nuclear briefing, endorsed a counterforce (eventually called a "limited war") plan, but quickly backed off, maintaining MAD as did later administrations, even when they publicly debated counterforce alternatives.[18] Strategists were always aware that any use of nuclear weapons could degenerate into "unrestrained slaughter"[19] of civilians since nuclear war is inherently unpredictable, no empirical data exists, and enemy behavior was the result of unpredictable models, as discussed in chapter 2. Countervalue advocates claimed that targeting cities was morally permissible on utilitarian grounds and pragmatically wise because the overwhelming violence of an attack against civilian populations would outweigh any military gains for an aggressor and thus best deter war,[20] while a counterforce posture would increase the pressure to launch first in a crisis so as not to be disarmed, thus increasing the probability of war through miscalculation or accident. The advocates of nuclear deterrence therefore justified their policy on instrumental, consequentialist moral grounds, arguing that some cost to the few (or in this case, the many) must be sustained to preserve the lives and freedoms of all.[21] The logical conclusion of countervalue strategic thinking seems counterintuitive: the Pentagon should want nuclear warheads targeted at undefended American cities because their vulnerability serves as collateral to reassure enemy states and prevent war.

The stability of Mutually Assured Destruction would become an argument used to oppose widespread civil defense initiatives and missile defenses. Such programs would be able to mitigate the damage of an adversary's response to American aggression, thus making their leaders distrustful of the United States and more likely to contemplate their own first strikes.[22] If the Soviets believed that an American nuclear attack could destroy their missile silos, bombers, and submarines, then their only reassurance could come from the knowledge that even a limited counterattack—a so-called "ragged response"—could still devastate American cities. If, however, civil defense programs could reduce expected casualties in those cities to an "acceptable" level, then the Soviet leadership would know that it could not deter an American nuclear attack. As a result, the USSR would have strong incentives to initiate a nuclear conflict in the hopes of catching the US unprepared, rather than waiting for an American strike to destroy Soviet nuclear capabilities before retaliation.[23] Other civil defense opponents such as Dwight Eisenhower's Secretary of State John Foster Dulles argued that building an effective US shelter system would undermine American alliances, amounting to a decision to "write off our friends in Europe."[24] In other words, American civilians must be ready to die to reassure European allies that American soldiers would be ready to die, too. Left unsaid was the question of exactly *which* civilians would die in a Soviet attack.

Imagining the destruction of cities and the means of their salvation performs much the same work as *fort-da*: rather than steel ourselves for loss, we imagine that we can calculate and control the awesome power of the Bomb that would otherwise seem so overwhelming. Imagining how some might be exposed to risk in order to save all, whether or not the plans are enacted, is an exercise in population management that gives a notion of control over the Bomb. The future, speculative nature of nuclear war planning allows multiple sites for enjoyment. First, planners can imagine that they might avoid war altogether through the right strategy, demonstrating the power of human rationality (nuclear deterrence) to overcome the threat of the Bomb. However, they can also imagine what a war would be like if it *did* occur, and the debate about countervalue and counterforce targeting was partly about this imagination. Talk of "damage limitation," for example, involved imagining that deterrence had already collapsed. Planners do not need to choose between alternate futures because it is the nature of risk to contemplate and master them all.

Every population is not equally exposed to risk, however. While the general principle of utilitarianism that underpins the calculation of lives should treat them all as equal, in practice some populations are more disposable than others. As Michael Dillon has argued, the initial step of calculating a value to life makes it possible to obviate the value of some lives entirely because it rejects the notion that life is incalculable by establishing an economy of exchange. Once lives can be valued in a finite manner and weighed against each other, devaluation is possible as well.[25] Because risk is not evenly distributed and all lives are not equal in the calculations of the powerful, the underlying dynamic of failed and feigned unicity has been manifested in culturally specific ways. Repeated investments accrete into durable formations, but those formations then channel how further investments are made. In other words, beneath the abstract language of nuclear planning lurks a set of racial and economic prejudices about which spaces and populations are worth saving and which are acceptable losses.

Debates over nuclear targeting and the value of different lives played out in the built environments of cities. It is not just the subject formed by the attempt to weave the Symbolic over the Real, but even the material environments we build. The sign is thus material in a very real sense: it produces subjects, their practices, and their physical surroundings. The city is one such sign, built in part by the powerful attachments negotiated under the threat of nuclear war. The metonymic connections concealed by the city as a nuclear target are all of the other investments that contribute to its material structure. In Cold War America, racial and economic inequality were some of the investments informing nuclear calculations.

Our Cities Must Fight

Class, race, and anti-urbanism were long bound up in the cultural reaction to civil defense. One of the most overtly cold-blooded results was the debate over "ethnic targeting" in the late 1970s and early 1980s. This policy would have attempted to disproportionately kill ethnic Russians in the event of a nuclear war with the hope that non-Russian peoples of the Soviet Union (Ukrainians, Baltic peoples, Kazakhs, Uzbeks, and so forth) would rise up and overthrow the state, which was understood (by some nuclear planners at least) to be a Russian-dominated continuation of the Tsarist Empire. Zbigniew Brzezinski allegedly interrupted a targeting discussion once to ask "Where are the plans for killing Russians?" When it was explained that all nuclear attacks would kill many Soviets, Brzezinski impatiently insisted, "I mean *Russian* Russians," and in doing so broke the taboo about openly promoting the direct killing of civilians.[26] Even the opposition to this policy was telling. David Cattell and George Quester argued it partly on the grounds that it was immoral, but also from an anxious white American racial perspective. If the United States targets ethnic Russians, might not the Soviet Union follow suit with its own increasingly accurate missiles? "Will we hear," they ask, "future discussions of how Soviet nuclear warheads are aimed at Scarsdale and not Harlem, at the San Fernando Valley and not the Spanish-speaking sections of East Los Angeles?"[27]

Cattell and Quester express a fear that began with the advent of strategic bombing against colonial targets around the turn of the twentieth century, when gas and explosives were used primarily by European powers against Africans and Asians. Sven Lindqvist documents the change that occurred when "under the surface calm, evil dreams began to rise." "The character of [European] fantasies changed," he writes. "Before there were airplanes, we had dreamed of triumph through bombing other races, other planets, other solar systems. But now that we really were bombing other races, we had nightmares of being bombed ourselves."[28] Planners were forced to concede that if they selected ethnic Russian targets on the basis of this identity as "Desired Ground Zeroes," the Soviets might do the same, and suddenly nuclear war seemed less palatable.[29] Cattell and Quester are not arguing that more people would die, but that the set of survivors might be different. This should be read alongside data collected by the Federal Civil Defense Administration suggesting that minorities would be disproportionately killed in a nuclear war. The result of its "continuity of government" efforts would be a state dominated by Republicans and white Dixiecrats. Recent immigrants, Jews, and other minorities were mostly urban in the early Cold War period, and thus likely to die in larger relative numbers. At one extreme, 67 percent of Protestants would survive the projected war. At the other, only 7 percent of Jews would live.[30] In theory, Grossman writes, "FCDA planning would have reestablished the contemporary social order of the early 1950s in a postnuclear era with one fundamental difference: the post-attack demographic reality that civilian defense planners used resembled Alexis de Tocqueville's homogenous America of the 1830s, not the country of the early 1950s."[31]

The racial order also influenced debates over bomb and fallout shelters. The first Federal Civil Defense Administrator was Millard Caldwell, a former governor of Florida who supported segregation and opposed the right of black Americans to vote.[32] Speaking at Caldwell's nomination hearing on January 15, 1951, Clarence Mitchell, director of the Washington Bureau of the National Association for the Advancement of Colored People, called the nomination "an insult to colored people," describing it as appeasement of white supremacists.[33] Mitchell and the NAACP leadership were particularly worried about what segregation would mean in the aftermath of a nuclear attack: "Here at home a national emergency may convert our large cities into battlegrounds. . . . If a bomb drops we do not want regulations that require citizens to run 10 blocks to a separate racial shelter when one marked for 'white only' is just around the corner. . . . [Caldwell's] record shows that he would not avoid dual standards, based on race. We, therefore, solemnly urge that his appointment be rejected."[34] Mitchell's concerns were well-founded. While segregation was never an official part of civil defense doctrine, it was quietly assumed in a number of plans formulated by individual states. Caldwell's strong support of states' rights against federal oversight helped to encourage this kind of planning.[35] This could be done in part by treating evacuation as simply a problem of moving people through space, referring to locations rather than the populations that lived in them or would be moved through them. Jonathan Lieb and Thomas Chapman studied one such plan in Savannah, Georgia, in which train cars would be used to evacuate schoolchildren. Although there was no mention of Jim Crow, Lieb and Chapman found that students from majority white schools were slated to be moved to communities with more resources for recovery.[36] Evacuation areas were effectively segregated, with thirty-nine of the forty-three sites receiving only black or only white children.[37] Civil defense was therefore viewed with suspicion by many black communities. During one drill in Mobile, Alabama, rumors spread that nuclear weapons would be employed deliberately to kill black people in resistance to school desegregation, causing a brief panic in the city.[38]

The national shelter program was more limited than might be apparent by the attention it received. Shelters were built, but ultimately the lion's share of preparation happened in the suburbs. Representative Martha Griffiths, a Democrat from Michigan, opposed urban shelter plans on the basis that "if the bombs fell at night" no one would be saved but "skid row characters" and "drunks."[39] Caldwell encouraged a strategy of "digging in" rather than evacuating, although the latter would become policy as part of America's highway programs later in the Eisenhower administration.[40] The 1951 FCDA propaganda film *Our Cities Must Fight* described the impulse to "take to the hills" as "pretty close to treason," "desertion, plain and simple" since in modern warfare, "each of us has his [*sic*] share of fighting to do." Enemies are constantly gauging our willingness to fight, or as the film bluntly puts it, "our capacity for sacrifice." The film downplays danger, claiming that "after an atomic airburst, the danger of lingering radiation and falling debris is over in a minute and a half."[41]

Ultimately, no American city had an effective, large-scale shelter system. An alternative program of industry dispersal was more successful. This was a plan to incentivize industries moving into suburbs and other locations where Soviet missiles were less likely to strike directly. Some precedent already existed in cities like Detroit, where the gigantic World War II–era Willow Run bomber plant was sited outside the city itself. Federal defense spending continued to make suburbs increasingly attractive after the war, partly with industry dispersal in mind.[42] Dispersal may not have been the primary cause of the white, middle-class relocation to suburbs, but did play a significant role in the construction of cities as dangerous spaces and suburbs as a potential solution.[43] Not only did federal financial incentives encourage dispersal, but the problems of urban civil defense created academic and professional connections between urban planners and defense intellectuals starting in the 1950s and 1960s. Both frequently published across disciplines on the problems posed to city infrastructure and planning by nuclear weapons. Beyond dispersal plans, this collaboration introduced military technologies and modes of thinking into the previously somewhat insular world of urban design, encouraging an ostensibly rational view of planning and human behavior.[44] This collaboration continues to shape cities as objects for global military targeting today. Thus began a new era of "military urbanism" in which cities even in the United States were seen "through the bombardier's eye."[45]

People were to escape these dispersed cities with automobiles. Highway construction took off during the Eisenhower administration justified in part by nuclear fear. Although economic considerations were a major factor in highway construction, civil defense against nuclear weapons also helped "sell highways to Congress and the nation."[46] Adapting lessons learned from difficulties bombing the German *Autobahn* during the Second World War, politicians argued that highway construction—particularly the kind that allowed people and vehicles in and out of cities quickly—was a survival necessity.[47] Sirens were installed around the country as highways were built to give locals warning of an impending Soviet attack. Beltways would be "Life Belts" permitting the US to recover quickly and "hit back" in the words of a *Life* magazine report on cyberneticist Norbert Wiener's plan for recovery.[48] Highways were public goods, but cars were not. City dwellers without the means to buy automobiles or the suburban contacts to help them relocate quickly would not benefit much from evacuation, an extension of the same class disparities that made the "best" shelters available only to the wealthy willing to build and finance their own.

Shelters, evacuation, and dispersal were all government policy at various times but only the latter two gained much federal support. There was very little evidence to suggest that any plan would work. The hydrogen bomb increased the potential for nuclear destruction by several orders of magnitude, and as arsenal sizes rapidly increased, plans for civilian protection yielded diminishing returns. Robert Moses, the infamous New York city planner, wrote an article opposing both large-scale civil defense measures and noting the impracticality of evacuation. Writing in the midst of highway expansions, Moses claimed that there were "Too many vehicles; too many people; no place to hide."[49] The suburbs, disproportionately white, were the imaginary site of postnuclear America's future, and what fallout protection programs were actually authorized concentrated their efforts there, a "built-in notice to millions of city dwellers that they [were] expendable," or in John Kenneth Galbraith's words, "a design for saving Republicans and sacrificing Democrats."[50]

Urban Sacrifice and the Wasteland Trope

The material organization resulting from nuclear defense policies helped to destroy American cities. Thomas Sugrue's study of industrial decline and social conflict in Detroit blames the dispersal of industry combined with an expanded highway system for allowing factories to relocate, limiting opportunity for the increasingly black, poor, and uneducated population of the Cold War inner city.[51] "As Detroit goes," wrote B. J. Widick in 1972, "so goes the country."[52] This maxim was unfortunately correct. Urban populations remained in place and therefore were increasingly denied manufacturing work, the basis for economic prosperity in Detroit, Cleveland, Pittsburgh, Chicago, and other cities that were rapidly transforming into the Rust Belt. Meanwhile, highways cut cities apart and demanded the destruction of (mostly poor) neighborhoods that stood in the way of construction. The physical infrastructure for industry dispersal and evacuation also facilitated the massive exodus undertaken by middle-class and white Americans. Especially in a climate where nuclear war was often considered very likely, if not inevitable, cities were always potential wastelands, almost already destroyed. Cities became sites of danger for those concerned with nuclear war, their desolation so certain that the present and future blurred together, as did the various elements of their supposed danger. For many survivalists, the threat of nuclear war blended with race riots and hatred of minorities into a generalized anti-urbanism.[53]

With the flight of population and wealth, the wasteland trope became a self-fulfilling prophecy. Detroit, as the most visible example, has been "so thoroughly humiliated by history, so emptied of the content, both material and human, that used to make this place *mean*, that it becomes questionable wither the city still exists," in the words of Jerry Herron.[54] Films such as *Four Brothers, Assault on Precinct 13, Narc*, and *True Romance* tell of a city plunged into anarchy by violent crime both organized and random. In *The Crow*, the city is literally hellish. *Robocop* portrays a future Detroit as almost ungovernable, saved only by a cyborg policeman constructed by a corrupt megacorporation. The cover of the award-winning documentary *Detropia* shows a man and a woman posed in front of one of Detroit's many abandoned houses. The image would look much like *American Gothic* except that both figures are wearing gas masks, a common trope in advertising for popular postnuclear video game series like *Fallout, Borderlands*, and *Metro*. These representations helped to change the city's image from the "Arsenal of Democracy" to "Wild West Detroit,"[55] a place where "the wheels came off the wagon of Western Civilization" according to the spokesman of a former Detroit mayor.[56] The habitual association in all forms of media between Detroit and violence has made the city a space of abjection that can be filled with any social evil, an internal zone of danger foreign to the rest of the country. Detroit is an ideograph, a powerful site of condensation for the fear and desire of urban destruction. The city's representation in mass media "stands for what everyone else fears and wants to be different from: a singular, cautionary disaster from which people elsewhere imagine they still have time to retreat."[57]

Recently, the ruins of Detroit have attracted "urban explorers" who seek out abandoned structures from the city's heyday in the 1950s and early 1960s, including fallout shelters. Explicit use of the wasteland trope is so common that religious organizations have picked it up as a call for salvation. The Christian Broadcasting Corporation in one recent example described this "urban wasteland" as a result of corruption rather than economic or racial conflict. "Welcome to Detroit, or what some call 'The Dead Zone.' It's an area of near-complete destruction many miles across," CBN stated. "Crime is the only growth industry, with murder being an everyday occurrence."[58] Similar associations of danger and decay are made with other cities, but Detroit is the metonymy for urban industrial decay. Even real estate listings sometimes declare that Detroit is a place for "homesteading," like the 19th Century American frontier. It is a signifier of powerful and conflicting affective investments, but these investments are maintained by a proximity to danger, much as the Bomb itself promises redemption only through violence.

The city wasteland trope transforms the victims of nuclear war—or neoliberal economics—into dangerous threats. Defense planners argued that hordes of refugees would leave big cities before or after a nuclear attack, straining the resources of the wealthier suburbs around them. This possibility led many public intellectuals, including religious leaders, to suggest that the ethical response of shelter owners confronted with the unprepared was to defend one's preparations, with lethal force if necessary. This "gun thy neighbor" ethic encouraged citizens to arm themselves not against potential Soviet invaders but against their own neighbors in the event that the desperate need of those neighbors became too intense. Suburban civil defense officials began to contemplate violence against their urban neighbors, as Bakersfield chief of police Horace Grayson did: "the greatest danger to Bakersfield would not be from an atomic bomb or its fallout, but from hundreds of thousands of displaced residents from the Los Angeles area, . . . They must be stopped south of town and shown a route to some kind of refuge on the desert."[59] Whites fleeing to suburbs in fear of race riots prepared the same way. A 1968 poll in the Detroit suburbs known as the "White Noose" found persistent fears of black invasion into these homogenous communities (99.5 percent white, according to the researchers), along with rumors of child murders and racial conflict.[60] Meanwhile, 63 percent of residents thought of buying guns,[61] a decision with obviously tragic consequences for nonwhite populations today.

It was a short step from this thinking to the idea that nuclear war might have an upside as "urban renewal."[62] Lawrence Hafstad, who was head of the Reactor Development Division of the Atomic Energy Committee before becoming vice president of General Motors, argued that the nuclear threat might be positive in a sense because it encouraged industries to relocate from city centers. "The atom bomb development," he wrote, "may come to be looked at in historical perspective . . . as 'Nature's slum clearance program.'"[63] In this thinking, atomic weapons would disproportionately destroy unproductive, undesirable populations, which were themselves making city spaces dangerous. David Wilson argues that "discardable" Rust Belt cities have globalized the trope of desolation and danger in which "poor black neighborhoods and populations need to be systematically isolated and managed as tainted and civic-damaging outcasts" in the name of "city survival."[64] Even the denial of insurance coverage had its bizarre parallel in nuclear warfare: that insurance companies deny coverage explicitly for nuclear attack lead Frances Ferguson to meditate on the sublime characteristics of nuclear war, unthinkable in the same way that uninsurable "acts of God" might be.[65] Racial segregation in these targeted cities was maintained partly by "redlining," or the denial of insurance to prospective minority (especially black) homebuyers seeking to move into white-dominated suburbs.

Nuclear policy alone did not give rise to the segregation, highways, suburbs, and interracial violence underpinning the notion of urban wasteland. Phil Reed, chair of the company board at General Electric, claimed that defense considerations were a supplement, but that his company's decision to decentralize production was primarily economic.[66] Highways were built and industries relocated in part for economic gain,[67] but as mentioned previously, the threat of nuclear war created an alibi in the form of transcendent, incomprehensible danger, a possibility so awful that it had to be avoided at all costs. Consequently, decisions framed as efforts to mitigate the nuclear threat were difficult to oppose because nothing could be more important than survival. Thus the Bomb could help to "sell highways to Congress and the nation," even though it was not the primary motivator for their development.[68] The Bomb and neoliberalism were intimately related, and security concerns often helped to shape national policy even when official justifications centered on the economy. As Ned O'Gorman has argued, during the period of Eisenhower's "New Look" military policy, economics came to conceal the national security apparatus, which nonetheless was foundational in the rise of the neoliberal security state.[69] Deliberate design would be almost impossible to prove in any savvy conspirator, but in Langdon Winner's words, "to recognize the political dimensions in the shapes of technology does not require that we look for conscious conspiracies or malicious intentions." The "deck is stacked" in favor of some interests over others such that neoliberal and defense ideologies—to the extent they are separate at all—provide mutual alibis for one another.[70]

What distracts attention while the deck is stacked is the operation of the unconscious, understood as the set of metonymic and metaphorical connections that are obscured by powerful sites of cathectic investment. Racial hatred and willingness to sacrifice the poor might underpin the urban transformations of the early Cold War period, but decisions by individuals and corporations to withdraw to the suburbs could be justified by the threat of nuclear war, an ever-present danger that helped conceal other motives. The Bomb intensified one set of explanations for sacrifice and in doing so managed to conceal others, even dispersing a set of tropes bearing an uncanny similarity to the white mythology of suburban flight. Cities were depicted as wastelands full of potential danger not just from the Bomb but from urban residents themselves who pose a threat to the (white) suburbs. As Sharon Zukin argues, industrial landscapes are a "moral order" in the sense that economic decisions also reflect cultural values.[71]

The Logic of Sacrifice

Through the wasteland trope, cities are united with another sacrificial nuclear landscape—the desert, site of American nuclear tests and common setting in the generic conventions of postapocalyptic fiction. Desert spaces, both magical and forbidding, "have" to be destroyed by the Bomb because the exigencies of national defense demand it.[72] But deserts are depicted as sterile landscapes, spaces free of human life that force us to contemplate what the world without us might be like. In them, we might see the possibility for something we cannot fully recuperate. Cities seem to lack this sense of otherworldly power because they are monuments to human artifice, but the shattered city is a testament to the power of the Bomb as a weapon capable of overwhelming even the most enduring human constructions. The city wasteland is made into a desert by nuclear war, but it was not always so. The narrative of Detroit is so powerful because it was once prosperous and now is fallen, paying for its sins, whether they are imagined as corruption, excess, and racial otherness by conservatives or the depredations of neoliberalism and the auto industry in the "place where capitalism failed" in Frank Rashid's phrase.[73]

My point here is not that there is a causal connection between the sacrifice of cities in nuclear imagination and their real abandonment—at least, not a strong one. Indeed, the lack of such a causal connection makes the resemblance between tropes of urban decay and nuclear apocalypse all the more striking. The natural laws of capitalism and the supposedly objective foundations of deterrence both seem to mandate that some populations will be sacrificed. The shadow of the Bomb provided an alibi for abandonment. The city as a nuclear target relied on many of the same tropes that circulated amongst white suburbanites, including marauding gangs of destitute city dwellers, abandoned wastelands incapable of supporting life, dangerous others, and the stark contrast of security and American values in the suburbs. All of these tropes could be animated by nuclear fear without acknowledging their parallel connections to white supremacist investments. By the same token, capital could flee on the basis of civil defense decentralization, making the now-unemployed urban population "collateral damage" rather than victims of neoliberal disregard for their welfare. The demand to know why there must be a sacrifice at all can be met with the melancholic reply that Slavoj Žižek characterizes as the knave's conservative mode of political engagement. The demand "why *must* there be sacrifice" is met by the sad lament, "*why* must there be sacrifice?" For the knave, the necessity for the loss is not in question. There is only space to sigh and wish it could be otherwise while we acknowledge that it cannot be so, generalizing the problem from the targeting of one group to an aspect of the immutable human condition.[74] This argument applies equally to nuclear deterrence and the neoliberal dislocation of industry in the Rust Belt. The available grounds for critique are limited by what is thinkable. Capitalism is not a fundamental, inevitable part of human social organization, but when presented as such, alternatives are necessarily constricted, as was the case with nuclear deterrence. Once the logic of inevitable sacrifice is accepted, political discourse is limited to a series of "least-bad" decisions rather than a fundamental reordering of political and economic power.

As the intersection of economic concerns, nuclear fear, and the built environment of cities like Detroit suggests, a psychoanalytic approach to the economy of desire should supplement, rather than preclude, other social theories about identity, fear, and violence. To say that the sign speaks through the subject is to argue that the range of tropes available to make meaning is limited by the unconscious, the economy of the Symbolic in which the subject is formed. It is a way of describing how particular cultural forms are shaped over time. Some signs bear more cathectic investment than others. Some "work" to a great degree and some don't. Formations like the city-as-wasteland trope cannot be explained away by reference to an underlying structure that spans everything empirically identifiable in the world, but they do hint at the necessity of accounting for imagination and trope. A focus on capitalism as the sole mover, for example, of urban sacrifice might not explain the particularities of civil defense nor why one population is put at risk while another is not. Psychoanalytic approaches should not replace explanations based on race, class, gender or other categories, but instead provide a set of analytic tools for describing the ways that subjects speak in the world, helping to provide a language accounting for which tropes become durable and which fade away. An account of the wasteland based on desire supplements racism and neoliberalism as explanations, identifying their common elements while not disavowing their differences.

While it may not be possible to subvert this motion of the drive entirely, it must be charted, brought to light, and criticized. The underpinnings of white supremacy and class violence that sustain fantasies of sacrifice are the "obscene supplement"[75] of both neoliberal urban abandonment and nuclear planning. As such, they sustain the structure of enjoyment only when kept hidden from everyday discourse. To expose them is a necessary, although not sufficient, means of delegitimizing the Symbolic order that is responsible for the (literally) concrete structure of the city in the United States, an order that must be disrupted for more radical strategies of redistribution and reparation to take root. Some Americans have always had the power and privilege to refuse sacrifice. Told that billions might die, they responded by insisting that they would make their own personal sacrifices not to be included amongst the dead. Communities formed, knitted together by survivalism and the collective fantasy of a society renewed by fire, where cities made into deserts could be rebuilt by true patriots unhindered by the loathsome otherness of their neighbors. If those who would die in an imagined nuclear war were already undesirable, the fantasy of nuclear war could have a strong appeal. Whites fleeing the cities did not just build shelters. The suburbs themselves *became* shelters.[76] In them, the relatively privileged could indulge in the fear of nuclear war while also enjoying the prospect in a Lacanian sense. Some grappled with the challenge of the Real that the figurative wasteland represented and imagined themselves seeding a new garden in its place. In nuclear fantasies, the sacrificial wasteland was an absence, whereas the reborn postapocalyptic community was a new presence. Instead of vowing to change the conditions that destroyed American cities or lead US leaders to contemplate genocide on a global scale, survivalist communities accepted the inevitability that impeccably rational models put forth and vowed that the bells of Hell might ring—for them, but not for me.[77] For in the prophecy of ashes, survivalists imagined a new world made pure by violence.

4

Da

Survival

> The point is generally misunderstood, but the objective of civilian defense is *not* merely to survive a nuclear war. By itself, such an activity is meaningless. Rather, *the aim of civil defense is to assure enough survivors so that the nation can be reconstructed and its social structure, fundamental morality, and traditions be preserved.*
>
> —Thomas L. Martin and Donald C. Latham, *Strategy for Survival* (emphasis in original)

The death drive is not exclusively about the desire to be destroyed. Jacques Lacan, interpreting Sigmund Freud, argued that there was only really one drive that contained both Eros and the death instinct. Death qualifies as a return to continuity, so the desire for death fits into this scheme, but it is not the only means of reaching out for the Real. Georges Bataille's interpretation was similar. Both eroticism and violence are essentially means of dissolving the borders of the subject, at least temporarily, in order to be in communion with something "more real" to which we usually do not have access. This is the tragic irony of the drive. No subject can experience the state of dissolution, since subjectivity is what makes meaningful experience possible. Our capacity to confuse reality with the Real through the loop of the subject and its enjoyment of subjectivity itself means that other symbols can stand in for the Real and serve as sites of cathexis, means to get a "taste" of something beyond the self without fully dismantling the subject, and even a route to enjoy failures of desire. Reproduction and destruction are symbolically linked: both express a desire for continuity. The desire to live on through future generations is one means of compensating for the individually exterminating inevitability of death, which every subject must confront. Thus, the fantasy of rebuilding alternates with that of destruction in a *fort-da* dynamic that gives the subject a point of investment.

The apocalypse is enjoyable largely because we imagine ways to control these conditions. Organized under the sign of survival, we imagine that a more authentic society might be rebuilt. We imagine catastrophe with horror, but there is also a whisper of desire underneath it: human society is one enormous mechanism to separate us from the Real, so if we live through the fire, we get to start over, closer to the land, closer to our nature, closer to the Real. We could form more genuine bonds with others and overcome the distance of reality. There might indeed be a silver lining to the mushroom cloud. Over the last seventy years in the United States, this desire has been expressed in fantasies of postapocalyptic renewal. While some populations are quietly slated for conditional sacrifice, other subjects define themselves around their imagined perseverance in a postnuclear world. Bearing strong similarities to the romanticized mythology of the American frontier, fictional narratives of postapocalyptic survival left persistent marks on American culture. Communities are organized around the texts, technologies, and practices of survival and the fantasy of rebuilding. Beginning with novels such as *Level Seven*, *A Canticle for Liebowitz*, *Farnham's Freehold*, *Dr. Bloodmoney*, and *Alas, Babylon*, postapocalyptic stories have remained influential in media. As Lacan mentions in passing, it is by "recounting a thousand fictions . . . on the subject of final things that we metaphorize, or tame, the confrontation with death and bring it into language."[1] *The Road* joins more right-wing, survivalist-community focused works such as *One Second After* and *Patriot Dawn,* in which survivalists imagine themselves tested against fantasized hordes of others who are often marked as racially or culturally different, as chapter 3 demonstrated, and the explosion of zombie stories accomplishes much the same.[2] In its combination of prophecy, moral instruction, and timelessness, the powerful cultural labor of postapocalyptic narrative stretches beyond explicit fiction and gestures toward a place previously reserved for myth.

This chapter focuses on survival, the counterpoint to the sacrifice discussed in chapter 3. If control over sacrificial zones represents power over absence, imagining survival creates a sense of power over presence. I will begin with a discussion of myth as a potential frame to interpret postapocalyptic survivor narratives. Mythic criticism, once popular amongst some rhetoricians, has largely fallen out of favor, but a reinterpretation of its psychoanalytic underpinnings might make it a useful avenue for exploration of the desire. Myth describes one kind of formation in the unconscious, a constellation of language that is repeatedly expressed in acts of speech, albeit with small differences in each instantiation. A brief examination of Cold War survivor fiction follows. Whereas the last chapter focused on the populations and spaces imagined as sacrifices in a nuclear war, this look at survivalism will emphasize the attendant myth of rebirth and regeneration that relatively privileged groups had imagined for themselves. Rather than attempt to examine this immense cultural production exhaustively, I focus on recurrent elements that thread their ways through many texts, focusing on common themes. The next section is an attempt to balance that breadth with a closer look at three recent right-wing survivalist novels to show the continued reverberations of the nuclear survival myth and the lasting disruptive power of the

Bomb. To demonstrate how this myth builds communities and defines subjects in unexpected ways, I will also examine survivalist dating websites. These, together with the hybrid human and electronic networks that constitute survivalist communities, suggest a contradiction between fear of the collapse of technological society and a dependence on it for identity and communication. This contradiction dissolves when survivalism is seen as a form of collective ritual rather than a wholly practical means of protection against catastrophe. Survivalist dating sites are mediated expressions of the desire for unmediated connection through fantasies of love and death. Far from the popular media image of naïve extremists, survivalists are good readers in a sense. The various signifiers of nuclear violence, from the horror of Trinity, the scenario planning of nuclear simulations, infinite-risk logic of the disarmament movement, to the city wasteland trope provide the resources for subjects to enjoy the end of the world. Ultimately, these various tropes detail one path of fantasy investment permitting individuals to imagine their own transcendence of language and society while retaining the capacity to enjoy them.

The Survival Myth

Elements of "mythic criticism" have been present in rhetoric at least since the 1960s. Michael Osborn argued in a 1967 essay that "archetypal metaphors" exist "immune to changes wrought by time" and "unaffected by cultural variation."[3] Osborn claimed that oppositions such as "light/dark" and "up/down" are universal metaphors grounded in human experience and basic motivation. Osborn's primary muse seems to be literary critic Northrop Frye, although his attempt to explain how universal categories stem from shared extralinguistic human attributes is also reminiscent of Carl Jung. Freud also argued that biology directly influences human experience, and through it, myth.[4] Freud and Jung initially differed over the importance of myth. Although Freud used myth even in his early work to explain his theories of repression and the unconscious, he criticized Jung for taking myth too seriously as an independent frame for psychoanalysis. Whereas Freud saw myth as a potential object of study for psychoanalysis, Jung saw the work of the field as itself mythic. Still, the opposition between these two perspectives is not as stark as it may seem. As Daniel Merkur argues, although Freud "adopted an ostensibly 'objective' perspective" and regarded Oedipus Rex as an allegory for the Oedipus complex, "he wrote publicly as though his theory . . . were being argued on the basis of Sophocles's text. Far from illustrating the Oedipus complex, Oedipus Rex became its proof text."[5] Freud also softened his position against myth later in life, taking it more seriously in books such as *Moses and Monotheism*.

Twentieth-century rhetorical scholarship on myth was primarily influenced by Jung. Jung's theory of myth relied on his interpretation of a collective human unconscious. Basic structures of thought inaccessible to the conscious mind are projected outward onto the world but they exist as categories that preexist any specific instantiation. Archetypes are one aspect of this projection, as underlying character concepts are used to interpret concrete phenomena. As Osborn would later argue, Jung believed these types and stories to be culturally and temporally universal.[6] Significantly for our purposes here, Jung explained the dynamics of the nuclear arms race through this mythic frame and the "shadow."[7] Jung became popularly known in the United States partly through the work of Joseph Campbell, who also drew from mythologist Mircea Eliade (who in fact collaborated with Jung and advanced a somewhat similar theory of archetypes). Campbell proposed that meaning "reveals itself" but one must first know the "grammar of symbols," for which there is "no better modern tool than psychoanalysis."[8]

The rhetorical theory of myth used by Janice Hocker Rushing and Thomas Frentz is adapted from Jung and Campbell's ideas. Rushing cites Campbell and the notion of the "culture hero" in her discussion of Reagan's Strategic Defense Initiative, for example, a significant project for nuclear criticism.[9] Rushing and Frentz argue for the place of myth in a field they saw as increasingly focused on ideological criticism, using Jung's work to argue for universal elements of narrative and an unconscious interiority that is expressed outward on the world. Even in 1991, these two scholars saw myth as being "marginalized," "dismissed," and "subordinated" in cultural and rhetorical studies.[10] This feeling was perhaps in part a response to a debate begun by Robert Rowland in the pages of *Communication Studies* a year prior, although others such as Barry Brummett, Osborn, and Martha Solomon stood by Rushing and defended the concept, eliciting a more moderate response from Rowland on the potential uses of myth.[11] Uses of myth in the same Jungian vein still occasionally crop up, such as James Darsey's citation of Jung in discussing the "journey" metaphor in President Barack Obama's discourse,[12] although Jung's universalism is less frequently defended.

In a little-known article published in *Medicine and War*, John Burry argued that nuclear war is, and must remain, a species of myth.[13] Nuclear survivor stories, surprisingly coherent as a category, might constitute a specific mythic tradition within this larger frame. Elements that are inessential to the plot are still frequently repeated between different works. Most of them exhibit similar characters, involve a hero's journey from one place to another, meditate on lawlessness, and describe new belief structures. These stories also tend to make the connection between speculative fiction and social commentary very clear. Because nuclear war was considered a real possibility throughout the second half of the twentieth century, the central element of postnuclear setting gave credibility to these stories that space operas, alien invasions, and monster movies lacked. While still speculative, therefore, nuclear survivor stories were plausible, putting them in a nonfalsifiable but persuasive category of their own, the possible but unreal. While the details of the individual stories were clearly invented, this sense of plausibility gave them purchase as imaginations of the future, and the daily threat of destruction with its myriad social consequences made moralizing possible in a way that other plausible speculative genres (e.g., "hard" sci-fi) could not always claim.

Some elements of rhetorical scholarship on myth find compelling support in nuclear war narratives. The characters in these stories do seem to fit archetypal molds. Indeed, many works of fiction seem to rely on archetypal identification. Alongside the "Wise Old Man," the "Culture Hero," and the "Shaman," we might add modern incarnations such as the "Greedy Capitalist," the "Lecherous Politician," or the "Vapid Reality TV Star." All of these character types perennially reappear carrying a certain cultural import and valence. In the context of nuclear fiction, the "Mad Scientist" (Bluthgeld in *Dr. Bloodmoney*, the titular character of *Dr. Strangelove*, Lufteufel in *Deus Irae*), the "Tough Wasteland Survivor" (Vic in *A Boy and His Dog*, the narrator of Fritz Lieber's *Night of the Long Knives*, the player-characters in all of the *Fallout* games), and the evil "Old Regime Survivor" (the Enclave of the *Fallout* games and the sentient computer of *I Have No Mouth and I Must Scream*, as well as Lufteufel and various *Fallout* characters) might qualify as archetypal.

The concept of the journey is also frequent enough to be a generic attribute (the player's quest in every *Fallout* game, Riddley's journey through postapocalyptic England in *Riddley Walker*, the journey to the sea in *The Road*, the race to Antarctica in *Down to the Sunless Sea*, various characters in *A Canticle for Leibowitz*, etc.). Ultimately most of these stories are tied together by a simple overarching theme: a nuclear war occurs, some people survive (often underground), and some kind of "good" new society arises, opposed by "bad" people. Most of these stories are written or created by Americans,[14] and this origin shows: most of these stories are essentially postapocalyptic Westerns with tough individualists surviving in a violent new frontier. In this sense, mythic treatments of nuclear war echo the earlier mythology of American continental expansion.

Myth is a useful conceptual category for identifying the impact of these tales, but it deserves some refinement. Traditional concepts of myth, even as they are applied by rhetoricians, tend to assume that it is "merely" metaphor standing in for some underlying truth that could be expressed literally. Just as trope can be seen as ornamental speech, so myth is primarily a genre of embellishment. Furthermore, many studies of myth that seek to identify some aspect beyond mere ornament rely on an interpretation of the subject as the bearer of some essential kernel of identity, a hidden interiority that is expressed through, rather than shaped by, language. This is evident in much work in the Jungian tradition: a set of archetypes preexist the subject and universally define the hidden collective consciousness. Both of these interpretations are at odds with the central theoretical arguments of this book—trope is not mere ornament because it describes the networks of the Symbolic that make meaning possible, and although signifiers do "speak through" subjects, they are not universal and timeless but rather reflect durable, serial affective investments without negating the importance of contingency.

A related problem is that Jungian theory of the unconscious assumes a deep structure to the unconscious. To argue that myths are unconscious tendencies projected outward assumes a prior, extralinguistic interior subject. A Lacanian approach works against this idea on the grounds that subjects are defined by discourses, without the need for another inaccessible universal order that could not, in any case, be proven to exist. In *Seminar III: The Psychoses*, Lacan argues that "nothing touching on the behavior of the human being as subject, or on anything in which he [*sic*] realizes himself, in which he quite simply is, can escape being bound by the laws of speech."[15] The unconscious is not some hidden interiority but is "continuous with the external dialogue," Lacan writes. It is the discourse of the Other understood as the Symbolic register, not of the internal self.[16] The sign speaks through us, and we are defined by what is said in the cacophony of the parlor like Kenneth Burke's famous "unending conversation" in *The Philosophy of Literary Form*. We are born into a linguistic order, participate in it without ever grasping the whole thing, and die before it is concluded.[17] This understanding of the Symbolic definition of the subject explains the persistence of myth and its effect on identity without reverting to the deep structures rejected by a properly rhetorical understanding of the unconscious. The evidence for an innate collective unconscious exists only as expressions in speech, which is also the evidence for the persistence of the signifier in Lacan's work, but the standard of parsimony should tilt us toward the latter.

This observation that the subject is shaped by language also complicates the model of communication on which Jungian myth interpretation relies. Campbell assumes that truth "reveals itself," or in other words, that it exists prior to its expression. This is the same argument that Sophia Heller uses to dismiss myth altogether: myth is "merely" metaphor, and once the underlying truth that it references is exposed, myth is irrelevant.[18] Three key assumptions here are that language can perfectly represent the world, that such a thing as "zero degree" language is possible, and that metaphor is merely ornamentation. As argued in previous chapters, language cannot communicate an unproblematic Real—the real by definition is what escapes symbolization. Efforts to construct mythic explanations of the world are exercises in reality, not the Real, meaning that they form human social reality but do so only through symbols which necessarily fail to capture the totality of the world external to human consciousness.[19] This doesn't deny that myth is *understood* as a revelation of underlying reality, but it does mean that what works its influence on mythmakers is not the Real but the set of symbolic ties that constitute reality, as distinguished by Lacan. The failure to adequate language with an objective, mind-independent world makes all speech metaphorical in some sense, while the basic constitution of the social world through trope suggests that we should always be skeptical of attempts to dismiss "mere" metaphor as solely ornamental.

Acknowledging that there is no detectable "deep structure" that determines the form of any particular myth, it is possible to think of myth as a durable constellation of metaphor and metonymy that forms the context for specific narratives shaped by its operation. Myth is the network of signification that organizes culturally durable narrative assemblages, a specific economy of meaning within the more general economy of mediation. Like stellar constellations, myths are durable but probably not timeless: their meaning and structure precedes any specific individual example but changes over time. Within this scheme, archetypes are simply ossified metaphors, sites of repeated investment that take on an illusory quality of permanence. William Marderness argues that myth is distinguished by its display of an analogy of form.[20] In this sense, it is a species of metalepsis, determining meaning through an enthymematic comparison of one set of metaphorical relationships to another. Audiences familiar with the larger story will fill in missing pieces, investing absences with meaning. Robert Ellwood argues that this is precisely what makes myth powerful. No myth can answer every question, so this "symbol in narrative form" requires the audience to participate.[21]

What might distinguish myth from genre is its relationship to the Real. Both myth and genre are characterized by serial repetitions of certain tropes in a narrative form which come to establish conventions for their type, but the two can be distinguished by the way subjects cathect to them. Myths are understood by their adherents to represent a hidden reality, like the deep structure which some (mistakenly) equate to the Real. Similarly, myths have an instructive aspect. They are supposed to be guides for behavior, as the title of one of Campbell's books suggests: *Myths We Live By*.[22] Rituals inspired by myth are products of human artifice, but ritual adherence serves to produce a sense of the Real as those who keep them can experience a connection with a mysterious order that greatly exceeds them.[23] Thus myth is a means of feigning unicity by incorporating the threatening Real into a predictable, mediated order, one that offers some reassurance in the face of the possibility of nothingness. As Eliade puts it, religion "expresses an unquenchable ontological thirst. Religious man [*sic*] thirsts for being. His terror of the chaos that surrounds his inhabited world corresponds to his terror of nothingness."[24] Like the sublime metaphor for Longinus, myth conceals the fact of its own artifice. Roland Barthes calls this "hide-and-seek," a move offering "an instantaneous reserve of history, a tamed richness, which it is possible to call and dismiss in a sort of rapid alternation."[25] This is the "alibi" of myth. Even as it constructs a narrative, it is always somewhere else, never present to be revealed as artifice.[26] This is true also in the community-forming properties of myth. Individual subjects do not so much build relations with one another through myth as they identify shared relations between themselves and the myth mirrored in others, although the sign in which they are mutually invested appears as a bond between them rather than a third term. In other words, they share a relation to the myth, not necessarily with one another, and thus identify through a relation of non-relation, or metaxy as Christian Lundberg puts it.[27]

To call postnuclear survival a "myth" is not a statement on the possible accuracy of survival plans, but instead draws attention to the power this arrangement of metaphors had to influence behavior and belief. Civil defense was revived in the early 1980s during the first Reagan administration when Cold War tensions (and urban social disparities) again came into the national spotlight.[28] According to apocalypse historian Frederic Baumgartner, awareness that the world might end became more intense in the Atomic Age than it ever had been before, even at the height of the Dark Ages.[29] A sense of impending judgment tied specifically to Revelation was evident in popular books like Hal Lindsey's *The Late Great Planet Earth* and among Reagan Administration officials, perhaps including the president himself.[30] Although civil defense remained limited, preparation for Armageddon still occurred. The ritual aspect of these preparations was evident in the repetition of rites meant to protect against the dangers of the Bomb, even ones met with a cynical reaction in some quarters, like duck-and-cover drills. Preparation was sometimes given an almost mystical quality. T. K. Jones, who bore the magisterial title of Deputy Under Secretary for Defense for Research and Engineering, Strategic and Theater Nuclear Forces, said in 1981, "If there are enough shovels to go around, everybody's going to make it. . . . It's the dirt that does it," hardly a reassuring statement, and one for which he was quickly silenced.[31] Jones's dirt and shovels are presented as talismans to ward against danger even though the increasing power of hydrogen bombs which made civil defense impractical by the 1960s had continued apace into the 1980s. Repetition and ritual are hallmarks of survivalism today, with many "preppers" practicing their plans and endlessly revising them for the apocalypse they imagine. The talismanic quality of simple items can be seen in the Department of Homeland Security's suggestion that Americans buy duct tape and plastic sheeting to defend against terrorist attacks.

Modern-day survivalism has become a highly visible cultural phenomenon, especially in the United States. Once considered the province of right-wing, uneducated, rural Christians, survivalism has perhaps benefited from the fad for local and boutique commercialism to reach new audiences. The popular National Geographic documentary series *Doomsday Preppers* showcased both "traditional" stereotypical preppers and younger, tech-savvy suburbanites. Popular films have featured preppers for years, from *Tremors* to *10 Cloverfield Lane*. Right-wing media figures such as Glenn Beck and Alex Jones frequently discuss topics of interest to these groups, and mainstream media occasionally covers them as well. Contemporary doomsday preppers sometimes reject the precise fears of their forebears (nuclear war, Soviet invasion, Biblical Armageddon), but they remain bound together by the same texts and ritual performances. Popular websites allow them to share information, fears, hopes, and even bragging photographs of their preparations ("preps"). These self-taken prep photos are particularly interesting as they display the commitment of the individual to the identity of doomsday prepper, the accumulation of ritualistic objects, and the importance of mimetic desire. These "shelfies" have supplemented the older rituals of military-style preparation and backwoods lore accumulation.

These (ostensibly) secular rituals suggest a repeated investment in apocalypse. The reward for adherence to the practices of survivalism is a chance to start society anew. Those who are prepared will survive, and they will be the ones to reestablish society with the corruption and distortions of the status quo swept away. As Senator Richard Russell said in 1968, "[i]f we have to start over again with another Adam and Eve, then I want them to be Americans and not Russians."[32] This is the real enjoyment of apocalyptic violence—it is, as Frederick Jessett wrote in the letter that opens chapter 3, a chance to indulge the fantasy that one's neighbors are gone and that the world can now be restored in whatever fashion we think best. The return to "true" American values was a perennial theme in the large number of postapocalyptic stories that are essentially Westerns concerned with what Richard Slotkin called "regeneration through violence."[33] Heroic, independent protagonists, mostly hypermasculine[34] and usually capable of intense violence, defend the frontier values of democracy, self-reliance, and hard work.

The nostalgia for the frontier and the "real" American life of the (white) suburbs was a common theme in fiction about civil defense and survival. This fiction was the regenerative supplement that accompanied destruction of otherized groups marked as sacrificial. Robert Heinlein's novel *Farnham's Freehold* is perhaps the best example of this whole dynamic in play. The titular character, Hugh Farnham, survives with his family, a few acquaintances, and a black servant in his suburban home bomb shelter, only to emerge into a pristine land with no evidence of war. Farnham is able to govern himself and his family however he pleases, including a frank acceptance of incest in a conversation with his daughter. Ultimately the group is discovered by technologically advanced strangers, only to discover that they have been transported into a distant future where people with dark skin who survived World War III rule the Earth. Discovering that whites are now kept as slaves and food for these villains, Farnham endeavors to travel back in time before the war and prepare himself with the means to prevent their domination of the Earth. His freehold is a libertarian dream, ready to defend white suburban values (while also transgressing them for pleasure) against threatening racial others. An extreme example for its time, the themes of white supremacy, racial fear, libertarian freedom, violent masculinity, and utopian communities flourishing after a nuclear war resonate with modern survivalist literature, as the next section will analyze in detail.[35]

Consistent with a suspicion of government that characterizes the American right wing, modest government civil defense programs were supplemented with much more vigorous private efforts by survivalists, along the lines of Farnham's fictional preparations. These fantasies represent judgment of one's enemies and vindication of one's beliefs, the obliteration of an oppressive order to make way for the birth of freedom. Again, the terror of nuclear war comes with its own attraction, but the mythic template laid by stories of the Bomb continues to serve as a site for communities to form around the sign of survival, and to large measure, the Bomb itself. Presented with an endless stream of predictions for the world's destruction over the last seventy years, survivalists have embraced their own version of Pascal's wager: the risk of destruction might be low, and the risk of survival might be low if nuclear war is to come, but any risk of survival makes the preparation effort a sacred mission. The Bomb revealed an indifferent universe that could function perfectly well without human beings. Survival myths helped to salve the horror of the Real by asserting a reason to struggle against death.

The promise of renewal is a means of access to the numinous power of the Bomb, or more generally, the dislocating sense that arises from a confrontation with a world where human civilization has been destroyed. It is easy to lampoon survivalist preparations as ineffective. Many prepare for a specific event—nuclear war, solar flare, supervolcano eruption, virus—rather than catastrophe in general. Many rely on bad science, optimistic assumptions about resource availability, or hopeless preparations out of scale with the events they are supposed to survive. This criticism misses the function of the survivalist myth as a means of access to the Real. Enjoyment is a product of ritual adherence—in other words, repetition. Survivalists don't seek to bring the comforts of society into a world of chaos. Rather, they continually practice living in a world *without* society, as it is currently understood, before any catastrophe has happened. They simulate a form of "genuine" sociality, an unmediated existence. They aren't trying to make things easy. They are enjoying the idea that conditions might be hard, giving them a chance to prove themselves and master the vagaries of nature just how they imagined early American pioneers to have done. Indeed, as Mary Manjikian argues, apocalyptic stories often appeal to those in positions of safety, rather than those most at risk.[36] To illustrate this point, the next section will explore the paradoxical ways that survivalist communities form with the help of technological media around the fantasy of a total obliteration of that same media and the society that it supports. To show the distant and pervasive ripples of the survival myth, I have chosen two perhaps unlikely networks to exemplify the fantasy: electromagnetic pulse fiction and Internet dating sites.

Feeling a Pulse

Nuclear fear created the framework for other kinds of apocalyptic technological visions, most of which now seem to include the fear that technology, like an angry God, will abandon us. Widespread electrical failure from solar flares or electromagnetic pulse (EMP) attacks is a recurrent theme in survivalist fiction.[37] EMP narratives are interesting both for the kind of work they do in organizing right-wing survivalist communities and because they show strong continuity with Cold War fears. Boosted by Y2K, 5/5/2000, and the Mayan doomsday hype of 2012, survivalist communities have knitted together through movies, television shows, press coverage, and the World Wide Web. Their concerns mirror those of Jacques Ellul or Paul Virilio to some extent, both of whom thought that an increasingly technologically integrated society faced the possibility of unpredictable accident and collapse. Its godlike structural position makes the Bomb a metonymic herald for the larger ills of technology and its omnipresence in modern life, as Ira Chernus argued, claiming that the Bomb was the primary organizing symbol of a machine society that demanded sacrifice and total control.[38] Much survivalist networking in the twenty-first century relies on the Internet and television, however. We are presented with another paradox: communities that set out to resist dependence on the global colonization of technique have become heavily reliant on electronic communication for their very identities. How do we explain why people who seek to live off the grid are largely connected by the system that they ostensibly fear and distrust?

In the *Left Behind* series of Christian apocalyptic novels, Lundberg finds a "readerly sadism" through which devout Christians who see themselves as members of a marginalized victim community can enjoy the suffering of their persecutors without violating Christian injunctions against violence. The series combines themes of persecution (outlaw Christian groups victimized by the Antichrist's regime), fear of global governance (the Antichrist, Nicolae Carpathia, takes power as leader of the United Nations), and graphic apocalyptic violence. Evangelical communities form around these texts not simply because they are shared, but because they are read in a particular way to forge common links in sadistic violence.[39] Evangelicals feel dispossessed by a dominant secular society that they interpret as hostile to their faith, but fantasies of revenge allow them to assert agency against it.[40] Although one traditional Freudian reading of violent fantasies suggests that they are a form of catharsis that prevents aggression from being externalized on living victims, Lundberg argues that apocalyptic texts form communities based on enjoyment of violence. The conditions of societal disintegration allow characters to enjoy advanced technology, killing, and worldly commerce because Armageddon suspends the normal rules of moral behavior.[41]

Three survivalist stories, all premised on the collapse of the North American electrical grid, display similar themes. The most widely read of these, William Forstchen's *One Second After*, is the first of a three-part series. The story takes place in an idyllic North Carolina town after an electromagnetic pulse caused by unknown agents destroys all modern electronics and throws the United States into nineteenth-century conditions. The main character, military history professor John Matherson, thinks that he lives in a "Norman Rockwell painting" even before the pulse.[42] Matherson's town of Black Mountain is one that progress has passed by, where folks still leave doors unlocked and an ice cream truck still makes the rounds in summer. When told that he "can't keep time back forever," Matherson wistfully suggests that he "can try."[43] Matherson dislikes text messaging because it lacks the authenticity of phone calls and worries about being "left behind," thanking God when his daughter's newfangled CD player dies.[44] When the pulse does hit, he observes that we were "all conditioned" by technology, so dependent that a "third-rate lunatic . . . with only one or two nukes" could "level the playing field against us."[45] Conservative ideology is plain throughout the book, although subtle by the standards of survivalist novels. Matherson asserts control as a somewhat reluctant military leader, carrying out executions of looters in the town square and ultimately organizing an army to fight off a gang of cannibalistic marauders from the big cities. Throughout the story he thinks of the lessons left by America's patriotic founders, a theme that powerfully influences contemporary right-wing extremist groups like the survivalist Patriot movement. Matherson works to bring industrial and communication technology back to Black Mountain even though he decries the failures of America's technological society.

It is the US Army that ultimately saves the day at the novel's conclusion. The scene is probably supposed to be reminiscent of American soldiers liberating Nazi-occupied Europe during the Second World War, although it is also made clear that the United States will never regain its position as the world's dominant power. Throughout the book, there is much praise for America's military legacy and various characters are veterans of wars ranging from World War II to the Second Gulf War. Survivalists in the hills turn out to be valued community members, echoing the help that persecuted Christians offer in *Left Behind*.[46] The execution scene, where Matherson shoots two unapologetic tattooed punks for looting, is almost a metonymy for the whole book: we who have sinned have been judged and condemned. Only violence can cleanse us. Liberal academics get their comeuppance: "They'll never make it now," says the president of Matherson's conservative Christian college. "I bet . . . they're sitting around like the French nobles did at Versailles even as the mob swarmed over the gates. I bet they're singing 'Give Peace a Chance,' even as they starve to death."[47] It's left up to conservative veterans and their followers to "rebuild America as we want it to be."[48]

One Second After thus shares significant elements with *Left Behind*, especially in its narrative of societal collapse, Christian reclamation, and the vindication of supposedly victimized conservatives. All of this is done without explicitly religious messages—no character in the book seems particularly devout, but conservative "Christian values" are essentially equivalent to the survivalist virtues of self-reliance, community, and sacrifice. Forstchen's book is also significant for the continuity with Cold War nuclear fear demonstrated by its substantial foreword and afterword. The afterword, written by US Navy Captain Bill Sanders, explains that the dangers of electromagnetic pulse are real, all resulting from our "technologically oriented society," the vulnerability of which "increases daily as our use and dependence on electronics continues to accelerate." The foreword, by conservative politician Newt Gingrich, explicitly links the story to *Alas, Babylon* and the movie *Testament*, "great classics of the Cold War" nuclear fear genre, which also influenced Gingrich himself.[49] The book is therefore situated in a longer history of survivalist destruction-and-rebirth fantasy, cultivating enjoyment in the suffering of enemies (starving liberal academics, violently executed "punk" looters, and gruesome battles and executions involving ex-criminal marauders). It is explicitly intended as a warning call for preparation.

More explicit still is James Knight's *The Pulse of Allah*, in which a conspiratorial Muslim Coalition unites the Islamic world, invades Europe, and launches an EMP attack on North America. Muslims are portrayed as rapists, murderers, cowards, and zealots who commit genocide in Israel and intend the same for Europeans. From a survivalist perspective, Knight's portrayal of Americans is more interesting. Within a week the US is reduced to rioting, murder, cannibalism, and rape as the "underclass" rebels. Liberals are again an object of scorn and fantasized revenge, as the same people who "regarded them [survivalists] as gun toting Neanderthals only days before" are suddenly the victims of bloody and humiliating depredations.[50] The government is equally bad, with the IRS, FAA, FEMA, and social welfare agencies described as variously meddling, breeding moral corruption, or simply ineffective. Americans are fallen. "Bloated government" is fortunately resolved by the pulse and attendant bloodshed.[51] The military, however, is universally praised, and the book is littered with unnecessary acronyms and technical weapons specs, nearly pornographic when compared with equally lurid descriptions of rape and sexual violence.[52] The author urges readers in a brief endnote to take the threat seriously, and states in the dedication that he hopes that the story "inspires you to be a bit more prepared so that you can take care of yourself" should society collapse.

Patriot Dawn, written by Max Velocity and available (like *Pulse of Allah*) for download through Amazon, is another example of hardcore, right-wing survivalist fantasy. The prologue details America's future collapse, beginning with the claim that the 2012 election "had been the mortal blow to the idea of America."[53] Following terrorist attacks, financial meltdown, and the collapse of America's electricity grid, Patriot organizations and conservative groups like the Tea Party are outlawed by the government, which has changed the American flag (in ways that resemble Obama's campaign logo) and restyled itself as "the Regime" after the South secedes again. Survivalist "preppers" are specifically targeted for murder or interment in "reeducation camps" if they are found to be stockpiling food.[54] All citizens are required to receive subcutaneous RFID chips, which is an echo of *Left Behind* and a long-standing Christian paranoia about the "mark of the Beast" described in Revelation, although *Patriot Dawn* is not explicitly religious.

The main characters, Jack and Caitlin Berenger, are two survivalists near Washington, DC, both ex-military, who fight a bloody battle with the rapacious forces of the Homeland Security Department and are forced to flee. They take refuge with an old Army Ranger colleague who is organizing military resistance against the government using supplies of food, ammunition, and other materiel stockpiled by likeminded survivalists before the collapse. The character's names are revealing. Jack Berenger (who seems to resemble *Platoon*'s Staff Sergeant Barnes, played by Tom Berenger) has a son named Andrew (Andrew, Jack's son). The two youngest children are Sarah and Connor, perhaps in reference to the tough survivalist Sarah Connor of the *Terminator* franchise. The most prominent nonwhite characters are a Latino rapist and former gang member serving the regime and the evil Director Woods, who sounds suspiciously like Reverend Jeremiah Wright except for his violent sexual proclivities and membership in the Nation of Islam.[55] The book valorizes US Army veterans much like *Pulse of Allah* and *One Second After*, although its characters feel no remorse killing those who side with the Regime. Along the way, a number of other references appear that may be intended for a survivalist audience—the name "Red Dawn" and the phrase "Okay, Let's Roll," for example.[56] The electronic book also contains ads for Max Velocity's tactical manuals and nonfiction prepper books.

Readerly sadism seems to be at work in all three novels. In each of them a small group of people distrusts technological society to some extent, takes the threat of collapse seriously, is ostracized for its efforts, and is vindicated when weak liberals, complacent consumers, and the dependent underclass are plunged into violence and dismay. Normal injunctions against violence are suspended, and characters are even allowed to mimic oppressive governments when they execute evildoers, steal supplies, or impose their own versions of martial law. The context in which these books operate suggests that an analysis based only on their textual properties could miss their larger significance as loci of investment for the enjoyment of violence. Both their medium of delivery and the larger network that defines it are important. All three books represent different parts of a spectrum that defines right-wing conservatism, especially as embodied in the Patriot movement, and more recently, extremist groups that have gained prominence after the 2016 election of Donald Trump. This millenarian survivalist movement coalesced in the early 1990s from elements in the gun rights, Christian fundamentalist, Aryan Nation, and evangelical apocalyptic movements. The Patriot and related militia groups are notable for being "arguably the first major US social movements to be organized primarily through overlapping, horizontal, nontraditional electronic media" such as videotape distribution, AM radio, and the Internet.[57] The Internet is not just a new means to transmit right-wing survivalist messages to potential recruits, insignificant beyond the content of its messages. A material account of mediation should attend to the community-shaping role of the Internet itself.

All three survivalist books mentioned here are available electronically on Amazon.com. A customer searching for *One Second After*, the most mainstream of the three, will be directed to a set of other publications automatically. Amazon includes features that display other books that customers bought along with or instead of the one revealed by a search, books "frequently bought together," and a range of products with similar descriptions. In this case, Amazon's algorithms will suggest a variety of nonfiction survivalist handbooks, Patriot-based electronic novels like *Patriot Dawn*, and even classic Cold War nuclear novels such as *Alas, Babylon*. Because Amazon sells a wide range of products, these suggestions are more than intertextual: they also include oxygen absorbers for food storage, DVDs, military medical kits, even nuclear simulation games like *First Strike*. Algorithms will refine suggestions over time based on what customers have rated or purchased, steadily expanding the range of survivalist products and media. Facebook groups like "Preppers World," "Preparing For SHTF," and "SHFT & Prepping Central," some with over a hundred thousand followers, then lead readers to endless articles about supposed signs of impending doom, from inflation in Russia to water shortages in California, often interspersed with pro-military or anti-Obama posts. With enough work, one eventually ends up with Shiguro Takada's *Contingency Cannibalism: Superhardcore Survivalism's Dirty Little Secret*.

The conditions of online commerce demonstrate how purely intertextual dissemination might benefit as an analytic tool from attention to the material forms of media, especially as commercial algorithms continue to develop in ways that resemble learning. Simulations make claims about the reality that they represent, but algorithms have a dual function. They pare down an overwhelming torrent of information, helping to navigate through the glut of data that we are inundated with. As Ken Hillis, Michael Petit, and Kylie Jarrett argue in their work on Google, algorithms also represent reality in a particular way—search results derived from them present a sense of reality, or at least what is "relevant" in it, and therefore mediate the social world.[58] Many products include vigorous forums where readers can meet likeminded peers or be directed toward other potential websites, purchases, and social media groups.[59] Further, Kindle books allow readers to highlight passages and see what other readers have highlighted as well. This feature implicitly guides practices of reading—in *One Second After*, readers are directed to passages that deride Mohandas Gandhi, extol "peace through superior firepower," recount seemingly practical survival advice, and explain how those dependent on medical technology are doomed after the pulse. In the popular highlights for *Pulse of Allah*, one is directed to warnings about Iran's real-world missile program, statements about gun control, and warnings that society is already "close to the edge." Searches in *Patriot Dawn* suggest tactical advice about vehicle convoys, the value of NATO standard 5.56mm ammunition, and equipment for evading thermal imaging. All of this suggests that attention to practices of reading should include the structure of media itself.

Hybrid linguistic and material connections are co-produced by consumers and automated processes. The Symbolic order's unconscious is partly mechanical, with human connections augmented by computer calculations designed to foster sometimes more literal investment. This is one way to understand Lacan's insight that the signifier speaks through us without a complete reduction to structuralism at the expense of agency. The Internet is a system of metonymic connections that can guide users to identify with specific things as elements of a broader identity, but the subject matters too. The choice of what to search, what to buy, and which of millions of competing identities, products, and practices to invest in is not predetermined. Still, communities exist around a set of associated signifiers, and the fantasy of complete consumer choice is false as availability, mimetic desire, and the logic of algorithmic advertising limits the conditions for choice to occur.

Communities do not only form around texts, but around a series of media and material objects. Instead of forming direct contacts with one another, it is possible to share a mutual connection with a medium or media object, like a dating site or survivalist message board. Algorithmic connections are so powerful partly because of their mystique—they learn and process for us, without requiring us to understand precisely how they work.[60] In some ways, this technology is revolutionary. Individuals can be put in direct contact with others thousands of miles away, and communities with relatively small absolute numbers can thrive by finding dispersed like-minded adherents. In another sense, however, this is nothing new: because subjects are inaugurated into a linguistic order that they did not choose and identify partly on the basis of concepts that long preexist them without the need for any specific human author, it could be argued that language has always operated like a computer algorithm to structure the conditions in which subjects exercise their autonomy, much like the rules of a game dictate possible moves without choosing for the player.

The implications of this form of connectivity are explored more fully in the conclusion, but it is important to note here that the structure of the survivalist myth has changed as the artifice of myth makes itself absent and the complex of human and mechanical reference and comparison does the same. Amazon's algorithms might still be understood as making fundamentally metonymic connections, but it is necessary to understand these tropes as principles of connection broadly, not just figural language. In this case, one might miss the full extent of a survivalist community animated by its enjoyment of violence, deeply concerned about the recession of technology from the world, and made real through the operation of that same technology with the help of corporate computer algorithms. In this sense technology has an aspect of the divine, promising to transcend humanity and reunite us with something like the godhead, giving it "a whiff of the holy" and a power to make connections seemingly without our direct involvement.[61] It helps to shape a society seen as fallen and corrupt by those who imagine its destruction, but also helps to mediate the communities that form around this imagination.

We'll All Go Together When We Go

Another aspect of survivalist sociality has attracted more popular attention of late: romance. The television show *Doomsday Preppers* interviews survivalists and rates their preparations according to "expert" analyses. The show is notable for its domestic, family-oriented themes. Households are the primary unit of analysis, and although the occasional tough ex-military loner shows up, the show focuses mostly on nuclear families or couples. A number of web clips are available on the National Geographic website.[62] "Backup upon Backup" features Johnny, his wife, and his sister-in-law (who is described as a "backup" *parent*, not a backup wife). "Doris Day of Doom" features a kindly older woman who involves her community in prepping activities, including the less-aggressive Sy Schotz, who insists that survivalists pay too much attention to weaponry. If roaming marauders show up, says Sy, he will just make them a nice meal and "charm them" (if this doesn't work or they don't prove "useful," however, he assures the viewer that he will poison them all or slit their throats as they sleep). A young woman featured in "Survival of the Fittest" plans to hole up in her apartment. As she holds her cat she demonstrates how her boyfriend intends to shoot it in the back of the skull.[63] The National Geographic website also features advertisements for Atlas Shelters, a company that promises to protect families in the case of Armageddon ("better prepared than scared"). While the show tends to poke fun at the outlandish aspects of doomsday preparation, National Geographic also offers a range of books, iPhone apps, survival advice, and speculative documentaries intended to prepare audiences for the breakdown of industrial civilization.

The show's depiction of happy (but prudent) families tends to be quite charitable. Never, for example, are profiled individuals shown to be overt white supremacists or members of violent Christian splinter groups, although as discussed above, these are strong themes in some survivalist communities. More openly mocking was a segment on Comedy Central's *The Colbert Report* entitled "End of the World of the Week." The show featured a report on SurvivalistSingles.com, an Internet dating site that caters to survivalists. Deriding the site as a place where singles can "Arma-get-it-on," Colbert lampooned several profiles and joked about the apparent incongruity between the search for love and preparations for the end of the world. That the selected profiles are fairly mainstream by the standards of SurvivalistSingles.com is not apparent in the episode.

SurvivalistSingles was one of several dating sites designed for survivalists. These, like the web of connections involving Amazon.com, help to establish survivalist communities and reveal a great deal about their membership.[64] SurvivalistSingles, whose motto was "Don't Face the Future Alone," at one point sported nearly 8,000 members, claiming to be the "fastest growing relationship site on the web."[65] The site also featured a somewhat generic graphic of two shadows, male and female, holding hands, which in context is perhaps eerily reminiscent of the carbon "shadows" of Hiroshima. A little over two-thirds of the site's members were male. Couples are also listed, although most of them seem more interested in starting offline survivalist communities than pursuing romantic interests. Many profiles overlapped with users at PrepperDating.com, an austere site with apparently many fewer members than SurvivalistSingles. Kwink.com, a site catering to niche groups, also has a survivalist page. Kwink is aimed at a larger audience although it contains many specialty groups (survivalists, self-described "beautiful people," vampires, and so forth).

These online groups represent the larger trend of dating sites that cater to specific niches. Besides obvious examples such as (possibly facetious) SeaCaptainDate.com, AshleyMadison (catering to married people seeking affairs, made notorious by a 2015 data hack), and Whispers4u.com (intended for people with disabilities), even mainstream sites have their own target audiences. eHarmony.com has roots in Christian evangelism;[66] OKCupid targets the hip urban crowd; and Adult Friend Finder, XXXMatch, and (originally) Tinder are for those who do not desire long-term relationships. Perhaps thousands of dating sites exist, and according to one executive interviewed by Dan Slater, a community of 60,000 is considered small even for a niche site.[67]

Although SurvivalistSingles and its imitators may be small by dating industry standards, the mere existence of these sites reveals interesting dynamics in the formation of survivalist communities. Presence on the Internet does not simply reflect the size of an offline community—it plays a role in establishing and legitimizing communities in the first place. PrepperDating.com included a "friend" system reminiscent of Facebook, its own practical survival forums, and advertising and links to survivalist products and pages. Many profiles on PrepperDating and SuvivalistSingles contained links to other Internet bulletin boards and forums, the most frequently linked of which is survivalistboards.com where members could find discussions about Christianity, conspiracy theories, and product advertisements from Condor Tactical Gear and other companies catering to security and paramilitary interests. SuvivalistSingles member AKPeakster, a 31-year-old woman, reports having read *One Second After* and fearing electromagnetic pulse attacks, as does Andrea Burke, who runs the site.[68]

Niche dating is about capitalizing on interests that might not be socially acceptable, creating a place where individuals can "mingle freely and furtively through a friendly flashing portal that screams: *See how many people are just like you?*"[69] When Rob Horning criticizes this view, arguing that online dating is about consuming the spectacle of dating rather than a "collaborative project riven with anxiety, negotiation, and compromise . . . taking the first tentative feints toward building a collective social unit,"[70] he overlooks the urgency of users like 56-year-old Stealth ("seeking Patriotic [*sic*] to watch my back as I will yours . . . [will] stand and fight oppression"), the loneliness of greyback ("Looking for the last love of my life"), the earnestness of jstme ("I am searching for my survivalist soul mate, a partner and companion") and even the rage and confusion of seriousfunfortwo ("Advanced Prepper. . . . Unfortunately very few of the Sheeple (women) out there understand why i [*sic*] do this and they prefer to remain ignorant to what goes on around them. . . . I am befuddled on [*sic*] how I might find a woman who shes [*sic*] my views on Prepping. It is a lifestyle and you both need to be on the same page"). It is hard to agree with critic Eva Illouz, who writes that "technology undermines . . . passion because of the way technology forces you to manage your relationships in a completely rational way and because of the way in which it creates a blasé attitude and cynical attitude towards the encounter."[71]

Illouz and Horning may well be correct to describe most of the people who use dating sites the way that they do. The argument here is not that these characterizations are necessarily wrong, but that they do not apply readily to survivalism. Survivalist dating sites are powerfully linked to a larger imagination of catastrophe and survival, connected by the material links of various media and different, sometimes conflicting, ideologies. People with disabilities—or even raunchy sea captains—are not linked by the intensity of belief in the coming apocalypse that urges lovers to kiss under the sword of Damocles rather than the mistletoe. For those who are preparing to be the world's last inhabitants after some catastrophe, the promise of finding love is a metonymy for overall fate of the human species. Some, like the 40-year-old woman blyssless, seem excited. "Blessings," she writes on her SurvivalistSingles profile. "The end of the world to me is a new begining [*sic*]. Im [*sic*] looking for someone who is looking forward to the coming tribulation and doesn't want to fight it alone." In her "favorite things" category, blyssless proclaims "I LOVE the HolyGhost! [*sic*]." Others worry that things are "going south," "about to get really problematic," or as many survivalists say, "the shit is going to hit the fan." Fear and welcoming bring users to the same places. Just as they rely on Amazon's algorithms to deliver lurid disaster pornography in the form of badly written pulp novels, survivalists online count on the matching functions of dating site algorithms to deliver them rugged souls with whom they can weather doomsday and once again go forth and multiply.

How does one both enjoy consuming the (imagined) suffering of billions of anonymous others and sometimes desperately hope to connect with one's soul mate among those same anonymous others? Recall the connection between Eros and Thanatos made by Bataille. Both are at heart a drive for continuity, and therefore a drive to exceed mediation. Alphonso Lingis argues that all community is based on the death of the other, and the possibility of human extinction must necessarily shape our subjectivities.[72] Individual connections of love happen, he writes, not to soothe the pain of the other or merely to help them die, but are premised on a desire "to substitute oneself for the other in his or her pain and dying," "to share the solitude of an event that is simultaneously and unthinkably his [*sic*] own most proper possibility and his radical dispossession."[73] This, perhaps, explains why survivalist dating profiles so often express the fear of "dying alone." It is not that we escape the bonds of mortality in love; it is that we imagine that when the world goes crashing down around us, we can at least die together. PadmeFaith, another Survivalist Singles user, put it succinctly: "Perhaps it won't happen for a long time," she wrote, "but it would be sad to go it alone."

Survivalists, like evangelicals, create specific communities to compensate for the inevitable breakdown of community writ large. We do, in practice, distinguish between friends and enemies, and there is no such thing as a frictionless global community, so groups respond to this failure by forging their own units which must necessarily contain an excluded "outside." Many—certainly not all—apocalyptic survival groups share the racist sentiments of *Farnham's Freehold*, where the terrifying reveal that encourages the main character to travel back in time to prevent a nuclear war is that technologically sophisticated nonwhite races dominate the Earth and cannibalize their white slaves after the US and USSR destroy each other. Hate groups enjoy hating others because to do so reaffirms one's own superiority and allows one to express sentiments that would otherwise be unacceptable in a broader social context.[74] For survivalist fiction, enjoying the economy of death often means a joy in the death of outsiders and a counterpoised remorse for the deaths of "good guys." What distinguishes survivalists from other apocalyptic groups is that their fantasy relies on gaining strength from these losses. Society does not end with them. It begins again. Baumgartner has argued that apocalypticism assuages the fear of death that accompanies natural deaths for some people. Infirmity and old age do not matter if the world will inevitably end soon, so the thought of apocalypse can serve to recuperate the traumatic emergence of the Real (death) even in other contexts.[75]

This may also explain why survivalist plans are often so obviously flawed. Among survivalists studied by sociologist Richard Mitchell, even those like George Kassner, who spent $700,000 building a fortified mountain retreat, are often quite impractical.[76] Survivalists do not all intend to survive. Instead, they find enjoyment in preparation. They consume the fantasy of survival. The technological links and media that form the survivalist community should be understood as proactive assertions of group identity, the affective investment in a particular identity that is not merely "a rejection or a protest against ordered social life" but an imaginative "reforming of social life."[77] The notion that survivalists may not be preparing fully for disaster even if they think they are is consistent with the idea of communities organized around death. When we seek to transgress the taboo against death, we do so by courting danger, by exposing our bodies to risk. Despite their professed fears of technological destruction and abandonment, survivalists may have a relationship with technique based not on fear but on boredom. Doomsday prepping, much like nuclear war gaming, allows the subject to experience a bit of taboo hardship and imagine death but still retreat to a safe space, free from harm, back in the mantle of the quotidian society, but with a sense of superiority over the unenlightened people who do ignore catastrophe. It is a way to play with doomsday and enjoy the fantasy of destruction without guilt.

As rationalization proceeds and technological societies seek to propagate comfort and safety, courting danger—taking a risk—becomes ever more difficult. Survivalism is a fantasy of danger bred from excessive safety.[78] Longing for the End of Days is really longing for a situation where our lives are not entirely safe, mediated, and comfortable, where danger still exists and death has meaning. Thus fresh_air_girl can write in her SurvivalistSingles profile "I'm not so freaked out about the end of the world, I am just tired of living in society the way it is." fresh_air_girl was 43-years-old at the time of the post, which is perhaps a bit below the mean age on SurvivalistSingles, unlike many other dating communities. The members of this group tend to be older, financially comfortable, white, and relatively secure, just as the survivalists interviewed by Mitchell were.[79] Survivalist prepping can be seen then as a ritual of adherence to the myth, and that myth itself as a representative of the sacred Real, a world that exists beyond the confines of human society and is heralded on Earth by the Bomb. Survivalist preparation understood as a cultural technology does two kinds of work: it allows its adherents to develop a sense of control (*automaton*) over their unpredictable fates (*tuché*), and at the same time, fantasize about what that unpredictable, authentic existence might be like—to get both *fort* and *da* at once. Preparing for the apocalypse isn't supposed to resist it by making (future) life easier. They are not trying to resist. They are trying to encounter resistance.

The sign of postapocalyptic survival made possible by the Bomb speaks through these various groups and knits them together, organized around the enjoyment of the imagined violence that started with the threat of nuclear attack and now extends from avian flu to zombies. The myth of survivalism, whether its practices and products would be helpful in the face of disaster or not, responds to the injunction to survive. The myth brings some sense of order to the world rent by the schism of the Bomb at Trinity and allows its subjects to enjoy the thought of urban destruction as an opportunity for renewal. It is a counterpart to simulating the apocalypse in war plans. Both allow subjects to enjoy a sense of control over the conditions of the world's presence and absence (the chaos of nuclear conflict or the obliteration of society), to have a fleeting taste of what might seem like the Real of the Bomb. Both try to tame the horror of human extinction, by fitting it into systemic rules on one hand, and preparing to defy it and start over on the other. Both are products of the allure and danger of risk. The war planner bluffs big to win, risking everything, while the survivalist tries to hedge their bets, imagining that after a bad bet there might still be a chance to win it all in the end once the weaker players have been wiped out. The nuclear age began with the overwhelming experience of the Real in nuclear explosions, which was then assimilated in the Symbolic economy of language, simulations, and games, and ultimately defied and venerated at once in the Imaginary of survivalism, itself made possible by the durable tropes and myths of the Symbolic, and repeated as a doomed, circuitous means of accessing the Real. This work of the death drive is the strongest thread weaving together the many disparate patches of nuclear imagination into one enduring cultural formation. It starts with the horror of the subject's frailty, and ends with the hubris of the subject's power.

Conclusion

Dragons on the Map

> Two menacing structures face each other today: the non-world of verbal machinery, which is out to dissolve everything into the noise of words, and the non-world of mechanized things, which, detached from language, is waiting only for a loud explosion to create a language of its own . . . so things crack and explode today as though they were trying to burst forth into sound—the sound of doom.
>
> —Max Picard, *The World of Silence*

After high school, I continued on to debate in college. In my last year, the national topic involved nuclear arms control. I would sometimes stay amongst the "U" call numbers in the basement of the Michigan State University Library all night reading books that hadn't been checked out since the 1980s, walking home in the early morning. As an adolescent, I had played role-playing games like *Dungeons & Dragons* and *Shadowrun*. My time with nuclear weapons scholarship was much the same. I memorized vast amounts of specialized terminology, sets of rules, fantastical locations like Yamantau Mountain and Pantex Plant, Eniwetok Atoll and Semipalatinsk. Nuclear strategy and *Dungeons & Dragons* perhaps have more similarities than differences. Both are about imagining worlds that might be, but aren't. Both are about sets of rules to determine outcomes, often involving horrible deaths, even the fate of the world. Both generate their procedures with little connection to empirical reality. They rely instead on the sense of wonder, of forces unseen and worlds made foreign, the thrill of simply *seeing if this works*. Parents in the 1980s worried about their children taking *D&D* too literally, perhaps even hurting someone. Some parents of debaters worried about nuclear war, too, but they don't seem to have made the connection between what their kids said in competitions and the grave words of politicians and generals on the evening news.

Every day on the way home from the library I would pass East Lansing's Seventh-Day Adventist Church in the half light of dawn. Even then, long after the Cold War ended, it had a prominent yellow-and-black "Fallout Shelter" sign bolted to its masonry, an old-fashioned triangular Civil Defense plate made of metal. Today that sign is gone. In its place is the deep-set rust stain that the sign left, indelibly marking its place in that triangular shape, an enthymeme of death and hope for anyone who remembers its old message. The sign is literally absent, but its distortion remains. The disarmament movement has dwindled too. There are no duck-and-cover drills; Bert the Turtle has gone the way of Lonesome George. But in the vast plains of America, updated nuclear silos still exist, alert as always, like swords among the plowshares. The Bomb is still with us. It's only the shelters that have disappeared.

This book has explored the distorting influence of the Bomb as a way to understand desire, namely the desire to experience the Real beyond mediation. Desire for an extralinguistic reality is perpetually frustrated by the limits of language and the media in which we live. Unable to escape the Symbolic and Imaginary registers of human experience, we forge our attachments to signifiers for the unspeakable. We misrecognize the uncanny elements of the Symbolic for the impossible Real. This is an issue raised by symbols in any form, as they must necessarily stand in for something that is absent. The connection between any particular signifier and what it represents may be arbitrary, but it is held together by our investment in the tie, a kind of implicit collective agreement necessary for language to convey meaning, to provide the resources for one speaking subject to address another. These agreements accrete into broader myths, sustained and shaped to create enduring cultural formations. Essentially, language works through a habitual confusion in which artifice is concealed by its own action. Even if the revelation of the Real cannot be transmitted in its full force from one subject to another, language can gesture beyond itself. I chose the Bomb to make this point partly because it is a particularly stark example of the numinous qualities of language, but it illustrates a more general sublime quality of communication.

Because the uncanny is never a complete substitute for the Real, the effort to reach it is frustrated and then repeated. Any object of desire understood as distinct from the subject must necessarily elude total incorporation because it stands in for a continuity that would unmake the subject. When we attain specific objects, the motion of the drive does not stop because each object stands in for something else in a signifying chain that has its final trajectory beyond the Symbolic order altogether. Perhaps such a unity with existence is possible, but if so, language cannot convey it. It is a currency that only serves up to a point. This basic dynamic is the first part of the death drive. We are pulled toward an unmediated experience of the world. When we encounter the inevitable obstacles of this quest, the next phase begins: the enjoyment of our efforts to control presence and absence, not because we enjoy either state (although we likely enjoy them both), but because we can compensate for frustration by attaching to the one condition we actually control—the capacity for enjoyment itself. Thus the *fort-da* game represents the arc of human desire, and at bottom, it is fundamentally rhetorical.

This formulation situates the death drive as problematic for communication studies, including media studies, cultural studies, and rhetoric. I have argued here that the death drive is not reducible to the desire, biological or otherwise, for death. Rather, it betrays the union of *Eros* and *Thanatos*: both are a desire for unmediated experience, for connection to all that the subject surrenders as the cost of its own coming into being. This current of desire is a product of the necessary conditions for the Symbolic, not the Real, even though it is a desire animated by the latter. The death drive is not a hidden structure that organizes the Real, but a dynamic observable in the Symbolic as it attempts to repair the rips and threadbare patches worn into it by the unimaginably vast world that exists outside our ken. The death drive itself might be silent and invisible, but its passage leaves a wake of distortions in language. The attempts to mediate what is beyond mediation comprise the only evidence available for the motion of the drive, and thus the proper tools to analyze it are found in communication studies. Things that seem inexpressible, and the desire to encounter them, have a powerful effect on the human world. To neglect this is to miss one important factor that shapes our communication. The mediation of desire is important because it is an attribute of signs that helps to explain why some might have traction and some might not.

The tradition most applicable to this understanding of the drive is the rhetorical tradition of the sublime. Edmund Burke, writing a century and a half before Sigmund Freud, identified the sublime as the interplay of two drives, one for pleasure and one for pain, but both present in the sublime in some measure, the latter more powerful because it is an "emissary" for that "king of terrors," death.[1] Burke borrowed from the tradition of Longinus which understood the sublime as an aspect of language, generally metaphor. It is to this understanding that I want to return, with a difference: communication is more than language, and the sublime is an aspect of communication. The advent of the atomic bomb elevated human expression to a qualitatively new degree. It became possible to communicate through fission and fusion, through nations destroyed in minutes, through genetic and environmental legacies marked on a millennial scale. Nuclear deterrence during the Cold War was a kind of dialogue between two parties expressed in a mixture of actions and words, with the possible destruction of a nuclear war as the largely enthymematic threat underpinning this exchange. Game theory had a related element of communication. It theorized about how messages should be sent and decoded in this dialogue, and what various signals might mean.

Today, the threats posed by synthetic biology, artificial intelligence, asteroid collisions, and a host of modern technological anxieties exist alongside nuclear anxiety. The discussion of these new threats follows paths that were first charted during the early nuclear era. They elicit horror and fascination in much the same way, and they have similar existential questions at their hearts. Derrida argued that nuclear war always exists textually in a sense because the actual material event of a species-destroying conflict would end history and society such that there would be no discourse left to address it. This observation could be generalized to other existential risks and the talk about them. The sublime functions for them, too. They evince the same kind of morbid fascination, talk of survival, and fantasies about rebuilding, as the continued popularity of apocalyptic science fiction amply shows. They contribute to the mythologies spawned by nuclear threats. The structural formations of nuclear fear might therefore shed some light on these new terrors. They too can be understood as examples of Burke's sublime mix of horror and desire, and analyzed with an eye to Longinus's work on the linguistic tools used to refer past the limits of language.

I would like to conclude by outlining the implications that I see in this project for communication studies and the politics of antinuclear activism. In keeping with my focus on the sublime elements of language, the ruptures of the Real in speech, and the compensatory means of "feigning unicity," I have chosen to focus mostly on rhetoric. This is not an effort to elevate rhetoric above the other subfields of communication. Rather, my goal has been to show how trope is more than "mere speech," but is inextricably tied to material practices and cultural processes. I once heard an eminent professor refer to rhetorical studies as the "imperialism of a small discipline." In focusing on the death drive and its expression in trope, I do not mean to add new forces to this conquering field and its universal aspirations. Instead, I want to demonstrate how the divisions between material, cultural, linguistic, and rhetorical phenomenon are artificial, much as the categories for describing nuclear war are products of artifice, always arbitrary in some sense. To the extent that various methods in communication are separate at all, rhetoric is one way of thinking about common problems that overlaps, supplements, strengthens, and benefits powerfully from other methods. Instead of the imperial metaphor, rhetoric is closer to the United Nations. It is an idealistic but always harried, frequently overlooked, and seldom appreciated means of seeking common bonds across enduring conflicts and differences. Its work will never be done, but nor should it ever stop. Rhetoric here describes the ways that language works to preserve a semblance of coherence when rifts emerge.

The significance of the Real suggests that omissions, breakdowns, and silence are important objects of study. We should not think of the inability to capture and translate something just as the failure of mediation but also the triumph of excess. The former centers the Symbolic order of human mediation as the key agent. The latter acknowledges that the universe outside our ken sometimes evades our grasp, as the various "new" materialisms have been quick to point out. The silence of Trinity was not just an absence of speech. It was the triumph of the Real, silence as its own revelation—an affirmative force. It is not necessary to ascribe agency to the Real to recognize that it is more than the space left outside of language. Neither should we ignore it because it is beyond our ability to translate. Its deformations alter the Symbolic, giving us outlines for speculation, even if we can never truly see what is behind the curtain. A theory of communication thus should at least speculate about what exceeds mediation because the network of signification cannot be described without some understanding, no matter how provisional, of its limits.

The word *theory* itself presents an opportunity for thinking about how rhetorical theory might benefit from more attention to the intersection of the Symbolic and the Real in sublime language. If the concept of the unconscious advanced in this book is correct, we should attend closely to the context of words in both their diachronic and synchronic relations. Etymology can be understood in this sense as an unconscious accretion over time—older meanings don't vanish so much as they remain evidence of what has been repressed in the itinerary of a signifier. Routes and roots are not unrelated. Nicolas of Cusa claimed that the word *theory* derived from *theoro*, "I see," which is also the origin of *Theos*, "God."[2] God looks on all things and sees them all, as does theory.[3] *Theoria* is the gaze that lights the shadows to reveal the world. This understanding of theory is like Georges Bataille's Sun of reason and truth, that rational source of enlightenment both figurative and literal. But the Sun is not exhausted by reason. There is also a rotten Sun, a harbinger of madness for those who stare at it too intensely.[4] The duality of the Sun for Bataille should recall the language used to describe nuclear testing. To affix ourselves to reason not only misses the lights that are outshone by the Sun's rays—as Longinus would have it—but also to court a larger catastrophe, akin to Jacques Lacan's notion of psychosis, in that we become unable to perceive how excessive faith in our abilities to track the world rationally is itself irrational.

This thread in the development of theory can be supplemented with another tradition, one derived from *téras* and later *therion*, the Greek origins of our word "monster." Monster, related to "demonstrate," was once a disruption, a *revelation*, an *apocalypse* in its original sense of these words as "unveiling." These words gradually came to represent *terror*, just as the revelation of the excesses beyond language can *terrify*, literally, fix one to the ground. Theory should not only trace the order of the world—it should be a *teratology*, an acknowledgment that the monstrous world "bites back," in Eugene Thacker's words. Teratology was once the "account of marvels."[5] It was sometimes pejorative: "when bold writers, fond of the sublime, intermix something great and prodigious in everything they write," it is not altogether a positive thing.[6] The word evokes the sublime in a rhetorical sense, linked with "prodigious monsters" of thought and desire.[7] As the psychoanalytic trend in rhetorical theory suggests, we can perhaps do more than explain how language works, how movements are organized, and how symbolic action occurs. We can also reveal the places where these things collapse into incoherence, and explore the mechanisms by which speaking subjects attempt to salvage their order.

The importance of the Real establishes the significance of the death drive for theories of communication. In Lacanian theory, the drive has generally been considered an aspect of the Symbolic order—the subject, formed through the alienation of the mirror phase, is driven to invest in objects (signifiers) that stand in for something lost that could make it whole. The formulation of the death drive in this book stresses the interaction of these elements of the Symbolic (and the Imaginary, in the case of the mirror stage and investments of meaning). This is in keeping with Lacan's own work but also Bataille's concept of continuity. The subject's initial formation marks it as discrete from everything else, which is the necessary condition for death since the demise of one individual is given significance only if that individual is marked off somehow as a subject in its own right. *Eros* drives the momentary unity of the self with another who stands in for the larger external world. *Thanatos* does the same in the more permanent state of death. What makes the two drive one is the common pull toward unmediated reality, a direct correspondence with and even momentary dissolution in the Real. Identifying the death drive as a desire to move beyond mediation shows the necessity of a broad view of communication. The connections that form between sites of investment for Lacan either proliferate meaning by referencing outward (e.g., metonymy) or condense meaning by establishing a particularly saturated connection, defining the sites involved by this strong relation (e.g., metaphor). These rhetorical tropes are typically used to analyze language, but they can be reframed to apply to mediation more generally, including the material aspect of specific media forms, like games.

In their canonical book *Remediation*, Jay David Bolter and Richard Grusin identify a seeming paradox in media. There are "contradictory imperatives for immediacy and hypermediacy . . . a double logic of *remediation*. Our culture wants both to multiply its media and to erase all traces of mediation: ideally, it wants to erase its media in the very act of multiplying them."[8] Both immediacy and hypermediacy have a long history—the first in the evolution of Western European painting, for example, and the second in illuminated medieval manuscripts.[9] The death drive enriches this observation by underpinning it with a theoretical explanation: we desire the Real (immediacy), but are frustrated in achieving it. Instead, we enjoy our seeming ability to control presence and absence, latching on to our own subjectivity and misrecognizing the Symbolic for the Real—hence the enjoyment of hypermediacy. These imperatives are contradictory in a sense, but they follow from one another according to the logic of the death drive. Hypermediacy can be mistaken for immediacy because media compose our reality—even though they do not capture the Real. Recall that Lacan's argument for the primacy of the death drive is partly that all drives seek their own extinction. In the desire for immediacy, media also seek their own extinction in a sense. The goal of mediation is much like artifice in rhetorical theory. We paradoxically desire both the well-constructed turn of phrase and the seemingly impromptu expression of genuine belief. Artful language can of course be appreciated precisely for this beauty and construction, but many times artifice is most profound when it appears not to be artificial at all. Similarly, the most complex and powerful media seek to instill the sense that we are not viewing media at all, but direct reality.

Bolter and Grusin define a medium as "that which remediates. It is that which appropriates the techniques, forms, and social significance of other media and attempts to rival or refashion them in the name of the real."[10] This definition essentially makes various media metaphors for one another, containers that reference other containers. If metaphor is remembered as *metapherein*, transfer between containers, then this process can be thought of as material metaphor. To say that remediation is the defining aspect of media as Bolter and Grusin do is consistent with metaphor as the "archetrope" of language, as J. Hillis Miller names it.[11] The common element is mediation itself. Remediation is metaphor, in which significance is transferred from one container to another, with the relationship of the two configuring the importance of the connection. Spoken metaphor is also a kind of remediation, and thus all speech must be, since words stand in for absent things. In metaphor, the importance of the vehicle is transferred to the tenor and vice versa, and both use language to stand in for something else—a concept, an object, a person, a place.

The dynamic of the death drive should suggest a different, more porous, theory of metaphor. One term does not replace another and simply suppress it. Rather, it allows its users to enjoy the absent term, which is always still present in the metaphor. The vehicle "countervalue," for example, stands in for the tenor "nuclear attack against civilians." This sense is not lost, but displaced. Metaphor is a dynamic process rather than a one-way substitution. One aspect is the replacement of one term by another, but this is not the end: the point of metaphor is that there is a cathectic investment in the *relationship between* two terms, the trait that enthymematically connects them. Concealment is one part of the process, but making the principle that connects the concealed tenor to the expressed vehicle present is another, a *fort-da* dynamic. It is the mediation between terms that serves to anchor enjoyment. The sublime aspect of metaphor is the charge of the Real, which makes a particular connection so bright as to conceal others, but the binary of present/absent is never so stark that alternative meanings, histories, and linkages are fully severed.

At the same time, a broad understanding of mediation has implications for metaphor and metonymy. These tropes are stunted when they are confined to language: not only does language stand in for other things, but different media create different conditions for investment. The simulated globe of *First Strike* stands in for the conglomeration of matter that constitutes the Earth itself just as the word "Earth" does in speech, but the degree of choice that video games allow permits a different kind of investment. For a subject to read about the radioactive wasteland of a postnuclear Earth is one thing, but for that subject to simulate its creation through their own choices is quite another. Metonymy, the proliferation of meaning that gestures from one trope out toward other contiguous signifiers, is mediated in different ways by changing technology. As the example of survivalist online communities shows, some of the labor of connection is now done by automated systems based on aggregated data. An Amazon review of *Farnham's Freehold* leads to a reviewer profile that leads to *One Second After*, where targeted ads lead to survival equipment, where reviews lead to message boards and message boards spin out across the Internet. Some of these selections are made by readers, while others are algorithmically generated, smoothing the paths between one type of symbolic link and another. Communities form in part around these spaces, connected not directly but by their shared relationship to a Facebook group, a particular electronic text, or a lifestyle. The electronic connections of the Internet make possible an itinerary that begins with *Farnham's Freehold* and ends with a marriage proposal made in a bunker.

The death drive as a desire for the Real also implicates antinuclear politics. As detailed in the introduction, much antinuclear scholarship adopts the "concealment thesis," the assumption that the nuclear weapons complex persists as it does because there is insufficient public deliberation. Deliberation is constrained in part because the language of nuclear war conceals its "reality," the horror of destruction. Thus Jonathan Schell graphically imagined destruction in *The Fate of the Earth*, Stephen Hilgartner, Richard C. Bell, and Rory O'Connor decry "nukespeak," and what Carol Cohn calls "technostrategic discourse" is the subject of thorough critique for its use of euphemism and mind-numbing arcane terminology. If the terms were changed, if "God terms" were replaced with "devil terms," as Barry Brummett suggests, then unimpeded debate might occur, and as Edward Schiappa argues, nuclear forces might be constrained. However, antinuclear scholarship in this vein has an uncanny resonance with the sublime discourse of the Bomb. It too seeks an appointment with the Real and makes nuclear imagination a site of enjoyment. As war games demonstrate, vivid imaginations of nuclear war are still just that—imaginations. Combining nuclear critique with graphic depictions of nuclear violence may simply assuage one's guilt about fascination with nuclear horror.

Bataille argued that the existence of taboos in language create, rather than hamper, the desire to do forbidden things. The excitement of doing something naughty is only possible if the desired pleasure is somehow off-limits. This helps to explain the link between sex and death in strategic terminology, which is the subject of Cohn's work on the language of defense intellectuals. Many nuclear euphemisms have a sexual connotation—"deep penetration," "spasm war," "hardening," and "bang for the buck," for example.[12] These terms certainly reflect a particular exercise of violent masculinity. What they also share with less sexually aggressive terms like "countervalue" is the attraction to a forbidden reality of nuclear war which remains distant from the speaker. A concept of the death drive as the desire for unmediated experience suggests that changing the language of expression for this taboo—perhaps even changing the patriarchal terms through which taboo and desire were expressed in the nuclear age—would not automatically change the investments that pin together nuclear warfare as a cultural technology. Instead, critique aimed at making the reality of nuclear war present in language contributes to the movement of desire that sustains our investment in the myths and tropes of nuclear war in the first place. Metaphor operates like the cycle of *fort-da*, where changing one signifier to make the signified term absent can itself be a source of enjoyment, a sense of power over presence and absence, with the original term returning from repression when it is filled in by an audience. We like to have our yellowcake and eat it too.

The danger of seeking the reality of nuclear warfare in language is that the inevitable failures of this project have already proven to have uncanny consequences. The fear of human extinction that struck George Kistiakowsky at Trinity and was developed by Schell's "infinite risk" formulation was a message inverted several times. All sacrifices are made acceptable by it, hence the death of some populations was rationalized in efforts to preserve others, with the underlying logic of neoliberalism and white supremacy unquestioned. Survivalists took the supreme value of human life as an injunction to live at all costs, and communities formed around the fruits of this (cathectic) labor. The gritty imagined world of nuclear warfare became a challenge and the promise of a new frontier, a strangely mediated means of escaping an overly mediated society. The themes of EMP novels show a prominent trend of anti-state sentiment in right-wing survivalism, which the rise of the "alt-right" has begun to channel toward institutional politics. Nuclear war, no matter how horrible or de-romanticized it is in antinuclear discourse, does not reach audiences in a vacuum. Postapocalyptic futures are not culturally discrete. So far, efforts to communicate the potential horror of nuclear war have resulted in a turn toward libertarian self-reliance and hostility to outgroups consistent with the general trend of neoliberalism to emphasize individual responsibility for survival in all contexts.

Even when the horror of nuclear war inspires political engagement, there is no guarantee that antinuclear initiatives result. As the discussion of Pascal's wager suggests, inspiring fear of nuclear war does not inevitably undermine deterrence—in fact, deterrence *requires* fear of nuclear conflict. Nuclear imaginatios might justify either disarmament or more aggressive nuclear policies. That Reagan's Strategic Defense Initiative was justified on these grounds should be a warning, according to Janne Nolan, because "the public's concern about nuclear weapons can be readily turned to fear. And this kind of public sentiment helped spawn the industry of nuclear deceit. . . . Calls to public activism with unspecific objectives may thus not be the best approach. Frightened Americans looking for solace are a great constituency for clever political strategists."[13] Project Plowshare and its more contemporary echoes suggest that fear can also be transformed easily into a promise of salvation. The valence of the Bomb switches easily for those beholden to its power; our reverence for it does not.

This book does not have an answer for Vladimir Lenin's most famous question. Nuclear warfare is still a possibility. Every few months a crisis occurs where the Bomb lurks in the shadows—the Korean DMZ, the Kashmir Line of Control, the Spratly Islands, the Kuril Islands, Iran, Israel, the Crimean Peninsula and Donbass. The major change from the Cold War might not be that nuclear war is less probable, or even less likely to wipe out humanity (if that was ever possible), but that it is no longer seen as the only likely threat capable of doing so. Climate change, itself identified and modeled with the help of simulations designed initially for modeling the effects of nuclear war, has become a more prominent issue. The term replaces "global warming" because it ostensibly reflects the Earth's reality more accurately. It shares much with the Bomb: apocalyptic predictions, survivor and disaster fiction, and the sense of humanity destroying itself through advancements in technology. Both issues have inspired much spilled ink, many conflicts between politicians, news media, and public figures, solemn efforts for international cooperation, and very little effective change. The brief, euphoric atmosphere of global unity as the Warsaw Pact states dissolved did not result in a permanent communion between the Earth's peoples. New divisions quickly emerged and old ones returned with a vengeance.

The many pledges for global cooperation from Kellogg-Briand to Bush-Gorbachev have all unraveled. Continuity and order in this sense appear to be impossible so far, and in their failures the contingency of the Real emerges. Despite all efforts to predict the future—from models to gut instinct—unexpected events continue to disrupt our plans. We still attempt to bridge these rifts, but we also seem to enjoy the vertigo that comes with staring into them. We are enjoined to stay on the bridge, to step back from the edge. After all, one single mistake could destroy everything, and the logic of infinite risk is part of the sign of survival that disciplines us when we drift too far toward the forbidden enjoyment of apocalyptic imagination. Survival may be an oversaturated signifier—nearly anything can be justified in its name, and the repressed other of extinction evinces fascination that goes beyond the needs of prudent concern.

The basic foundation of deterrence is the threat of nuclear retaliation, ultimately against cities. The United States, attacked by Russia or China, would detect incoming weapons and launch its own in return before they could be lost ("use it or lose it," in Cold War parlance). With enemy missiles already in the air, it would be pointless to destroy their empty silos, so at least implicitly the threat is against tens of millions of people who might not even know that the war had started. In other words, the basic national strategy of NATO, Russia, China, and other nuclear states relies on planning to commit genocide on an unprecedented scale against people that each of them argues are oppressed by their own government. The only rational reason to threaten a nuclear war is to prevent a nuclear war. Thus, nuclear weapons threaten survival in the name of protecting it. Every atrocity and degradation of life that does not threaten human extinction is tolerable to prevent one that does, in a "tyranny of survival."[14] In this sense, nuclear planners were right all along. Several powers, each distrusting the others, are locked together in a situation that is suboptimal for all of them with no escape in sight.

Nuclear strategists treated human survival like poker, but to seek a justification for this policy is closer to three-card monte. Each time one policy is developed, the goal of security moves somewhere else. The investment in survival cannot be rational if it is self-defeating. More fundamentally, its value is a human one. Despite the immense importance we attach to life, there is no objective value to it outside a human frame. *Why survive at all*? This question is no longer forbidden. Speculative realism, cosmic horror, pessimistic philosophy, and various materialisms all grapple with it. If there is some cosmic plan for humanity in the Real, it eludes us. Any assertion of value—that we are intelligent life, that death brings suffering, that we are obliged to future generations, and so forth—simply leads to another "why," in the kind of game toddlers play almost as soon as they learn to speak. Efforts to avoid nuclear war, both through deterrence and disarmament, rely on supposedly rational means to reach a goal that is fundamentally irrational. One reaction has been "virulent nihilism," as in Nick Land's book of that name,[15] or Thomas Ligotti's declaration that human existence is "malignantly useless" and consciousness a "long con." Ray Brassier, who wrote an introduction to Ligotti's book, expresses similar sentiments in *Nihil Unbound*.[16] If there is no reason for survival, why bother? Why keep looking for something we will never find? The insights of the death drive seem to lead to a very bleak conclusion: we cannot live in the Real, at least not in a way meaningful to others. We are condemned to seek after an object that we cannot have, endlessly falling short, endlessly cracking the artifice of the Symbolic walls that contain us, and, seeing the light filter through, repairing them rather than tearing them down. Along the way, we turn on each other and do great violence to ourselves and others. While it takes everyone together to create a peaceful world, it takes one alone to reintroduce violence to it and start the cycle anew.

It is in this place of despair from which we should understand the politics of the death drive. Because it is an inevitable byproduct of discontinuous subjectivity, the drive cannot be wished away. We will probably always desire continuity that we cannot have and the object from which we are rent by our separation from the world as a whole. Todd McGowan argues that a recognition of the death drive's inevitability might not remake the material structure of society—at least not immediately—but it could have a profound effect on the way we understand enjoyment. Instead of questing after impossible utopias and deferring fulfillment to a place always just over the horizon, we must learn to love imperfection, uncertainty, and ambiguity. Instead of cathecting solely to the objects of our pursuit, we must learn to enjoy the frustrations of the death drive in ways that don't condemn others for its inevitable failure. Instead of seeking to overcome every limit as an obstacle to enjoyment (as I have argued we do with the limits of language in the Real), we have to enjoy the limits themselves as obstacles to the movement of the drive. Desire may be inevitable, but we can change the way we orient ourselves toward the frustrations and repetitions of the drive, learning to enjoy the partial challenges of our limits instead of deferring enjoyment for the achievement of some utopian state that we will never reach.[17]

Paradoxically enough, some doomsday preppers might already be doing this. To build a shelter and plan to kill the neighbors is one thing. To simply camp with one's friends and families, learn to enjoy growing one's own food, and work to build more resilient and inclusive communities in the face of scarcity is another. The problem is essentially temporal.[18] What makes survivalism coalesce around violence is the understanding that the world needs to end for society to be remade. Suddenly prepping becomes just work, a means to an end—utility in Bataille's sense. Although there is obviously enjoyment in the sense of affective investment in the practices and tropes of survival, it remains organized around the "big payoff" of a world-shattering disaster, and thus enjoyment is mostly deferred and attachment forms to the disaster itself, fabulously textual as it may be. What ruins the game of *fort-da* is the same thing that ruins other rule-bound games. As Roger Caillois argues, the assumption that games must then result in something else, some "real world" benefit, turns them into work and sometimes directs them to violence. To avoid the "corruption" of games, play must be an end in itself, something useless in the sense of Bataille's sovereign poetry.[19]

The sublime is a language suited for this change. The sense of being in the presence of silence, an active force that exceeds language, breeds both terror and fascination, but what results from these encounters is not determined in advance. Instead of deferring enjoyment for the eventual mastery of all contingent experience in mediation, the sublime draws a limit to the value of language used for productive work. Lacan focuses on two primary tropes, both of which operate to connect discrete signifiers. Metaphor acts as a formal structure of transfer, something that belongs squarely in the Symbolic as it operates prior to specific meanings. Metonymy overlaps more closely with the Imaginary—it is the site of rigid investments that leave little room for movement, like the delusions experienced by psychotics. The sublime suggests a third possibility, an intersection of Symbolic and Real. *Catachresis*, mentioned in chapter 1, marks an inherent failure. The trope works by revealing the dissonance between two things in a comparison. It gestures toward the inadequacy of speech, and therefore must be enjoyed precisely in its limitations and misfires. To read catachresis is to appreciate that the frustrations and aporiae of language are a source of beauty we can attain, while the absent objects of our desire (and reference) are not. Bataille's distinction between poetry and the language of utility revolves around a similar observation. Poetry, in his sense, does not aim to *do* anything by organizing the world differently. It is expression without utility that can still be a site of sovereign enjoyment.[20] In Otto's language, this is to recognize that the *mysterium tremens* can be a source of awe and wonder without becoming also a target of mastery and domestication.

The sublime is not a sufficient principle for any politics. It is useful as a practice of reading, both to identify how some investments cause political solutions to serially fail and also how we might learn to enjoy these limits without a frenzied rush to new utopias. Ned O'Gorman's argument that the sublime can have no politics because it cannot make practical differentiations is correct if one understands politics to be about the allocation of scarce resources and rhetoric to be about this conception of politics, and is a valuable warning in any case.[21] But as Bataille defines it, politics is concerned with the handling of surfeit, not scarcity.[22] The teratology of rhetoric I suggest as a supplement—not a replacement—to instrumental politics is also directed toward excess rather than scarcity. Nuclear war is a problem of excess in a double sense: the excess of reality that is the Real, and the excess of energy that thermonuclear processes provide for warfare. Regarding our attempts to control excess as tragic poetry rather than rational imperatives might help combat some of the hubris that makes nuclear policy so dangerous. Reading postnuclear futures as things that beggar our faculties rather than demand our allegiances might help to change how our investments in apocalypse are stitched together and what kind of communities they produce.

Sublime language will not help arms control specialists much in figuring out the details of nuclear arms verification measures—or help the Pentagon determine which Russian ICBM fields to target, for that matter. It won't even fully account for the discourses that surround these projects. Instead, an explicit recognition of the sublime characteristics of language should help us to accept the limits of our ability to map the world and reincorporate its breakdowns, and to appreciate these inevitable failures for what they are. The sublime as teratology—like psychoanalysis—complements traditional approaches of rhetoric and media studies but cannot supplant them without remainder. Its focus on irrationality and desire does not encompass everything. Rather, the idea of rhetorical teratology helps to account for the limit cases of communication and the ways in which these limits seep into the everyday. It's not a map. It's an effort to explain why "here be dragons" is scrawled on the edges, and why some of us read that not as a warning but as a promise.

Notes

Introduction

1. Circular error probability (CEP) is a measure of missile accuracy; TEL stands for transporter erector launcher, which is a portable missile system; and EW/GCI is early warning/ground-controlled interception, a kind of air defense.

2. Jonathan Schell, *The Fate of the Earth* (New York: Alfred Knopf, 1982).

3. Don DeLillo, *End Zone* (New York: Penguin Books, 1986).

4. James Woolsey, "Hearing of the Senate Select Committee on Intelligence Subject: Nomination of R. James Woolsey to Become Director of Central Intelligence," *Federal News Service*, February 2, 1993.

5. All Political Ads, "Will This Brand New Hillary Clinton Ad Sway the Election?" YouTube, October 7, 2016, https://www.youtube.com/watch?v=lha5Gk-yCbw; All Political Ads, "The Girl from the Haunting 'Daisy' Ad Is Back . . . ," YouTube, October 31, 2016, https://www.youtube.com/watch?v=npNqT3N1XoQ.

6. Bruce Blair, "What Exactly Would It Mean to Have Trump's Finger on the Nuclear Button?" *Politico Magazine*, June 11, 2016, http://www.politico.com/magazine/story/2016/06/2016-donald-trump-nuclear-weapons-missiles-nukes-button-launch-foreign-policy-213955.

7. Bruce Blair et al., "Joint Statement by Former Nuclear Launch Officers," *Washington Post* apps, n.d., http://apps.washingtonpost.com/g/documents/world/read-the-letter-from-former-nuclear-launch-officers-opposing-trump/2176/.

8. Nik DeCosta-Klipa, "At New Hampshire Rally, President Obama Pounces on Report That Donald Trump Got His Twitter Access Taken Away," *Boston Globe*, November 7, 2016, https://www.boston.com/news/politics/2016/11/07/at-new-hampshire-rally-president-obama-pounces-on-report-that-donald-trump-got-his-twitter-access-taken-away.

9. On the four discourses, see Jacques Lacan, *The Other Side of Psychoanalysis*, bk. 17 of *The Seminar of Jacques Lacan*, trans. Russell Grigg (New York: W. W. Norton, 2007).

10. Jacques Lacan, *The Psychoses*, bk. 3 of *The Seminar of Jacques Lacan*, trans. Russell Grigg (New York: W. W. Norton, 1993), 14.

11. Elaine Scarry, *Thermonuclear Monarchy: Choosing between Democracy and Doom* (New York: W. W. Norton, 2014).

12. Jacques Derrida, "No Apocalypse, Not Now (Full Speed Ahead, Seven Missiles, Seven Missives)," *Diacritics* 14, no. 2 (1984): 20–31.

13. Pseudo-Dionysius, *The Complete Works*, trans. Colm Luibheid (New York: Paulist Press, 1987), 50, 150.

14. The capitalized "Symbolic" refers to the order of language that composes the "reality" of the human world. Along with the Real and the Imaginary, the Symbolic is one of the three orders of experience in Lacanian psychoanalysis. For the importance of this term in rhetoric, see Christian O. Lundberg, "The Royal Road Not Taken: Joshua Gunn's 'Refitting Fantasy: Psychoanalysis, Subjectivity and Talking to the Dead' and Lacan's Symbolic Order," *Quarterly Journal of Speech* 90, no. 4 (2004): 495–500; and Christian O. Lundberg, *Lacan in Public: Psychoanalysis and the Science of Rhetoric* (Tuscaloosa: University of Alabama Press, 2012), 87.

15. Derrida, "No Apocalypse, Not Now"; Robert Jay Lifton, *Death in Life: Survivors of Hiroshima* (Chapel Hill: University of North Carolina Press, 1991); Robert Jay Lifton and Richard Falk, *Indefensible Weapons: The Political and Psychological Case against Nuclearism* (New York: Basic Books, 1992).

16. Stephen Hilgartner, Richard C. Bell, and Rory O'Connor, *Nukespeak* (New York: Penguin Books, 1983).

17. Carol Cohn, "Sex and Death in the Rational World of Defense Intellectuals," *Signs* 12, no. 4 (Summer 1987): 687–718.

18. David Cratis Williams, "Nuclear Criticism: In Pursuit of a 'Politically Enabling' Deconstructive Voice," *Journal of the American Forensic Association* 24 (Winter 1988): 193–205.

19. Barry Brummett, "Perfection and the Bomb: Nuclear Weapons, Teleology, and Motives," *Journal of Communication* 39, no. 1 (1989): 85–95.

20. Bryan C. Taylor, "'A Hedge against the Future': The Post–Cold War Rhetoric of Nuclear Weapons Modernization," *Quarterly Journal of Speech* 96, no. 1 (2010): 1–24; Bryan C. Taylor, ed., *Nuclear Legacies: Communication, Controversy, and the U.S. Nuclear Weapons Complex* (Lanham, MD: Lexington Books, 2007); Bryan C. Taylor, "'Our Bruised Arms Hung Up as Monuments': Nuclear Iconography in Post–Cold War Culture," *Critical Studies in Media Communication* 20, no. 1 (2003); Bryan C. Taylor, "Nuclear Weapons and Communication Studies: A Review Essay," *Western Journal of Communication* 62, no. 3 (1998): 1–34.

21. Ned O'Gorman, "The Sensibility of the State: Operation Ivy and the Appearance of the Cold War 'Super,'" *Rhetoric & Public Affairs* 19, no. 1 (2016): 1–44; Ned O'Gorman and Kevin Hamilton, "Visualities of Strategic Vision: Lookout Mountain Laboratory and the Deterrent State from Nuclear Tests to Vietnam," *Visual Studies* 30, no. 2 (2015): 195–208; Ned O'Gorman, "Eisenhower and the American Sublime," *Quarterly Journal of Speech* 94, no. 1 (2008): 44–72.

22. Gerard J. DeGroot, *The Bomb: A Life* (Cambridge, MA: Harvard University Press, 2004), 2.

23. Edward Schiappa, "The Rhetoric of Nukespeak," *Communication Monographs* 56 (September 1989): 253.

24. Brummett, "Perfection and the Bomb."

25. Charles Kauffman, "Names and Weapons," *Communication Monographs* 56 (September 1989): 273–85.

26. Williams, "Nuclear Criticism."

27. Schiappa, "Rhetoric of Nukespeak," 286.

28. Ibid., 254.

29. Derrida, "No Apocalypse, Not Now," 20–31.

30. Cohn, "Sex and Death."

31. Jacques Lacan, *Écrits: The First Complete Edition in English*, trans. Bruce Fink (New York: W. W. Norton, 2006), 6–48.

32. Mary Manjikian, *Apocalypse and Post-Politics: The Romance of the End* (Lanham, MD: Lexington Books, 2014), 139.

33. Robert Jay Lifton, *The Nazi Doctors: Medical Killing and the Psychology of Genocide* (New York: Basic Books, 1986); Robert Jay Lifton and Eric Markusen, *The Genocidal Mentality: Nazi Holocaust and the Nuclear Threat* (New York: Basic Books, 1990); Lifton and Falk, *Indefensible Weapons*.

34. Masahide Kato, "Nuclear Globalism: Traversing Rockets, Satellites, and Nuclear War via the Strategic Gaze," *Alternatives: Global, Local, Political* 18, no. 3 (1993): 339.

35. "Fantasy" as used here refers to the Lacanian concept that a particular relation—that of fantasy—sustains a subject's relation to an object. This idea fits into the broader order of the Imaginary, which also includes meaning and other attachments to specific signifiers which themselves are part of a larger economy (the Symbolic). In communication studies, this concept is elaborated by the fine work of Joshua Gunn. See, for example, Joshua Gunn, "Refitting Fantasy: Psychoanalysis, Subjectivity, and Talking to the Dead," *Quarterly Journal of Speech* 90, no. 1 (2004): 1–23; and Joshua Gunn, "Maranatha," *Quarterly Journal of Speech* 98, no. 4 (November 2012): 359–85.

36. Ira P. Chernus, *Dr. Strangegod: On the Symbolic Meaning of Nuclear Weapons* (Columbia: University of South Carolina Press, 1986), 31.

37. Kenneth Burke, *Language as Symbolic Action: Essays on Life, Literature, and Method* (Berkeley: University of California Press, 1966), 22.

38. Excellent work in communication studies on the concept of the Real already exists. See Barbara Biesecker, "Rhetorical Studies and the 'New' Psychoanalysis: What's the Real Problem? or Framing the Problem of the Real," *Quarterly Journal of Speech* 84, no. 2 (1998): 222–40; Barbara Biesecker, "Prospects of Rhetoric for the Twenty-First Century: Speculations on Evental Rhetoric Ending with a Note on Barack Obama and a Benediction by Jacques Lacan," in *Reengaging the Prospects of Rhetoric: Current Conversations and Contemporary Challenges*, ed. Mark J. Porrovecchio (New York: Routledge, 2010), 16–36; and Kevin Johnson and Jennifer Asenas, "The Lacanian Real as a Productive Supplement to Rhetorical Critique," *Rhetoric Society Quarterly* 43, no. 2 (2013): 155–76.

39. Georges Bataille, *Erotism: Death and Sensuality*, trans. Mary Dalwood (San Francisco: City Lights Books, 1986), 12–13.

40. Martin Heidegger, *The Question concerning Technology and Other Essays*, trans. William Lovitt (New York: Garland, 1977), 135.

41. Eugene Thacker, *In the Dust of This Planet*, vol. 1 of *Horror of Philosophy* (Winchester, UK: Zero Books, 2011), 4.

42. Jacques Lacan, *The Four Fundamental Concepts of Psychoanalysis*, trans. Alan Sheridan (New York: W. W. Norton, 1978), 53–54.

43. Sigmund Freud, *Beyond the Pleasure Principle*, trans. James Strachey (New York: W. W. Norton, 1961), 13–17.

44. Jacques Lacan, "Columbia University: Lecture on the Symptom," in *Culture/Clinic 1: Applied Lacanian Psychoanalysis*, ed. Jacques-Alain Miller and Maire Jaanus (Minneapolis: University of Minnesota Press, 2013), 13.

45. John Durham Peters, *Speaking into the Air: A History of the Idea of Communication* (Chicago: University of Chicago Press, 1999), 2.

46. Ira P. Chernus, *Nuclear Madness: Religion and Philosophy of the Nuclear Age* (Albany: SUNY Press, 1991), 59.

47. Edmund Burke, *A Philosophical Enquiry into the Origin of Our Ideas of the Sublime and Beautiful* (Oxford: Oxford University Press, 2008).

48. Immanuel Kant, *Critique of Judgment*, trans. Werner Pluhar (Indianapolis, IN: Hackett, 1987).

49. Phillip Shaw, *The Sublime (The New Critical Idiom)* (New York: Routledge, 2006).

50. The true identity of Longinus is not known, and thus the moniker Pseudo-Longinus is sometimes used. I will follow more recent convention and refer to the author as Longinus.

51. Longinus, *On Great Writing (On the Sublime)*, trans. G. M. A. Grube (Indianapolis, IN: Hackett, 1991), 4.

52. Ibid., 29.

53. Lundberg, *Lacan in Public*, 52.

54. The unconscious, following Lacan, is not the subject's hidden interior life but the network of signifiers that determine the subject's world and interior thoughts, internalized from without rather than welling up from within. This concept is explored more fully in subsequent chapters.

55. Timothy Morton, *Hyperobjects: Philosophy and Ecology after the End of the World* (Minneapolis: University of Minnesota Press, 2013).

56. Quentin Meillassoux, *After Finitude: An Essay on the Necessity of Contingency*, trans. Ray Brassier (London: Continuum, 2008).

57. Ivan Oelrich, *Missions for Nuclear Weapons after the Cold War*, Federation of American Scientists Occasional Paper No. 3 (Washington, DC: Federation of American Scientists, January 2005), 46.

58. Pseudo-Dionysius, *Complete Works*, 53.

Chapter 1

1. Eugen Weber, *Apocalypses: Prophets, Cults and Millennial Beliefs throughout the Ages* (London: Hutchinson, 1999), 39.

2. Jay Rubenstein, *Armies of Heaven: The First Crusade and the Quest for Apocalypse* (New York: Basic Books, 2011), xiii.

3. See, for example, Stephen O'Leary, *Arguing the Apocalypse: A Theory of Millennial Rhetoric* (Oxford: Oxford University Press, 1994); and Barry Brummett, *Contemporary Apocalyptic Rhetoric* (New York: Praeger, 1991).

4. DeGroot, *The Bomb*, 62.

5. Ferenc Szasz, *The Day the Sun Rose Twice: The Story of the Trinity Site Nuclear Explosion, July 16, 1945* (Albuquerque: University of New Mexico Press, 1984), 83.

6. Lansing Lamont, *Day of Trinity* (New York: Atheneum, 1965), 3.

7. A. Costandina Titus, *Bombs in the Backyard: Atomic Testing and American Politics* (Reno: University of Nevada Press, 2001), 61–62.

8. Edwin McMillan, "Trinity Test, July 16 1945 Eyewitness Report by Edwin McMillan," NuclearFiles.org, accessed 2015, http://www.nuclearfiles.org/menu/key-issues/nuclear-weapons/history/pre-cold-war/manhattan-project/trinity/eyewitness-edwin-mcmillan_1945-07-16.htm.

9. Cyril Smith, "Trinity Test, July 16 1945 Eyewitness Report by Cyril S. Smith," NuclearFiles.org, accessed 2015, http://www.nuclearfiles.org/menu/key-issues/nuclear-weapons/history/pre-cold-war/manhattan-project/trinity/eyewitness-cyril-smith_1945-07-16.htm.

10. Ernest Lawrence, "The Atomic Bomb Test," in *The Bomb*, ed. Keith Eubank (Malabar, FL: Krieger , 1991), 168–69.

11. Melba Scott, with Carol Ahlgren, "Witness to an Atomic Test," *Nebraska History* 77 (1996): 40. Brackets in original.

12. Ibid., 41.

13. Robert Campbell, with Mary Palevsky, "Interview with Robert Campbell," *Nevada Test Site Oral History Project* (Las Vegas: UNLV Libraries, 2007), 41.

14. E.g., Otto Robert Frisch, "O. R. Frisch Eyewitness Account of Trinity Test July 1945," in *The American Atom: A Documentary History of Nuclear Policies from the Discovery of Fission to the Present*, 2nd ed., ed. Philip Cantelon, Richard Hewlett, and Robert Williams (Philadelphia: University of Pennsylvania Press, 1991), 46.

15. Jeremy Bernstein, "A Mushroom Cloud, Recollected," *NYR Daily* (blog), *New York Review of Books*, March 23, 2010, http://www.nybooks.com/daily/2010/03/23/a-mushroom-cloud-recollected/.

16. Farrell, qtd. in Leslie Groves, *Now It Can Be Told: The Story of the Manhattan Project* (New York: Da Capo Press, 1962), 436.

17. Max Picard, *The World of Silence*, trans. Stanley Godman (Chicago: Henry Regnery, 1952), 121. In the field of rhetoric this work has been taken up by Cheryl Glen. See Cheryl Glen, *Unspoken: A Rhetoric of Silence* (Carbondale: Southern Illinois University Press, 2004).

18. Richard Lee Miller, *Under the Cloud: The Decades of Nuclear Testing* (The Woodlands, TX: Two-Sixty Press, 1991), 46. Emphasis in original.

19. Paul Boyer, *By the Bomb's Early Light: American Thought and Culture at the Dawn of the Atomic Age* (New York: Pantheon Books, 1985), 3–4.

20. Schell, *Fate of the Earth*, 4.

21. Tom Eyers, *Lacan and the Concept of the "Real"* (New York: Palgrave Macmillan, 2012), 1.

22. Slavoj Žižek, *The Plague of Fantasies* (London: Verso, 2008), 83.

23. Johnson and Asenas, "Lacanian Real," 155–76.

24. Lacan, *Écrits*, 78.

25. The mirror stage is a metaphor for the process of subject formation and the ongoing role of identification with external signifiers. It should not be understood literally as a stage in child development, although individuals must indeed go through it to attain the conditions for selfhood.

26. Lundberg, *Lacan in Public*, 39.

27. Lacan, *Écrits*, 79.

28. Lundberg, *Lacan in Public*, 87.

29. Jacques Lacan, *Anxiety*, bk. 10 of *The Seminar of Jacques Lacan*, ed. Jacques-Alain Miller, trans. A. R. Price (Cambridge: Polity Press, 2014), 15.

30. Lacan, *Écrits*, 260–64.

31. Lundberg, *Lacan in Public*, 2–3.

32. William Leonard Laurence, *Dawn over Zero: The Story of the Atomic Bomb* (A. A. Knopf, 1946), 12.

33. Conant, qtd. in Alex Wellerstein, "James B. Conant on Trinity (1945)," *Restricted Data: The Nuclear Secrecy Blog*, July 16, 2012, http://blog.nuclearsecrecy.com/2012/07/16/conant-on-trinity-1945/.

34. Laurence, *Dawn over Zero*, 11.

35. Scott, "Witness," 43.

36. Thacker, *Dust of This Planet*, 4.

37. Todd Gitlin, *The Sixties: Years of Hope, Days of Rage* (New York: Bantam Books, 1993), 22.

38. Ibid., 23.

39. Howard Philips Lovecraft, *Selected Letters*, vol. 2, *1925–1929*, ed. August Derleth and Donald Wandrei (Sauk City, WI: Arkham House, 1965), 172.

40. Ibid., 172.

41. Thomas Ligotti, *The Conspiracy against the Human Race: A Contrivance of Horror* (New York: Hippocampus Press, 2010).

42. Georges Bataille, "Hegel, Death and Sacrifice," *Yale French Studies* 78 (1990): 15.

43. Chernus, *Dr. Strangegod*, 29–30.

44. Jacques Lacan, *The Triumph of Religion Preceded by Discourse to Catholics*, trans. Bruce Fink (Cambridge: Polity, 2013), 64–65.

45. David Noble, *The Religion of Technology: The Divinity of Man and the Spirit of Invention* (New York: Penguin Books, 1999).

46. Patrick Wright, *Tank* (Penguin Books, 2000), 154.

47. Robert Jungk, *Brighter than a Thousand Suns: A Personal History of the Atomic Scientists*, trans. James Cleugh (San Diego: Harcourt, 1958), 201.

48. Lamont, *Day of Trinity*, 12.

49. Farrell, qtd. in Groves, *Now It Can Be Told*, 436.

50. Bernstein, "Mushroom Cloud."

51. Rudolf Otto, *The Idea of the Holy: An Inquiry into the Non-rational Factor in the Idea of the Divine and Its Relation to the Rational* (Mansfield Center, CT: Martino, 2010).

52. Ibid., 10. The phrase also appears in Job's reaction to Leviathan.

53. Ibid., 21.

54. Ibid., 31.

55. Ibid., 16.

56. Lacan, *Anxiety*, 6.

57. Jason Colavito, *Ancient Atom Bombs: Fact, Fraud, and the Myth of Prehistoric Nuclear Warfare* (self-pub., 2011), 23.

58. John Brandenburg, "Evidence of a Massive Thermonuclear Explosion on Mars in the Past, the Cydonian Hypothesis, and Fermi's Paradox," *Journal of Cosmology* 24, no. 13 (2014): 12229–80.

59. Meillassoux, *After Finitude*, 14.

60. E.g., Fred Knelman, *Reagan, God, and the Bomb* (Toronto: McClelland and Stewart, 1985). For critical reviews of apocalyptic literature, see Frank Kermode, *The Sense of an Ending: Studies in the Theory of Fiction* (New York: Oxford University Press, 1967); and David Dowling, *Fictions of Nuclear Disaster* (Iowa City: University of Iowa Press, 1987).

61. Noble, *Religion of Technology*, 3–13.

62. Claire Troes Schaus, *What Price Survival? An Essay on the Ultimate Destiny of Mankind* (New York: Exposition Press, 1967), 30–34, 123.

63. Wilbur Smith, *This Atomic Age and the Word of God* (Boston: W. A. Wilde, 1948), 44.

64. Ibid., 307.

65. Jason Leopold, "'Jesus Loves Nukes': Air Force Cites New Testament, Ex-Nazi, to Train Officers on Ethics of Launching Nuclear Weapons," Truthout, July 27, 2011, http://www.truth-out.org/news/item/2356:jesus-loves-nukes-air-force-cites-new-testament-exnazi-to-train-officers-on-ethics-of-launching-nuclear-weapons.

66. Charles Seife, *Sun in a Bottle: The Strange History of Fusion and the Science of Wishful Thinking* (New York: Penguin, 2008), 57.

67. Debra Rosenthal, *At the Heart of the Bomb* (Reading, MA: Addison-Wesley, 1990), 55.

68. Sigmund Freud, *The Standard Edition of the Complete Psychological Works of Sigmund Freud*, trans. James Strachey, Anna Freud, Alix Strachey, and Alan Tyson (London: Hogarth Press, 1955), 17:244.

69. Lacan, *Anxiety*, 65.

70. Ibid., 53.

71. Ibid., 41.

72. Ibid., 53.

73. Žižek, *Plague of Fantasies*, 83.

74. Longinus, *On Great Writing*, 4.

75. Ibid., 29.

76. Joshua Gunn and David Beard, "On the Apocalyptic Sublime," *Southern Communication Journal* 65 no. 4 (2000): 275.

77. Julia Kristeva, *Powers of Horror: An Essay on Abjection*, trans. Leon S. Roudiez (New York: Columbia University Press, 1982), 11–12.

78. Lundberg, *Lacan in Public*, 85.

79. Ibid., 52.

80. Denis Donoghue, *Metaphor* (Cambridge, MA: Harvard University Press, 2014), 52–53.

81. Ibid., 59.

82. For a more complete account of affect in Lacan's work, see Colette Soler, *Lacanian Affects*, trans. Bruce Fink (New York: Routledge, 2016).

83. Valerie Kuletz, *Tainted Desert: Environmental and Social Ruin in the American West* (New York: Routledge, 1998), 260–61.

84. Samuel Glasstone and Philip J. Dolan, *The Effects of Nuclear Weapons*, 3rd ed. (Washington, DC: US Government Printing Office, 1977), 442–43, 604–8.

85. Thomas Sebeok, *Communication Measures to Bridge Ten Millennia* (Columbus, OH: Battelle Memorial Institute Office for Nuclear Waste Isolation, 1984), 2.

86. Ibid., 24.

87. Paul de Man, "The Epistemology of Metaphor," in *On Metaphor*, ed. Sheldon Sacks (Chicago: University of Chicago Press, 1978), 19.

88. Joseph Cirincione, *Bomb Scare: The History and Future of Nuclear Weapons* (New York: Columbia University Press, 2007), 25.

89. Leonard Reiffel, *A Study of Lunar Research Flights* (Kirtland Air Force Base, NM: Air Force Special Weapons Center, June 19, 1959).

90. "From a Shocking New Book: Facts and Fallacies of World War III," *Popular Science*, July 1961, 180.

91. Scott Kirsch, *Proving Grounds: Project Plowshare and the Unrealized Dream of Nuclear Earthmoving* (New Brunswick, NJ: Rutgers University Press, 2005), 3.

92. Ibid., 148.

93. Edward Teller et al., *The Constructive Uses of Nuclear Explosives* (New York: McGraw-Hill, 1968).

94. Seife, *Sun in a Bottle*, 60.

95. Kirsch, *Proving Grounds*, 38–39.

96. Seife, *Sun in a Bottle*, 68–72.

97. Arjun Makhijani and Hisham Zerriffi, *Dangerous Thermonuclear Quest* (Takoma Park, MD: Institute for Energy and Environmental Research, July 1998), 2–3.

98. Ned O'Gorman, "The Political Sublime: An Oxymoron," *Millennium* 34 (2005): 891. See the conclusion of this book for a discussion of the relationship between the sublime and the political.

99. Adam Weinstein, "VIDEO: Nuke the Oil Spill?" *Mother Jones*, May 24, 2010, http://www.motherjones.com/blue-marble/2010/05/nuke-bomb-oil-spill-cleanup-crazy-russia-gulf-bp.

100. Chris Landsea, "Subject: C5c) Why Don't We Try to Destroy Tropical Cyclones by Nuking Them?" National Oceanic and Atmospheric Administration, Hurricane Research Division, http://www.aoml.noaa.gov/hrd/tcfaq/C5c.html.

101. National Aeronautics and Space Administration, *2006 Near-Earth Object Survey and Deflection Study* (Washington, DC: NASA, December 2006), 15.

102. See Makhijani and Zerriffi, *Dangerous Thermonuclear Quest.*

103. International Atomic Energy Agency, "Information Circular: Treaty on the Non-Proliferation of Nuclear Weapons," INFCIRC/140, April 22, 1970, 3.

104. Bataille, *Erotism*, 274–75.

105. Andrew Robinson, "The Political Theory of Constitutive Lack: A Critique," *Theory & Event* 8, no. 1 (2005), https://doi.org/10.1353/tae.2005.0016.

106. Jacques Derrida, *Archive Fever: A Freudian Impression*, trans. Eric Prenowitz (Chicago: University of Chicago Press, 1996).

107. Lacan, *Psychoses*, 82.

108. The frequent use of "obliteration" in nuclear texts is interesting from an etymological perspective. The word derives from the Latin *literra*, "letter," and prefix "ob-," meaning "against." To obliterate then is to destroy the letter. The prefix "ob-," however, has another meaning, much rarer, of "to go towards," as in "obdulcorate" (to make sweeter). "Obliterate" could therefore mean to rush toward the letter, rather than to be against it. The word appears to be its own antonym, but the context of mixed desire and terror of nuclear destruction makes it a perfect choice. A similar observation can be made about "desolation" and "destruction." The prefix "de-" has opposite meanings in the two words (desolation: toward solitude; destruction: away from structure) so that "desolation" and "destruction" might mean "away from/towards solitude" and "elimination of/rush to structure." A more complete argument for the importance of etymology can be found in the conclusion of this book.

109. Ron Hirschbein, *Massing the Tropes: The Metaphorical Construction of American Nuclear Strategy* (Westport, CT: Praeger Security International, 2005), 61.

Chapter 2

1. Lacan, *Écrits*, 7.

2. Ibid., 21.

3. Giardina was also reported smoking cigarette butts scavenged from ashtrays—literally sifting through the ashes.

4. Robert Burns, "Gambling Nuke Commander Linked to Fake Poker Chips," Salon.com, November 22, 2014, http://www.salon.com/2014/11/22/gambling_nuke_commander_linked_to_fake_poker_chips/.

5. Žižek, *Plague of Fantasies*, 35–36.

6. Cecil Haney, "Statement of Admiral C. D. Haney Commander United States Strategic Command before the Senate Committee on Armed Services," February 27, 2014, https://www.armed-services.senate.gov/imo/media/doc/Haney_02-27-14.pdf.

7. Ibid., 6.

8. Lacan, *Four Fundamental Concepts*, 53–54.

9. Lacan, *Écrits*, 28–29.

10. Fred Kaplan, *The Wizards of Armageddon* (New York: Simon and Schuster, 1983), 391.

11. Langdon Winner, *The Whale and the Reactor: A Search for Limits in an Age of High Technology* (Chicago: University of Chicago Press, 1986) 145.

12. Sharon Ghamari-Tabrizi, *The Worlds of Herman Kahn: The Intuitive Science of Thermonuclear War* (Cambridge, MA: Harvard University Press, 2005), 8.

13. Alex Abella, *Soldiers of Reason: The RAND Corporation and the Rise of the American Empire* (Orlando, FL: Harcourt, 2008), 51–53.

14. Ghamari-Tabrizi, *Worlds of Herman Kahn*, 149.

15. Kaplan, *Wizards of Armageddon*, 269.

16. Ibid., 270. Emphasis in original.

17. Arbella, *Soldiers of Reason*, 35.

18. Joseph Raatz, "War Game Helps Reinvigorate Nuclear Strategic Thinking," Air Force Global Strike Command, December 20, 2013, http://www.afgsc.af.mil/News/Article-Display/Article/629692/war-game-helps-reinvigorate-nuclear-strategic-thinking/.

19. Thomas Allen, *War Games: The Secret World of the Creators, Players, and Policy Makers Rehearsing World War III Today* (New York: McGraw-Hill, 1987), 78; Ghamari-Tabrizi, *Worlds of Herman Kahn*, 8

20. Kaplan, *Wizards of Armageddon*, 87.

21. Ghamari-Tabrizi, *Worlds of Herman Kahn*, 160–61.

22. Alan Beyerchen, "Clausewitz, Nonlinearity, and the Unpredictability of War," *International Security* 17, no. 3 (Winter 1992/93): 59–90; Mark Buchanan, *Ubiquity: Why Catastrophes Happen* (New York: Three Rivers Press, 2000), 62.

23. Fred Charles Iklé, "The Prevention of Nuclear War in a World of Uncertainty," *Policy Sciences* 7 (1976): 246.

24. Matthew McKinzie et al., *The U.S. Nuclear War Plan: A Time for Change* (New York: Natural Resources Defense Council, June 2001), ix–xi.

25. Allen, *War Games*, 7.

26. Ibid., 64. Emphasis added.

27. Edward Berger, Harvey Boulay, and Betty Zisk, "Simulation and the City: A Critical Overview," *Simulation & Gaming* 1 (1970): 416.

28. Garry Brewer and Martin Shubik, *The War Game: A Critique of Military Problem Solving* (Cambridge, MA: Harvard University Press, 1979), 3–8.

29. It could still be objected that *games* often model systems that aren't real, like magic or nonexistent sci-fi weapons. It could be argued that these imaginary systems are metaphorical representations of something else, making the game an example of metalepsis, or that apparently nonreferential games like *Tetris* are simply vague metaphors, but in the context of nuclear war games, no such gymnastics are necessary. The kind of nuclear war that we usually model does not itself exist as lived empirical reality. As one civilian shouted at an Air Force officer during a heated debate on nuclear strategy, "General, I have fought as many nuclear wars as you have" (Arbella, *Soldiers of Reason*, 138).

30. Ian Bogost, *Persuasive Games: The Expressive Power of Videogames* (Cambridge, MA: MIT Press, 2007), 3.

31. Although one *can* read the story as a tragedy, perhaps centered on Gollum's epic journey to reclaim his stolen ring, which ends with his death at the hands of the thief's nephew and the defeat of Sauron, whose tireless work to bring order to Middle Earth

was doomed from the start. There is also Kirill Yeskov's sequel from the orc perspective focused on the tyranny of the Fellowship and their inheritors.

32. Espen Aarseth, *Cybertext: Perspectives on Ergodic Literature* (Baltimore, MD: Johns Hopkins University Press, 1997), 4.

33. Brummett, "Perfection and the Bomb," 91–92.

34. "SIOP" is the American Single Integrated Operational Plan, now outdated. "RSIOP" is the "Red Single Integrated Offensive Plan," the hypothetical enemy plan against which SIOP was tested in games. The "Red" in this title is a reference to the "Red Team" that simulates an enemy in Pentagon war games, not (directly) the Communist ideology of the Warsaw Pact. It is worth noting the fact, however, that the "O" in the American SIOP stands for "Operational," while the "O" in the simulated Soviet plan stands for "Offensive" (Allen, *War Games*, 25).

35. Allen, *War Games*, 18.

36. Paul Bracken, *The Second Nuclear Age: Strategy, Danger, and the New Power Politics* (New York: Henry Holt, 2012), 20.

37. Lacan, *Écrits*, 236.

38. Allen, *War Games*, 40.

39. Ibid., 267.

40. Pieczenik, qtd. in ibid., 250. Italics in original.

41. Bracken, *Second Nuclear Age*, 82–88.

42. Freud, *Beyond the Pleasure Principle*, 16–17.

43. Norbert Wiener, *God & Golem, Inc.: A Comment on Certain Points Where Cybernetics Impinges on Religion* (Cambridge, MA: MIT Press, 1964), 24–25.

44. Ibid., 26–27.

45. Roger Caillois, *Man, Play and Games*, trans. Meyer Barash (Urbana: University of Illinois Press, 2001), 5.

46. Ibid., 8–9.

47. Lundberg, *Lacan in Public*, 114.

48. Brewer and Shubik, *War Game*, 25.

49. Lacan, *Triumph of Religion*, 60.

50. David Aaron, "Playing with Apocalypse," *New York Times Magazine*, December 29, 1985, 2.

51. McKinzie et al., *U.S. Nuclear War Plan*, ix.

52. Ibid., 1.

53. Emmanuel Lund, "Preview: First Strike Plunges Us into a Cold War Scenario," AppsZoom, February 7, 2014, http://www.appszoom.com/magazine/preview-first-strike-plunges-us-into-a-cold-war-scenario_2529.

54. Harry Slater, "The Firing Line: 5 questions for Blindflug Studios on First Strike," Pocket Gamer, March 17, 2014, http://www.pocketgamer.co.uk/r/iPad/First+Strike/news.asp?c=58211.

55. "Mr. Obama and Mr. Putin Should Play First Strike," *// B%-L#OG»...* (blog), First Strike, December 4, 2013, http://www.firststrike.mobi/2013/12/04/mr-obama-and-mr-putin-should-play-first-strike/.

56. *// B%-L#OG»...* (blog), First Strike, http://www.firststrike.mobi/blog/.

57. Matthew Thomas Payne, "Marketing Military Realism in Call of Duty 4: Modern Warfare," *Games and Culture* 7 (2012): 305–11.

58. Blindflug Studios, *First Strike* (video game), iOS, v. 1.0.3 (Zurich: Feinheit GmbH, 2014).

59. "First Strike: Final Hour," Steam, May 4, 2017, http://store.steampowered.com/app/587000/First_Strike_Final_Hour/.

60. "Mr. Obama."

61. Ian Bogost, *Unit Operations: An Approach to Videogame Criticism* (Cambridge, MA: MIT Press, 2006), 136.

62. Chris Priestman, "Hands-On with First Strike—Nuclear War Is Devastating but It Sure Is Fun," Pocket Gamer, February 17, 2014, http://www.pocketgamer.co.uk/r/iPad/First+Strike/news.asp?c=57465.

63. Harry Slater, "First Strike," Pocket Gamer, March 13, 2014, http://www.pocketgamer.co.uk/r/iPad/First+Strike/review.asp?c=58126.

64. Abella, *Soldiers of Reason*, 159.

65. Owen Faraday, "Review: First Strike," Pocket Tactics, March 17, 2014, http://www.pockettactics.com/reviews/review-first-strike/.

66. Lory Gil, "First Strike Game Review: Start a Nuclear War from Your iPad," *iDownloadBlog*, March 21, 2014, http://www.idownloadblog.com/2014/03/21/first-strike-game-review/.

67. Owen Faraday, "Stop Worrying and Love the Bomb: First Strike Is Out Worldwide," Pocket Tactics, March 12, 2014, http://www.pockettactics.com/articles/stop-worrying-love-bomb-first-strike-worldwide/.

68. Christopher Goetz, "Tether and Accretions: Fantasy as Form in Videogames," *Games and Culture* 7 (2012): 423.

69. Freud, *Complete Psychological Works*, 17:244. See the discussion of this passage in chapter 1.

70. Jason Carl Ruddy, "First Strike (iOS) Review," Kaiju Pop, March 12, 2014, http://kaijupop.com/2014/03/first-strike-ios-review/.

71. Ibid.

72. Bogost, *Unit Operations*, 6.

73. Ibid., 32–35.

74. Lundberg, *Lacan in Public*, 9.

75. Ibid., 22.

76. Lundberg, *Lacan in Public*, 4–5.

77. Lacan, *Four Fundamental Concepts*, 53–56.

78. Lacan, *Écrits*, 44.

79. Allen, *War Games*, 142.

80. Abella, *Soldiers of Reason*, 25.

81. Ibid., 134.

82. Jeff Jordan, introduction to *Gambling on God: Essays on Pascal's Wager*, ed. Jeff Jordan (Lanham, MD: Rowman and Littlefield, 1994), 1.

83. Blaise Pascal, *Pensées*, trans. W. F. Trotter (New York: E. P. Dutton, 1957), 67–69.

84. Nuclear winter is a theory, itself based on volcanic and impact-event theories extrapolated in climate simulations, that a nuclear war would produce so much smoke and debris along with ecological changes that it would temporarily blot out the sun, causing an extended period of darkness on Earth where low temperatures and lack of sunlight would imperil life on Earth. In another example of the metastasis of simulation, nuclear winter models were the basis for the GCMs used for calculations of global warming, which as they became more sophisticated, were then used again to calculate nuclear winter effects. For a critical history of the concept, see Lawrence Badash, *A Nuclear Winter's Tale: Science and Politics in the 1980s* (Cambridge, MA: MIT Press, 2009).

85. Schell, *Fate of the Earth*, 95.

86. Pseudo-Dionysius, *Complete Works*, 52–53.

87. Roy Sorensen, "Infinite Decision Theory," in Jordan, *Gambling on God*, 141.

88. Andrea Gagliarducci, "At Vienna Conference, Holy See Renews Call for Nuclear Disarmament," Catholic News Agency, December 16, 2014, http://www.catholicnewsagency.com/news/at-vienna-conference-holy-see-renews-call-for-nuclear-disarmament-14771/.

89. Eliezer Yudkowsky, "Cognitive Biases Potentially Affecting Judgment of Global Risks," in *Global Catastrophic Risks*, ed. Nick Bostrom and Milan Ćirković (New York: Oxford University Press, 2008), 106–7.

90. Richard Adams, *Watership Down: A Novel* (New York: Scribner, 2009), 475.

91. Dennis Pamlin and Stuart Armstrong, *Global Challenges: 12 Risks That Threaten Human Civilisation* (Oxford: Global Challenges Foundation, February 2015), 33.

92. Heidegger, *Question concerning Technology*, 135.

93. Ibid., 136.

94. Schell, *Fate of the Earth*, 116.

95. John Kleinig, *Valuing Life* (Princeton, NJ: Princeton University Press, 1991), 196–97.

96. Another possible inversion of this argument is found in Ligotti's claim that the capacity to reproduce is precisely why the species should be destroyed—doing so prevents the suffering that results from being born against one's will and essentially condemned to the knowledge, and inevitability, of one's own death. See Ligotti, *Conspiracy*.

97. "Campaign Spot: Peace Little Girl (1964)," The History Channel, accessed 2012, http://www.history.com/topics/us-presidents/presidential-elections/videos/campaign-spot-peace-little-girl-1964.

98. Lee Edelman, *No Future: Queer Theory and the Death Drive* (Durham, NC: Duke University Press, 2004), 18.

99. Kaplan, *Wizards of Armageddon*, 78.

100. Ron Suskind, *The One Percent Doctrine: Deep inside America's Pursuit of Its Enemies since 9/11* (New York: Simon & Schuster, 2006), 62.

101. John Mueller, *Atomic Obsession: Nuclear Alarmism from Hiroshima to Al-Qaeda* (Oxford: Oxford University Press, 2010), 19–20.

102. Nick Bostrom, "Astronomical Waste: The Opportunity Cost of Delayed Technological Development," *Utilitas* 15, no. 3 (2003): 311.

103. Joseph Caldwell, "On Human Population, Global Nuclear War and the Survival of Planet Earth" (self-pub. essay, October 26, 2000), https://www.rairarubiabooks.com/related-pdf-1-on-human-population-global-nuclear-war-and-the-survival-of-planet-earth.html.

104. Mac Slavo, "Video: Model Shows How Ebola Will Spread: 'It Only Takes One Infected Individual Making It through a Checkpoint,'" Infowars, September 10, 2014, https://www.infowars.com/video-model-shows-how-ebola-will-spread-it-only-takes-one-infected-individual-making-it-through-an-airport-checkpoint/.

105. Crazy Monkey Games, *Pandemic 2* (video game), July 18, 2008, http://www.crazymonkeygames.com/Pandemic-2.html.

106. MOBS Lab, "Assessing the International Spreading Risk Associated with the 2014 West African Ebola Outbreak," Northeastern University Laboratory for the Modeling of Biological and Socio-technical Systems, copyright 2017, http://www.mobs-lab.org/ebola.html.

107. Abraham Riesman, "Ebola News Gives Me a Guilty Thrill. Am I Crazy?" *Pacific Standard*, October 23, 2014, https://psmag.com/social-justice/ebola-news-gives-guilty-thrill-crazy-93002.

Chapter 3

1. Roland Barthes, *The Semiotic Challenge*, trans. Richard Howard (Berkeley: University of California Press, 1994), 19[illegible].

2. Raymond Williams, *Literature and Marxism* (Oxford: Oxford University Press, 1997), 132.

3. Rey Chow, *The Age of the World Target: Self-Referentiality in War, Theory, and Comparative Work* (Durham, NC: Duke University Press, 2006), 12.

4. E.g., ibid., 42–43.

5. Matthew Jones, *After Hiroshima: The United States, Race and Nuclear Weapons in Asia, 1945–1965* (Cambridge: Cambridge University Press, 2010), 2–3.

6. Sam Keen, *Faces of the Enemy: Reflections of the Hostile Imagination* (San Francisco: Harper & Row, 1986), 84–85.

7. Nick Turse, *Kill Anything That Moves: The Real American War in Vietnam* (New York: Picador, 2013), 49–51.

8. Dean MacCannell, "Baltimore in the Morning . . . After: On the Forms of Post-Nuclear Leadership," *Diacritics* 14, no. 2 (Summer 1984): 34.

9. Ibid., 45.

10. Ibid., 34.

11. Lundberg, *Lacan in Public*, 52.

12. Richard Overy, *Why the Allies Won* (New York: W. W. Norton, 1995), 112–13.

13. William Martel and Paul Savage, *Strategic Nuclear War: What the Superpowers Target and Why* (New York: Greenwood Press, 1986), 6.

14. David Rosenberg, "The Origins of Overkill: Nuclear Weapons and American Strategy, 1945–1960," in *Strategy and Nuclear Deterrence: An International Security Reader*, ed. Steven Miller (Princeton, NJ: Princeton University Press, 1984), 169.

15. John Finnis, Joseph Boyle, and Germain Grisez, *Nuclear Deterrence, Morality and Realism* (Oxford: Clarendon Press, 1987), 138–39.

16. McKinzie et al., *U.S. Nuclear War Plan*, 15.

17. Martel and Savage, *Strategic Nuclear War*, 138.

18. Jeffrey Richelson, "Population Targeting and U.S. Strategic Doctrine," in *Strategic Nuclear Targeting*, ed. Desmond Ball and Jeffrey Richelson (Ithaca, NY: Cornell University Press, 1986), 240–42. The claim that weapons would be targeted precisely against military targets with low civilian deaths has been frequently repeated with new technologies, such as "smart" bombs and Predator/Reaper drones, despite the regular confirmation of "collateral damage."

19. Martel and Savage, *Strategic Nuclear War*, 130.

20. John Kultgen, *In the Valley of the Shadow: Reflections on the Morality of Nuclear Deterrence* (New York: Peter Lang, 1999), 266–69.

21. Robert Tucker, "Morality and Deterrence," in *Nuclear Deterrence: Ethics and Strategy*, ed. Russell Hardin, John Mearsheimer, Gerald Dworkin, and Robert Goodin (Chicago: University of Chicago Press, 1985), 53.

22. Charles Glaser, *Analyzing Strategic Nuclear Policy* (Princeton, NJ: Princeton University Press, 1990), 117; Dean Wilkening, Kenneth Watman, Michael Kennedy, and Richard Darilek, *Strategic Defenses and Crisis Stability* (Santa Monica, CA: RAND Corporation, 1989), 32–35.

23. It is far from clear that the Soviet leadership believed in the value of its own vulnerability as a salve for American fears. Not only did the USSR have an enormous civil defense shelter program, but when the 1972 Anti-Ballistic Missile Treaty allowed one

missile defense base for each party, the Soviets built one around Moscow (Galosh). The United States built its missile defense base around an ICBM field in North Dakota.

24. Kenneth Rose, *One Nation Underground: The Fallout Shelter in American Culture* (New York: New York University Press, 2001), 32.

25. Michael Dillon, "Another Justice," *Political Theory*, 27, no. 2 (April 1999): 165.

26. Thomas Powers, "Choosing a Strategy for World War III," *Atlantic Monthly*, November 1982, 86.

27. David Cattell and George Quester, "Ethnic Targeting: Some Bad Ideas," in Ball and Richelson, *Strategic Nuclear Targeting*, 282.

28. Sven Lindqvist, *A History of Bombing*, trans. Linda Haverly Rugg (New York: The New Press, 2001), 71.

29. The reciprocation argument was also made about civil defense. Its basic narcissism is suggested by the dearth of examples of its inverse; i.e., it was seldom suggested that Soviet policy would be modeled by the United States, but frequently suggested that American policy would be modeled by the Soviet Union. "Desired ground zeroes" is in Richelson, "Population Targeting," 241.

30. Andrew Grossman, "Segregationist Liberalism: The NAACP and Resistance to Civil-Defense Planning in the Early Cold War, 1951–1953," *International Journal of Politics, Culture, and Society* 13, no. 3 (2000): 491.

31. Ibid., 479.

32. Patrick Sharp, *Savage Perils: Racial Frontiers and Nuclear Apocalypse in American Culture* (Norman: University of Oklahoma Press, 2007), 196–97.

33. United States Congress, Senate Committee on Armed Services, *Nomination of Millard Frank Caldwell, Jr., to be Federal Civil Defense Administrator: Hearing before Subcommittee, 82d Congress, 1st Session, January 15, 1951* (Washington, DC: US Government Printing Office, 1951), 2.

34. Ibid., 6.

35. Grossman, "Segregationist Liberalism," 482–83.

36. Jonathan Lieb and Thomas Chapman, "Jim Crow, Civil Defense, and the Hydrogen Bomb: Race, Evacuation Planning, and the Geopolitics of Fear in 1950s Savannah, Georgia," *Southeastern Geographer* 51, no. 4 (Winter 2011): 588.

37. Ibid., 586.

38. Rose, *One Nation Underground*, 110.

39. Ibid., 206.

40. Grossman, "Segregationist Liberalism," 484.

41. Anthony Rizzo, dir., *Our Cities Must Fight* (Archer Productions, 1951), film.

42. Sarah Peterson, *Planning the Home Front: Building Bombers and Communities at Willow Run* (Chicago: University of Chicago Press, 2013), 1–7.

43. Jennifer Light, *From Warfare to Welfare: Defense Intellectuals and Urban Problems in Cold War America* (Baltimore, MD: Johns Hopkins University Press, 2003), 44.

44. Ibid., 3–5.

45. Stephen Graham, *Cities under Siege: The New Military Urbanism* (London: Verso, 2011), 14.

46. Tom Lewis, *Divided Highways: Building the Interstate Highways, Transforming American Life* (Ithaca, NY: Cornell University Press, 2013), 107.

47. Ibid., 90; Graham, *Cities under Siege*, 14.

48. "How U.S. Cities Can Prepare for Atomic War," *Life*, December 18, 1950, 78–80.

49. Robert Moses, "The Civil Defense Fiasco," *Harpers*, November 1, 1957, 31.

50. Rose, *One Nation Underground*, 160.

51. Thomas Sugrue, *The Origins of the Urban Crisis: Race and Inequality in Postwar Detroit* (Princeton, NJ: Princeton University Press, 1996), 3–6.

52. B. J. Widick, *Detroit: City of Race and Class Violence* (Chicago: Quadrangle Books, 1972), v.

53. James Coates, *Armed and Dangerous: The Rise of the Survivalist Right* (New York: Hill and Wang, 1987), 9.

54. Jerry Herron, *After Culture: Detroit and the Humiliation of History* (Detroit, MI: Wayne State University Press, 1993), 14. Emphasis in original.

55. Scott Martelle, *Detroit: A Biography* (Chicago: Chicago Review Press, 2012), 227.

56. Ze'ev Chafets, *Devil's Night and Other True Tales of Detroit* (New York: Random House, 1990), 26.

57. Herron, *After Culture*, 100.

58. Chuck Holton, "The Dead Zone: Detroit Becomes Urban Wasteland," CBN News, April 9, 2013, http://www.cbn.com/cbnnews/us/2013/april/the-dead-zone-detroit-becomes-urban-wasteland/?mobile=false.

59. Rose, *One Nation Underground*, 100.

60. Donald Warren, "Community Dissensus: Panic in Suburbia," in *A City in Racial Crisis: The Case of Detroit Pre- and Post- the 1967 Riot*, ed. Leonard Gordon (Dubuque, IA: W. C. Brown, 1971), 124.

61. Ibid., 137.

62. John Kossik, *63 Alfred Street, Where Capitalism Failed: The Life and Times of a Venetian Gothic Mansion in Downtown Detroit* (self-pub., 2010), 117.

63. Lawrence Hafstad, "If an H-bomb Hits—a Report by Top Scientists," *U.S. News and World Report*, March 2, 1956, 42.

64. David Wilson, *Cities and Race: America's New Black Ghetto* (London: Routledge, 2007), 5.

65. Frances Ferguson, "The Nuclear Sublime," *Diacritics* 14, no. 2 (Summer 1984): 4–5.

66. Light, *Warfare to Welfare*, 26.

67. Ibid., 11.

68. Ibid., 6; Lewis, *Divided Highways*, 107.

69. Ned O'Gorman, *The Iconoclastic Imagination: Image, Catastrophe, and Economy in America from the Kennedy Assassination to September 11* (Chicago: University of Chicago Press, 2016), 177–79.

70. Winner, *Whale and the Reactor*, 25–26.

71. Sharon Zukin, *Landscapes of Power: From Detroit to Disneyworld* (Berkeley: University of California Press, 1991), 254.

72. See Kuletz, *Tainted Desert*.

73. Kossik, *63 Alfred Street*, 115.

74. Žižek, *Plague of Fantasies*, 56–57.

75. Ibid., 35–36.

76. I am indebted to Dr. Eric King Watts for this observation.

77. I am paraphrasing a British First World War military song.

Chapter 4

1. Jacques Lacan, *Formations of the Unconscious*, bk. 5 of *The Seminar of Jacques Lacan*, ed. Jacques-Alain Miller, trans. Russell Grigg (Cambridge: Polity Press, 2017), 34.

2. On zombies, see Eric King Watts, "Postracial Fantasies, Blackness, and Zombies," *Communication and Critical/Cultural Studies* 14, no. 4 (2017): 317–33.

3. Michael Osborn, "Archetypal Metaphor in Rhetoric: The Light-Dark Family," *Quarterly Journal of Speech* 53, no. 2 (1967): 116.

4. Robert Ellwood, *Tales of Darkness: The Mythology of Evil* (London: Continuum, 2009), 87.

5. Daniel Merkur, *Psychoanalytic Approaches to Myth: Freud and the Freudians* (New York: Routledge, 2005), 7.

6. Carl Jung, *The Essential Jung*, ed. Anthony Storr (Princeton, NJ: Princeton University Press, 1983), 65.

7. Ibid., 396–99.

8. Joseph Campbell, *The Hero with a Thousand Faces* (Princeton, NJ: Princeton University Press, 1973), vii.

9. Janice Hocker Rushing, "Ronald Reagan's 'Star Wars' Address: Mythic Containment of Technical Reasoning," *Quarterly Journal of Speech* 72, no. 4 (1986): 429.

10. Janice Hocker Rushing and Thomas S. Frentz, "Integrating Ideology and Archetype in Rhetorical Criticism," *Quarterly Journal of Speech* 77, no. 4 (1991): 387.

11. See *Communication Studies* 41, no. 2 (1990).

12. James Darsey, "Barack Obama and America's Journey," *Southern Communication Journal* 74, no. 1 (2009): 89.

13. John M. Burry, "Nuclear War as a Myth: The Politics of Preventive Medicine," *Medicine and War* 3 (1987): 177–80.

14. Although many exceptions exist, including *Mad Max*, *Down to the Sunless Sea*, and *On the Beach*, as well as Russian and Soviet works like *Metro 2033* and *The Slynx*.

15. Lacan, *Psychoses*, 84.

16. Ibid., 112.

17. Burke, *Language as Symbolic Action*, 110–11.

18. Sophia Heller, *The Absence of Myth* (Albany: SUNY Press, 2006), 1–5.

19. Lundberg, *Lacan in Public*, 25–26.

20. William Marderness, *How to Read a Myth* (Amherst, NY: Humanity Books, 2009), 23–24.

21. Ellwood, *Tales of Darkness*, 4–7.

22. "Genre" and "myth" do not have to be understood as entirely distinct categories for this argument to work. What we learn from interpreting something *as* myth might differ from what would be learned treating it *as* a representative of a genre, but I do not mean to draw some impervious boundary between the two. They are distinguished here as means of interpretation, not as formally distinct categories.

23. Mircea Eliade, *The Sacred and the Profane: The Nature of Religion*, trans. Willard Trask (New York: Harcourt, Brace & World, 1959), 28.

24. Ibid., 64.

25. Roland Barthes, *Mythologies*, trans. Annette Lavers (New York: Hill and Wang, 1972), 118.

26. Ibid., 123–24.

27. Lundberg, *Lacan in Public*, 101–3.

28. Allan Winkler, *Life under a Cloud: American Anxiety about the Atom* (Oxford: Oxford University Press, 1993), 124–33.

29. Frederic Baumgartner, *Longing for the End: A History of Millennialism in Western Civilization* (New York: St. Martin's Press, 1999), 213.

30. Knelman, *Reagan, God, and the Bomb*, passim.

31. Robert Scheer, *With Enough Shovels: Reagan, Bush and Nuclear War* (New York: Random House, 1982), 18.

32. "Russell Urges Antimissile Force so Nation Can Rebuild in Event of 'Nuclear Exchange' with Soviet," *New York Times*, November 22, 1968, 9.

33. Richard Slotkin, *Regeneration through Violence: The Mythology of the American Frontier* (New York: Harper Perennial, 1996).

34. For a treatment of hypermasculine fantasies in doomsday prepping, see Casey Ryan Kelly, "The Man-pocalpyse: Doomsday Preppers and the Rituals of Apocalyptic Manhood," *Text and Performance Quarterly* 36 (2016): 95–114.

35. For an analysis of antiblack violence in contemporary survivalist fantasies, see Watts, "Postracial Fantasies."

36. Manjikian, *Apocalypse and Post-Politics*, 7.

37. The 1962 nuclear test Starfish Prime revealed that the electromagnetic pulse (EMP) effect of nuclear explosions had been greatly underestimated. EMP-caused electrical surges disable electronic equipment over a potentially large area of the Earth's surface, depending on yield, altitude, and other attributes of the explosion, and thus suggest that even a "small" nuclear attack could be used to destroy an entire country's economy.

38. Chernus, *Dr. Strangegod*, 136–37.

39. Christian O. Lundberg, "The Pleasure of Sadism: A Reading of the *Left Behind* Series," in *Media and the Apocalypse*, ed. Kylo-Patrick Hart and Annette Holba (New York: Peter Lang, 2009), 117–20.

40. Ibid., 127.

41. Ibid., 127. For a complementary reading of *Passion of the Christ* from a psychoanalytic perspective—also treated by Lundberg in *Lacan in Public*—see Joshua Gunn, "Maranatha."

42. William Forstchen, *One Second After* (New York: Forge, 2009), 18.

43. Ibid., 20–22.

44. Ibid., 36–30.

45. Ibid., 64.

46. Ibid., 159.

47. Ibid., 212.

48. Ibid., 215.

49. Ibid., 12.

50. James Knight, *The Pulse of Allah* (self-pub., 2012), 106.

51. Ibid., 296. This sentiment recalls a similar musing in *Alas, Babylon* when two main characters are cheered up after a Soviet-US nuclear war by the thought that they no longer have to pay income taxes.

52. Ibid., 106, 196, 303.

53. Max Velocity, *Patriot Dawn: The Resistance Rises* (self-pub., 2012), 1.

54. Ibid., 13–14. The fear of preppers being targeted by government is another common one online. A minor panic was started when some prepping websites claimed that rainwater collection had been outlawed. See also Calum Matheson, "'What Does Obama Want of Me?' Anxiety and Jade Helm 15," *Quarterly Journal of Speech* 102, no. 2 (2016): 133–49.

55. Velocity, *Patriot Dawn*, 126.

56. "Okay, let's roll" may be a reference to the final words of Todd Beamer, who apparently led the attempt to disrupt the hijacking of United Airlines Flight 93 on September 11, 2001.

57. Chip Berlet and Matthew Lyons, *Right-Wing Populism in America: Too Close for Comfort* (New York: Guilford Press, 2000), 289.

58. Ken Hillis, Michael Petit, and Kylie Jarrett, *Google and the Culture of Search* (New York: Routledge, 2013), 20.

59. In the course of researching and writing this chapter, the content of advertising I am exposed to through Google, Amazon, and eBay has changed as the algorithms they run note my activity and tailor promotions. I have been prompted to buy, for example, 32,000 servings of food in an "Emergency Cube" from Costco to sustain a family of four for a year without electricity; a "doomsday axe" through Amazon, which comes in "Toxic Green Fallout Edition" and, for "lady preppers," the "Pink Tomboy Edition"; and, to prove that the algorithms aren't perfect, Fallout Boy concert tickets through eBay.

60. Mark Andrejevic, *Infoglut: How Too Much Information Is Changing the Way We Think and Know* (New York: Routledge, 2013), 14–15.

61. Hillis, Petit, and Jarrett, *Google*, 144–45.

62. Each episode is broken into smaller segments, some of which are online as short clips. I have chosen to reference Internet clips here rather than television programs in the hope that they will be more easily accessible to readers.

63. National Geographic, "Doomsday Preppers," National Geographic Society, accessed 2013, http://channel.nationalgeographic.com/doomsday-preppers/video-gallery/.

64. All three survivalist dating sites discussed here allowed nonmembers to view at least some parts of member profiles—full ones in the case of PrepperDating.com and SurvivalistSingles.com. The latter site also publishes fairly extensive membership data, although exact figures cannot be calculated due to "dead" and redundant profiles.

65. Numbers as of late December 2014. Having checked these numbers periodically for eighteen months prior, I saw the group grow by roughly 2,000 members, although I have never seen more than one online at a time. All profiles on SurvivalistSingles were displayed for the public and do not require a log-in or site membership to view. SurvivalistSingles and PrepperDating appear to be defunct at the time of writing, but other groups still exist, as do specialized survivalist lists on kwink.com.

66. Dan Slater, *Love in the Time of Algorithms: What Technology Does to Meeting and Mating* (New York: Penguin Group, 2013), 87.

67. Ibid., 45–50.

68. Melissa Breyer, "Survivalist Singles, a Dating Site for those Expecting an Apocalypse," Treehugger, April 3, 2012, https://www.treehugger.com/culture/doomsday-dating-matchmaking-sites-survivalists.html.

69. Slater, *Love*, 137.

70. Rob Horning, "Single Servings," *New Inquiry*, February 12, 2013, https://thenewinquiry.com/single-servings/.

71. Eva Illouz, "Love in the Time of Capital," interview by Jesse Tangen-Mills, *Guernica*, June 1, 2010.

72. Alphonso Lingis, *Deathbound Subjectivity* (Bloomington: Indiana University Press, 1989), 176–77.

73. Ibid., 190.

74. Michael Waltman and John Haas, *The Communication of Hate* (New York: Peter Lang, 2011), 2.

75. Baumgartner, *Longing for the End*, 264.

76. Richard Mitchell, *Dancing at Armageddon: Survivalism and Chaos in Modern Times* (Chicago: University of Chicago Press, 2002), 4.

77. Ibid., 9.

78. Ibid., 210–12.

79. Ibid., 9, 200.

Conclusion

1. Burke, *Philosophical Enquiry*, 36.

2. Nicolas of Cusa, *Selected Spiritual Writings*, trans. H. Lawrence Bond (New York: Paulist Press, 1997), 213. That Nicolas was likely wrong about this etymology arguably makes it that much more interesting as repressed meaning.

3. Ibid., 237.

4. Georges Bataille, *Visions of Excess: Selected Writings, 1927–1939*, trans. Allan Stoekl (Minneapolis: University of Minnesota Press, 1985), 57–58.

5. *Concise Oxford English Dictionary* (11th ed., 2008), s.v. "teratology."

6. Nathan Bailey, *An Universal Etymological English Dictionary* [. . .] (Knapton, 1731), s.v. "teratology."

7. Joseph Shipley, *The Origins of English Words: A Discursive Dictionary of Indo-European Roots* (Baltimore, MD: Johns Hopkins University Press, 2001), 197.

8. Jay David Bolter and Richard Grusin, *Remediation: Understanding New Media* (Cambridge, MA: MIT Press, 1999), 5. Emphasis in original.

9. Ibid., 11–12.

10. Ibid., 65–66.

11. J. Hillis Miller, *Others* (Princeton, NJ: Princeton University Press, 2001), 66.

12. Cohn, "Sex and Death," 693.

13. Janne Nolan, *Guardians of the Arsenal: The Politics of Nuclear Strategy* (New York: Basic Books, 1989), 283.

14. Daniel Callahan, *The Tyranny of Survival and Other Pathologies of Civilized Life* (New York: Macmillan, 1973), 92–100.

15. Nick Land, *The Thirst for Annihilation: Georges Bataille and Virulent Nihilism* (London: Routledge, 1992).

16. Ray Brassier, *Nihil Unbound: Enlightenment and Extinction* (Basingstoke, UK: Palgrave Macmillan, 2007).

17. Todd McGowan, *Enjoying What We Don't Have: The Political Project of Psychoanalysis* (Lincoln: University of Nebraska Press, 2013), 283–86.

18. For excellent work on the politics of time and its differential experience among disparate identities, see Sarah Sharma, *In the Meantime: Temporality and Cultural Politics* (Durham, NC: Duke University Press, 2014).

19. Caillois, *Man, Play and Games*, 44.

20. Bataille, "Hegel, Death and Sacrifice," 25.

21. O'Gorman, "Political Sublime," 889.

22. Georges Bataille, *The Accursed Share: An Essay on General Economy*, vol. 1, *Consumption*, trans. Robert Hurley (New York: Zone Books, 1988), 24–26.

Works Cited

Aaron, David. "Playing with Apocalypse." *New York Times Magazine*, December 29, 1985.

Aarseth, Espen. *Cybertext: Perspectives on Ergodic Literature*. Baltimore, MD: Johns Hopkins University Press, 1997, 4.

Abella, Alex. *Soldiers of Reason: The RAND Corporation and the Rise of the American Empire*. Orlando, FL: Harcourt, 2008.

Adams, Richard. *Watership Down: A Novel*. New York: Scribner, 2009.

Allen, Thomas. *War Games: The Secret World of the Creators, Players, and Policy Makers Rehearsing World War III Today*. New York: McGraw-Hill, 1987.

All Political Ads. "The Girl from the Haunting 'Daisy' Ad Is Back . . ." YouTube, October 31, 2016. https://www.youtube.com/watch?v=npNqT3N1XoQ.

———. "Will This Brand New Hillary Clinton Ad Sway the Election?" YouTube, October 7, 2016. https://www.youtube.com/watch?v=lha5Gk-yCbw.

Andrejevic, Mark. *Infoglut: How Too Much Information Is Changing the Way We Think and Know*. New York: Routledge, 2013.

Badash, Lawrence. *A Nuclear Winter's Tale: Science and Politics in the 1980s*. Cambridge, MA: MIT Press, 2009.

Bailey, Nathan. *An Universal Etymological English Dictionary* [. . .]. Knapton, 1731.

Barthes, Roland. *Mythologies*. Translated by Annette Lavers. New York: Hill and Wang, 1972.

———. *The Semiotic Challenge*. Translated by Richard Howard. Berkeley: University of California Press, 1994.

Bataille, Georges. *The Accursed Share: An Essay on General Economy*. Vol. 1, *Consumption*, translated by Robert Hurley. New York: Zone Books, 1988.

———. *Erotism: Death and Sensuality*. Translated by Mary Dalwood. San Francisco: City Lights Books, 1986.

———. "Hegel, Death and Sacrifice." *Yale French Studies* 78 (1990): 9–28.

———. *Visions of Excess: Selected Writings, 1927–1939*. Translated by Allan Stoekl. Minneapolis: University of Minnesota Press, 1985.

Baumgartner, Frederic. *Longing for the End: A History of Millennialism in Western Civilization*. New York: St. Martin's Press, 1999.

Berger, Edward, Harvey Boulay, and Betty Zisk. "Simulation and the City: A Critical Overview." *Simulation & Gaming* 1 (1970): 411–28.

Berlet, Chip, and Matthew Lyons. *Right-Wing Populism in America: Too Close for Comfort*. New York: Guilford Press, 2000.

Bernstein, Jeremy. "A Mushroom Cloud, Recollected." *NYR Daily* (blog), *New York Review of Books*, March 23, 2010. http://www.nybooks.com/daily/2010/03/23/a-mushroom-cloud-recollected/.

Beyerchen, Alan. "Clausewitz, Nonlinearity, and the Unpredictability of War." *International Security* 17, no. 3 (Winter 1992/93): 59–90.

Biesecker, Barbara. "Prospects of Rhetoric for the Twenty-First Century: Speculations on Evental Rhetoric Ending with a Note on Barack Obama and a Benediction by Jacques Lacan." In *Reengaging the Prospects of Rhetoric: Current Conversations and Contemporary Challenges*, edited by Mark J. Porrovecchio, 16–36. New York: Routledge, 2010.

———. "Rhetorical Studies and the 'New' Psychoanalysis: What's the Real Problem? or Framing the Problem of the Real." *Quarterly Journal of Speech* 84, no. 2 (1998): 222–40.

Blair, Bruce. "What Exactly Would It Mean to Have Trump's Finger on the Nuclear Button?" *Politico Magazine*, June 11, 2016. http://www.politico.com/magazine/story/2016/06/2016-donald-trump-nuclear-weapons-missiles-nukes-button-launch-foreign-policy-213955.

Blair, Bruce, Michael Miller, William A. DeGroodt, John Noonan, Harvey R. Greenberg, James Robertson, Geoffrey Kanner, Edward Warren, Louis Mark Lussky, and Brian Weeden. "Joint Statement by Former Nuclear Launch Officers." *Washington Post* apps, n.d. http://apps.washingtonpost.com/g/documents/world/read-the-letter-from-former-nuclear-launch-officers-opposing-trump/2176/.

Blindflug Studios. *First Strike* (video game). iOS, v. 1.0.3. Zurich: FEINHEIT GmbH, 2014. *// B%-L#OG»...* (blog). First Strike. http://www.firststrike.mobi/blog/.

Bogost, Ian. *Persuasive Games: The Expressive Power of Videogames*. Cambridge, MA: MIT Press, 2007.

———. *Unit Operations: An Approach to Videogame Criticism*. Cambridge, MA: MIT Press, 2006.

Bolter, Jay David, and Richard Grusin. *Remediation: Understanding New Media*. Cambridge, MA: MIT Press, 1999.

Bostrom, Nick. "Astronomical Waste: The Opportunity Cost of Delayed Technological Development." *Utilitas* 15, no. 3 (2003): 308–14.

Boyer, Paul. *By the Bomb's Early Light: American Thought and Culture at the Dawn of the Atomic Age*. New York: Pantheon Books, 1985.

Bracken, Paul. *The Second Nuclear Age: Strategy, Danger, and the New Power Politics*. New York: Henry Holt, 2012.

Brandenburg, John. "Evidence of a Massive Thermonuclear Explosion on Mars in the Past, the Cydonian Hypothesis, and Fermi's Paradox." *Journal of Cosmology* 24, no. 13 (2014): 12229–80.

Brassier, Ray. *Nihil Unbound: Enlightenment and Extinction*. Basingstoke, UK: Palgrave Macmillan, 2007.

Brewer, Garry, and Martin Shubik, *The War Game: A Critique of Military Problem Solving*. Cambridge, MA: Harvard University Press, 1979.

Breyer, Melissa. "Survivalist Singles, a Dating Site for Those Expecting an Apocalypse." Treehugger, April 3, 2012. https://www.treehugger.com/culture/doomsday-dating-matchmaking-sites-survivalists.html.

Brummett, Barry. *Contemporary Apocalyptic Rhetoric*. New York: Praeger, 1991.

———. "Perfection and the Bomb: Nuclear Weapons, Teleology, and Motives." *Journal of Communication* 39, no. 1 (1989): 85–95.

Buchanan, Mark. *Ubiquity: Why Catastrophes Happen*. New York: Three Rivers Press, 2000.

Burke, Edmund. *A Philosophical Enquiry into the Origin of Our Ideas of the Sublime and Beautiful*. Oxford: Oxford University Press, 2008.

Burke, Kenneth. *Language as Symbolic Action: Essays on Life, Literature, and Method*. Berkeley: University of California Press, 1966.

Burns, Robert. "Gambling Nuke Commander Linked to Fake Poker Chips." Salon.com, November 22, 2014. http://www.salon.com/2014/11/22/gambling_nuke_commander_linked_to_fake_poker_chips/.

Burry, John M. "Nuclear War as a Myth: The Politics of Preventive Medicine." *Medicine and War* 3 (1987): 177–80.

Caillois, Roger. *Man, Play and Games*. Translated by Meyer Barash. Urbana: University of Illinois Press, 2001.

Caldwell, Joseph. "On Human Population, Global Nuclear War and the Survival of Planet Earth." Self-published essay, October 26, 2000. https://www.rairarubiabooks.com/related-pdf-1-on-human-population-global-nuclear-war-and-the-survival-of-planet-earth.html.

Callahan, Daniel. *The Tyranny of Survival and Other Pathologies of Civilized Life*. New York: Macmillan, 1973.

"Campaign Spot: Peace Little Girl (1964)." The History Channel, accessed 2012, http://www.history.com/topics/us-presidents/presidential-elections/videos/campaign-spot-peace-little-girl-1964.

Campbell, Joseph. *The Hero with a Thousand Faces*. Princeton, NJ: Princeton University Press, 1973.

Campbell, Robert, with Mary Palevsky. "Interview with Robert Campbell." *Nevada Test Site Oral History Project*. Las Vegas: UNLV Libraries, 2007.

Cattell, David, and George Quester. "Ethnic Targeting: Some Bad Ideas." In *Strategic Nuclear Targeting*, edited by Desmond Ball and Jeffrey Richelson, 267–84. Ithaca, NY: Cornell University Press, 1986.

Chafets, Ze'ev. *Devil's Night and Other True Tales of Detroit*. New York: Random House, 1990.

Chernus, Ira P. *Dr. Strangegod: On the Symbolic Meaning of Nuclear Weapons*. Columbia: University of South Carolina Press, 1986.

———. *Nuclear Madness: Religion and Philosophy of the Nuclear Age*. Albany: SUNY Press, 1991.

Chow, Rey. *The Age of the World Target: Self-Referentiality in War, Theory, and Comparative Work*. Durham, NC: Duke University Press, 2006.

Cirincione, Joseph. *Bomb Scare: The History and Future of Nuclear Weapons*. New York: Columbia University Press, 2007.

Coates, James. *Armed and Dangerous: The Rise of the Survivalist Right*. New York: Hill and Wang, 1987.

Cohn, Carol. "Sex and Death in the Rational World of Defense Intellectuals." *Signs* 12, no. 4, (Summer 1987): 687–718.

Colavito, Jason. *Ancient Atom Bombs: Fact, Fraud, and the Myth of Prehistoric Nuclear Warfare*. Self-published, 2011.

Concise Oxford English Dictionary. 11th ed. 2008.

Crazy Monkey Games. *Pandemic 2* (video game). July 18, 2008. http://www.crazymonkeygames.com/Pandemic-2.html.

Darsey, James. "Barack Obama and America's Journey." *Southern Communication Journal* 74, no. 1 (2009): 88–103.

DeCosta-Klipa, Nik. "At New Hampshire Rally, President Obama Pounces on Report That Donald Trump Got His Twitter Access Taken Away." *Boston Globe*, November 7, 2016. https://www.boston.com/news/politics/2016/11/07/at-new-hampshire-rally-president-obama-pounces-on-report-that-donald-trump-got-his-twitter-access-taken-away.

DeGroot, Gerard J. *The Bomb: A Life*. Cambridge, MA: Harvard University Press, 2004.

DeLillo, Don. *End Zone*. New York: Penguin Books, 1986.

de Man, Paul. "The Epistemology of Metaphor." In *On Metaphor*, edited by Sheldon Sacks, 11–28. Chicago: University of Chicago Press, 1978.

Derrida, Jacques. *Archive Fever: A Freudian Impression*. Translated by Eric Prenowitz. Chicago: University of Chicago Press, 1996.

———. "No Apocalypse, Not Now (Full Speed Ahead, Seven Missiles, Seven Missives)." *Diacritics* 14, no. 2 (1984): 20–31.

Dillon, Michael. "Another Justice." *Political Theory* 27, no. 2 (April 1999): 155–75.

Donoghue, Denis. *Metaphor*. Cambridge, MA: Harvard University Press, 2014.

Dowling, David. *Fictions of Nuclear Disaster*. Iowa City: University of Iowa Press, 1987.

Edelman, Lee. *No Future: Queer Theory and the Death Drive*. Durham, NC: Duke University Press, 2004.

Eliade, Mircea. *The Sacred and the Profane: The Nature of Religion*. Translated by Willard Trask. New York: Harcourt, Brace & World, 1959.

Ellwood, Robert. *Tales of Darkness: The Mythology of Evil*. London: Continuum, 2009.

Eyers, Tom. *Lacan and the Concept of the "Real."* New York: Palgrave Macmillan, 2012.

Faraday, Owen. "Review: First Strike." Pocket Tactics, March 17, 2014. http://www.pockettactics.com/reviews/review-first-strike/.

———. "Stop Worrying and Love the Bomb: First Strike Is Out Worldwide." Pocket Tactics, March 12, 2014. http://www.pockettactics.com/articles/stop-worrying-love-bomb-first-strike-worldwide/.

Ferguson, Frances. "The Nuclear Sublime." *Diacritics* 14, no. 2 (Summer, 1984): 4–10.

Finnis, John, Joseph Boyle, and Germain Grisez. *Nuclear Deterrence, Morality and Realism*. Oxford: Clarendon Press, 1987.

"First Strike: Final Hour." Steam, May 4, 2017. http://store.steampowered.com/app/587000/First_Strike_Final_Hour/.

Forstchen, William. *One Second After*. New York: Forge, 2009.

Freud, Sigmund. *Beyond the Pleasure Principle*. Translated by James Strachey. New York: W. W. Norton, 1961.

———. *The Standard Edition of the Complete Psychological Works of Sigmund Freud*. Vol. 17, translated by James Strachey, Anna Freud, Alix Strachey, and Alan Tyson. London: Hogarth Press, 1955.

Frisch, Otto Robert. "O. R. Frisch Eyewitness Account of Trinity Test July 1945." In *The American Atom: A Documentary History of Nuclear Policies from the Discovery of Fission to the Present*, 2nd ed., edited by Philip Cantelon, Richard Hewlett, and Robert Williams, 46–47. Philadelphia: University of Pennsylvania Press, 1991.

"From a Shocking New Book: Facts and Fallacies of World War III." *Popular Science*, July 1961, 92–95, 178–81.

Gagliarducci, Andrea. "At Vienna Conference, Holy See Renews Call for Nuclear Disarmament." Catholic News Agency, December 16, 2014. http://www.catholicnewsagency.com/news/at-vienna-conference-holy-see-renews-call-for-nuclear-disarmament-14771/.

Ghamari-Tabrizi, Sharon. *The Worlds of Herman Kahn: The Intuitive Science of Thermonuclear War*. Cambridge, MA: Harvard University Press, 2005.

Gil, Lory. "First Strike Game Review: Start a Nuclear War from Your iPad." *iDownloadBlog*, March 21, 2014. http://www.idownloadblog.com/2014/03/21/first-strike-game-review/.

Gitlin, Todd. *The Sixties: Years of Hope, Days of Rage*. New York: Bantam Books, 1993.

Glaser, Charles. *Analyzing Strategic Nuclear Policy*. Princeton, NJ: Princeton University Press, 1990.

Glasstone, Samuel, and Philip J. Dolan. *The Effects of Nuclear Weapons*. 3rd ed. Washington, DC: US Government Printing Office, 1977.

Glen, Cheryl. *Unspoken: A Rhetoric of Silence*. Carbondale: Southern Illinois University Press, 2004.

Goetz, Christopher. "Tether and Accretions: Fantasy as Form in Videogames." *Games and Culture* 7 (2012): 419–40.

Graham, Stephen. *Cities under Siege: The New Military Urbanism*. London: Verso, 2011.

Grossman, Andrew. "Segregationist Liberalism: The NAACP and Resistance to Civil-Defense Planning in the Early Cold War, 1951–1953." *International Journal of Politics, Culture, and Society* 13, no. 3 (2000): 477–97.

Groves, Leslie. *Now It Can Be Told: The Story of the Manhattan Project*. New York: Da Capo Press, 1962.

Gunn, Joshua. "Maranatha." *Quarterly Journal of Speech* 98, no. 4 (November 2012): 359–85.

———. "Refitting Fantasy: Psychoanalysis, Subjectivity, and Talking to the Dead." *Quarterly Journal of Speech* 90, no. 1 (2004): 1–23.

Gunn, Joshua, and David Beard. "On the Apocalyptic Sublime." *Southern Communication Journal* 65, no. 4 (2000): 269–86.

Hafstad, Lawrence. "If an H-bomb Hits—a Report by Top Scientists." *U.S. News and World Report*, March 2, 1956.

Haney, Cecil. "Statement of Admiral C. D. Haney Commander United States Strategic Command before the Senate Committee on Armed Services." February 27, 2014. https://www.armed-services.senate.gov/imo/media/doc/Haney_02-27-14.pdf.

Heidegger, Martin. *The Question concerning Technology and Other Essays*. Translated by William Lovitt. New York: Garland, 1977.

Heller, Sophia. *The Absence of Myth*. Albany: SUNY Press, 2006.

Herron, Jerry. *After Culture: Detroit and the Humiliation of History*. Detroit, MI: Wayne State University Press, 1993.

Hilgartner, Stephen, Richard C. Bell, and Rory O'Connor. *Nukespeak*. New York: Penguin Books, 1983.

Hillis, Ken, Michael Petit, and Kylie Jarrett. *Google and the Culture of Search*. New York: Routledge, 2013.

Hirschbein, Ron. *Massing the Tropes: The Metaphorical Construction of American Nuclear Strategy*. Westport, CT: Praeger Security International, 2005.

Holton, Chuck. "The Dead Zone: Detroit Becomes Urban Wasteland." CBN News, April 9, 2013. http://www.cbn.com/cbnnews/us/2013/april/the-dead-zone-detroit-becomes-urban-wasteland/?mobile=false.

Horning, Rob. "Single Servings." *New Inquiry*, February 12, 2013. https://thenewinquiry.com/single-servings/.

"How U.S. Cities Can Prepare for Atomic War." *Life*, December 18, 1950, 77–86.

Iklé, Fred Charles. "The Prevention of Nuclear War in a World of Uncertainty." *Policy Sciences* 7 (1976): 245–50.

Illouz, Eva. "Love in the Time of Capital." Interview by Jesse Tangen-Mills. *Guernica*, June 1, 2010.

International Atomic Energy Agency. "Information Circular: Treaty on the Non-Proliferation of Nuclear Weapons." INFCIRC/140, April 22, 1970.

Jessett, Frederick. "Shelters and Self." Letter to *Christian Century*, December 13, 1961, 1496.

Johnson, Kevin, and Jennifer Asenas. "The Lacanian Real as a Productive Supplement to Rhetorical Critique." *Rhetoric Society Quarterly* 43, no. 2 (2013): 155–76.

Jones, Matthew. *After Hiroshima: The United States, Race and Nuclear Weapons in Asia, 1945–1965*. Cambridge: Cambridge University Press, 2010.

Jordan, Jeff. Introduction to *Gambling on God: Essays on Pascal's Wager*, edited by Jeff Jordan, 1–10. Lanham, MD: Rowman and Littlefield Publishers, 1994.

Jung, Carl. *The Essential Jung*. Edited by Anthony Storr. Princeton, NJ: Princeton University Press, 1983.

Jungk, Robert. *Brighter than a Thousand Suns: A Personal History of the Atomic Scientists*. Translated by James Cleugh. San Diego: Harcourt, 1958.

Kant, Immanuel. *Critique of Judgment*. Translated by Werner Pluhar. Indianapolis, IN: Hackett, 1987.

Kaplan, Fred. *The Wizards of Armageddon*. New York: Simon and Schuster, 1983.

Kato, Masahide. "Nuclear Globalism: Traversing Rockets, Satellites, and Nuclear War via the Strategic Gaze." *Alternatives: Global, Local, Political* 18, no. 3 (1993): 339–60.

Kauffman, Charles. "Names and Weapons." *Communication Monographs* 56, no. 3 (September 1989): 273–85.

Keen, Sam. *Faces of the Enemy: Reflections of the Hostile Imagination*. San Francisco: Harper & Row, 1986.

Kelly, Casey Ryan. "The Man-pocalpyse: Doomsday Preppers and the Rituals of Apocalyptic Manhood." *Text and Performance Quarterly* 36 (2016): 95–114.

Kermode, Frank. *The Sense of an Ending: Studies in the Theory of Fiction*. New York: Oxford University Press, 1967.

Kirsch, Scott. *Proving Grounds: Project Plowshare and the Unrealized Dream of Nuclear Earthmoving*. New Brunswick, NJ: Rutgers University Press, 2005.

Kleinig, John. *Valuing Life*. Princeton, NJ: Princeton University Press, 1991.

Knelman, Fred. *Reagan, God, and the Bomb*. Toronto: McClelland and Stewart, 1985.

Knight, James. *The Pulse of Allah*. Self-published, 2012.

Kossik, John. *63 Alfred Street, Where Capitalism Failed: The Life and Times of a Venetian Gothic Mansion in Downtown Detroit*. Self-published, 2010.

Kristeva, Julia. *Powers of Horror: An Essay on Abjection*. Translated by Leon S. Roudiez. New York: Columbia University Press, 1982.

Kuletz, Valerie. *Tainted Desert: Environmental and Social Ruin in the American West*. New York: Routledge, 1998.

Kultgen, John. *In the Valley of the Shadow: Reflections on the Morality of Nuclear Deterrence*. New York: Peter Lang, 1999.

Lacan, Jacques. *Anxiety*. Bk. 10 of *The Seminar of Jacques Lacan*, edited by Jacques-Alain Miller, translated by A. R. Price. Cambridge: Polity Press, 2014.

———. "Columbia University: Lecture on the Symptom." In *Culture/Clinic 1: Applied Lacanian Psychoanalysis*, edited by Jacques-Alain Miller and Maire Jaanus, 8–16. Minneapolis: University of Minnesota Press, 2013.

———. *Écrits: The First Complete Edition in English*. Translated by Bruce Fink. New York: W. W. Norton, 2006.

———. *Formations of the Unconscious*. Bk. 5 of *The Seminar of Jacques Lacan*, edited by Jacques-Alain Miller, translated by Russell Grigg. Cambridge: Polity Press, 2017.

———. *The Four Fundamental Concepts of Psychoanalysis*. Translated by Alan Sheridan. New York: W. W. Norton, 1978.

———. *The Other Side of Psychoanalysis*. Bk. 17 of *The Seminar of Jacques Lacan*, translated by Russell Grigg. New York: W. W. Norton, 2007.

———. *The Psychoses*. Bk. 3 of *The Seminar of Jacques Lacan*, translated by Russell Grigg. New York: W. W. Norton, 1993.

———. *The Triumph of Religion Preceded by Discourse to Catholics*. Translated by Bruce Fink. Cambridge: Polity, 2013.

Lamont, Lansing. *Day of Trinity*. New York: Atheneum, 1965.

Land, Nick. *The Thirst for Annihilation: Georges Bataille and Virulent Nihilism*. London: Routledge, 1992.

Landsea, Chris. "Subject: C5c) Why Don't We Try to Destroy Tropical Cyclones by Nuking Them?" National Oceanic and Atmospheric Administration, Hurricane Research Division. http://www.aoml.noaa.gov/hrd/tcfaq/C5c.html.

Laurence, William Leonard. *Dawn over Zero: The Story of the Atomic Bomb*. New York: A. A. Knopf, 1946.

Lawrence, Ernest. "The Atomic Bomb Test." In *The Bomb*, edited by Keith Eubank, 167–69. Malabar, FL: Krieger, 1991.

Leopold, Jason. "'Jesus Loves Nukes': Air Force Cites New Testament, Ex-Nazi, to Train Officers on Ethics of Launching Nuclear Weapons." Truthout, July 27, 2011. http://www.truth-out.org/news/item/2356:jesus-loves-nukes-air-force-cites-new-testament-exnazi-to-train-officers-on-ethics-of-launching-nuclear-weapons.

Lewis, Tom. *Divided Highways: Building the Interstate Highways, Transforming American Life*. Ithaca, NY: Cornell University Press, 2013.

Lieb, Jonathan, and Thomas Chapman. "Jim Crow, Civil Defense, and the Hydrogen Bomb: Race, Evacuation Planning, and the Geopolitics of Fear in 1950s Savannah, Georgia." *Southeastern Geographer* 51, no. 4 (Winter 2011): 578–95.

Lifton, Robert Jay. *Death In Life: Survivors of Hiroshima*. Chapel Hill: University of North Carolina Press, 1991.

———. *The Nazi Doctors: Medical Killing and the Psychology of Genocide*. New York: Basic Books, 1986.

Lifton, Robert Jay, and Richard Falk, *Indefensible Weapons: The Political and Psychological Case against Nuclearism*. New York: Basic Books, 1982.

Lifton, Robert Jay, and Eric Markusen. *The Genocidal Mentality: Nazi Holocaust and the Nuclear Threat*. New York: Basic Books, 1990.

Light, Jennifer. *From Warfare to Welfare: Defense Intellectuals and Urban Problems in Cold War America*. Baltimore, MD: Johns Hopkins University Press, 2003.

Ligotti, Thomas. *The Conspiracy against the Human Race: A Contrivance of Horror*. New York: Hippocampus Press, 2010.

Lindqvist, Sven. *A History of Bombing*. Translated by Linda Haverly Rugg. New York: The New Press, 2001.

Lingis, Alphonso. *Deathbound Subjectivity*. Bloomington: Indiana University Press, 1989.

Longinus. *On Great Writing (On the Sublime)*. Translated by G. M. A. Grube. Indianapolis, IN: Hackett, 1991.

Lovecraft, Howard Philips. *Selected Letters*. Vol 2, *1925–1929*, edited by August Derleth and Donald Wandrei. Sauk City, WI: Arkham House, 1965.

Lund, Emmanuel. "Preview: First Strike Plunges Us into a Cold War Scenario." AppsZoom,

February 7, 2014. http://www.appszoom.com/magazine/preview-first-strike-plunges-us-into-a-cold-war-scenario_2529.

Lundberg, Christian O. *Lacan in Public: Psychoanalysis and the Science of Rhetoric*. Tuscaloosa: University of Alabama Press, 2012.

———. "The Pleasure of Sadism: A Reading of the *Left Behind* Series." In *Media and the Apocalypse*, edited by Kylo-Patrick Hart and Annette Holba, 97–128. New York: Peter Lang, 2009.

———. "The Royal Road Not Taken: Joshua Gunn's 'Refitting Fantasy: Psychoanalysis, Subjectivity and Talking to the Dead' and Lacan's Symbolic Order." *Quarterly Journal of Speech* 90, no. 4 (2004): 495–500.

MacCannell, Dean. "Baltimore in the Morning . . . After: On the Forms of Post-Nuclear Leadership." *Diacritics* 14, no. 2 (Summer 1984): 32–46.

Makhijani, Arjun, and Hisham Zerriffi. *Dangerous Thermonuclear Quest*. Takoma Park, MD: Institute for Energy and Environmental Research, July 1998.

Manjikian, Mary. *Apocalypse and Post-Politics: The Romance of the End*. Lanham, MD: Lexington Books, 2014.

Marderness, William. *How to Read a Myth*. Amherst, NY: Humanity Books, 2009.

Martel, William, and Paul Savage. *Strategic Nuclear War: What the Superpowers Target and Why*. New York: Greenwood Press, 1986.

Martelle, Scott. *Detroit: A Biography*. Chicago: Chicago Review Press, 2012.

Matheson, Calum. "'What Does Obama Want of Me?' Anxiety and Jade Helm 15." *Quarterly Journal of Speech* 102, no. 2 (2016): 133–49.

McGowan, Todd. *Enjoying What We Don't Have: The Political Project of Psychoanalysis*. Lincoln: University of Nebraska Press, 2013.

McKinzie, Matthew, Thomas B. Cochran, Robert S. Norris, and William M. Arkin. *The U.S. Nuclear War Plan: A Time for Change*. New York: Natural Resources Defense Council, June 2001.

McMillan, Edwin. "Trinity Test, July 16 1945 Eyewitness Report by Edwin McMillan." NuclearFiles.org, accessed 2015. http://www.nuclearfiles.org/menu/key-issues/nuclear-weapons/history/pre-cold-war/manhattan-project/trinity/eyewitness-edwin-mcmillan_1945-07-16.htm.

Meillassoux, Quentin. *After Finitude: An Essay on the Necessity of Contingency*. Translated by Ray Brassier. London: Continuum, 2008.

Merkur, Daniel. *Psychoanalytic Approaches to Myth: Freud and the Freudians*. New York: Routledge, 2005.

Miller, J. Hillis. *Others*. Princeton, NJ: Princeton University Press, 2001.

Miller, Richard Lee. *Under the Cloud: The Decades of Nuclear Testing*. The Woodlands, TX: Two-Sixty Press, 1991.

Mitchell, Richard. *Dancing at Armageddon: Survivalism and Chaos in Modern Times*. Chicago: University of Chicago Press, 2002.

MOBS Lab. "Assessing the International Spreading Risk Associated with the 2014 West African Ebola Outbreak." Northeastern University Laboratory for the Modeling of Biological and Socio-technical Systems, copyright 2017. http://www.mobs-lab.org/ebola.html.

Morton, Timothy. *Hyperobjects: Philosophy and Ecology after the End of the World*. Minneapolis: University of Minnesota Press, 2013.

Moses, Robert. "The Civil Defense Fiasco." *Harpers*, November 1, 1957.

"Mr. Obama and Mr. Putin Should Play First Strike." *//B%-L#OG»...* (blog). First Strike.

December 4, 2013. http://www.firststrike.mobi/2013/12/04/mr-obama-and-mr-putin-should-play-first-strike/.

Mueller, John. *Atomic Obsession: Nuclear Alarmism from Hiroshima to Al-Qaeda*. Oxford: Oxford University Press 2010.

National Aeronautics and Space Administration. *2006 Near-Earth Object Survey and Deflection Study*. Washington, DC: NASA, December 2006. https://www.hq.nasa.gov/office/pao/FOIA/NEO_Analysis_Doc.pdf.

National Geographic. "Doomsday Preppers." National Geographic Society, accessed 2013. http://channel.nationalgeographic.com/doomsday-preppers/video-gallery/.

Nicolas of Cusa. *Selected Spiritual Writings*. Translated by H. Lawrence Bond. New York: Paulist Press, 1997.

Noble, David. *The Religion of Technology: The Divinity of Man and the Spirit of Invention*. New York: Penguin Books, 1999.

Nolan, Janne. *Guardians of the Arsenal: The Politics of Nuclear Strategy*. New York: Basic Books, 1989.

Oelrich, Ivan. *Missions for Nuclear Weapons after the Cold War*. Federation of American Scientists Occasional Paper No. 3. Washington, DC: Federation of American Scientists, January 2005.

O'Gorman, Ned. "Eisenhower and the American Sublime." *Quarterly Journal of Speech* 94, no. 1 (2008): 44–72.

———. *The Iconoclastic Imagination: Image, Catastrophe, and Economy in America from the Kennedy Assassination to September 11*. Chicago: University of Chicago Press, 2016.

———. "The Political Sublime: An Oxymoron." *Millennium* 34 (2005): 889–915.

———. "The Sensibility of the State: Operation Ivy and the Appearance of the Cold War 'Super.'" *Rhetoric & Public Affairs* 19, no. 1 (2016): 1–44.

O'Gorman, Ned, and Kevin Hamilton, "Visualities of Strategic Vision: Lookout Mountain Laboratory and the Deterrent State from Nuclear Tests to Vietnam." *Visual Studies* 30, no. 2 (2015): 195–208.

O'Leary, Stephen. *Arguing the Apocalypse: A Theory of Millennial Rhetoric*. Oxford: Oxford University Press, 1994.

Osborn, Michael. "Archetypal Metaphor in Rhetoric: The Light-Dark Family." *Quarterly Journal of Speech* 53, no. 2 (1967): 115–26.

Otto, Rudolf. *The Idea of the Holy: An Inquiry into the Non-rational Factor in the Idea of the Divine and Its Relation to the Rational*. Mansfield Center, CT: Martino, 2010.

Overy, Richard. *Why the Allies Won*. New York: W. W. Norton, 1995.

Pamlin, Dennis, and Stuart Armstrong. *Global Challenges: 12 Risks That Threaten Human Civilisation*. Oxford: Global Challenges Foundation, February 2015. https://api.globalchallenges.org/static/wp-content/uploads/12-Risks-with-infinite-impact.pdf.

Pascal, Blaise. *Pensées*. Translated by W. F. Trotter. New York: E. P. Dutton, 1957.

Payne, Matthew Thomas. "Marketing Military Realism in Call of Duty 4: Modern Warfare." *Games and Culture* 7 (2012): 305–11.

Peters, John Durham. *Speaking into the Air: A History of the Idea of Communication*. Chicago: University of Chicago Press, 1999.

Peterson, Sarah. *Planning the Home Front: Building Bombers and Communities at Willow Run*. Chicago: University of Chicago Press, 2013.

Picard, Max. *The World of Silence*. Trans. Stanley Godman. Chicago: Henry Regnery, 1952.

Powers, Thomas. "Choosing a Strategy for World War III." *Atlantic Monthly*, November 1982, 82–110.

Priestman, Chris. "Hands-On with First Strike—Nuclear War Is Devastating but It Sure Is Fun." Pocket Gamer, February 17, 2014. http://www.pocketgamer.co.uk/r/iPad/First+Strike/news.asp?c=57465.

Pseudo-Dionysius. *The Complete Works*. Translated by Colm Luibheid. New York: Paulist Press, 1987.

Raatz, Joseph. "War Game Helps Reinvigorate Nuclear Strategic Thinking." Air Force Global Strike Command, December 20, 2013. http://www.afgsc.af.mil/News/Article-Display/Article/629692/war-game-helps-reinvigorate-nuclear-strategic-thinking/.

Reiffel, Leonard. *A Study of Lunar Research Flights*. Kirtland Air Force Base, NM: Air Force Special Weapons Center, June 19, 1959.

Richelson, Jeffrey. "Population Targeting and U.S. Strategic Doctrine." In *Strategic Nuclear Targeting*, edited by Desmond Ball and Jeffrey Richelson, 234–49. Ithaca, NY: Cornell University Press, 1986.

Riesman, Abraham. "Ebola News Gives Me a Guilty Thrill. Am I Crazy?" *Pacific Standard*, October 23, 2014. https://psmag.com/social-justice/ebola-news-gives-guilty-thrill-crazy-93002.

Rizzo, Anthony, dir. *Our Cities Must Fight*. Archer Productions, 1951. Film.

Robinson, Andrew. "The Political Theory of Constitutive Lack: A Critique." *Theory & Event* 8, no. 1 (2005). https://doi.org/10.1353/tae.2005.0016.

Rose, Kenneth. *One Nation Underground: The Fallout Shelter in American Culture*. New York: New York University Press, 2001.

Rosenberg, David. "The Origins of Overkill: Nuclear Weapons and American Strategy, 1945–1960." In *Strategy and Nuclear Deterrence: An International Security Reader*, edited by Steven Miller, 113–81. Princeton, NJ: Princeton University Press, 1984.

Rosenthal, Debra. *At the Heart of the Bomb*. Reading, MA: Addison-Wesley, 1990.

Rubenstein, Jay. *Armies of Heaven: The First Crusade and the Quest for Apocalypse*. New York: Basic Books, 2011.

Ruddy, Jason Carl. "First Strike (iOS) Review." Kaiju Pop, March 12, 2014. http://kaijupop.com/2014/03/first-strike-ios-review/.

Rushing, Janice Hocker. "Ronald Reagan's 'Star Wars' Address: Mythic Containment of Technical Reasoning." *Quarterly Journal of Speech* 72, no. 4 (1986): 415–33.

Rushing, Janice Hocker, and Thomas S. Frentz. "Integrating Ideology and Archetype in Rhetorical Criticism." *Quarterly Journal of Speech* 77, no. 4 (1991): 385–406.

"Russell Urges Antimissile Force so Nation Can Rebuild in Event of 'Nuclear Exchange' with Soviet." *New York Times*, November 22, 1968.

Scarry, Elaine. *Thermonuclear Monarchy: Choosing between Democracy and Doom*. New York: W. W. Norton, 2014.

Schaus, Claire Troes. *What Price Survival? An Essay on the Ultimate Destiny of Mankind*. New York: Exposition Press, 1967.

Scheer, Robert. *With Enough Shovels: Reagan, Bush and Nuclear War*. New York: Random House, 1982.

Schell, Jonathan. *The Fate of the Earth*. New York: Alfred Knopf, 1982.

Schiappa, Edward. "The Rhetoric of Nukespeak." *Communication Monographs* 56 (September 1989): 253–72.

Scott, Melba, with Carol Ahlgren. "Witness to an Atomic Test." *Nebraska History* 77 (1996): 33–44. http://www.nebraskahistory.org/publish/publicat/history/full-text/NH1996AtomicTest.pdf.

Sebeok, Thomas. *Communication Measures to Bridge Ten Millennia*. Columbus, OH: Battelle Memorial Institute Office for Nuclear Waste Isolation, 1984.

Seife, Charles. *Sun in a Bottle: The Strange History of Fusion and the Science of Wishful Thinking*. New York: Penguin, 2008.

Sharma, Sarah. *In the Meantime: Temporality and Cultural Politics*. Durham, NC: Duke University Press, 2014.

Sharp, Patrick. *Savage Perils: Racial Frontiers and Nuclear Apocalypse in American Culture*. Norman: University of Oklahoma Press, 2007.

Shaw, Phillip. *The Sublime (The New Critical Idiom)*. New York: Routledge, 2006.

Shipley, Joseph. *The Origins of English Words: A Discursive Dictionary of Indo-European Roots*. Baltimore, MD: Johns Hopkins University Press, 2001.

Slater, Dan. *Love in the Time of Algorithms: What Technology Does to Meeting and Mating*. New York: Penguin Group, 2013.

Slater, Harry. "The Firing Line: 5 Questions for Blindflug Studios on First Strike." Pocket Gamer, March 17, 2014. http://www.pocketgamer.co.uk/r/iPad/First+Strike/news.asp?c=58211.

———. "First Strike." Pocket Gamer, March 13, 2014, http://www.pocketgamer.co.uk/r/iPad/First+Strike/review.asp?c=58126.

Slavo, Mac. "Video: Model Shows How Ebola Will Spread: 'It Only Takes One Infected Individual Making It through a Checkpoint.'" Infowars, September 10, 2014. https://www.infowars.com/video-model-shows-how-ebola-will-spread-it-only-takes-one-infected-individual-making-it-through-an-airport-checkpoint/.

Slotkin, Richard. *Regeneration through Violence: The Mythology of the American Frontier*. New York: Harper Perennial, 1996.

Smith, Cyril. "Trinity Test, July 16 1945 Eyewitness Report by Cyril S. Smith." NuclearFiles.org., accessed 2015. http://www.nuclearfiles.org/menu/key-issues/nuclear-weapons/history/pre-cold-war/manhattan-project/trinity/eyewitness-cyril-smith_1945-07-16.htm.

Smith, Wilbur. *This Atomic Age and the Word of God*. Boston: W. A. Wilde, 1948.

Soler, Colette. *Lacanian Affects*. Translated by Bruce Fink. New York: Routledge, 2016.

Sorensen, Roy. "Infinite Decision Theory." In *Gambling on God: Essays on Pascal's Wager*, edited by Jeff Jordan, 139–59. Lanham, MD: Rowman and Littlefield Publishers, 1994.

Sugrue, Thomas. *The Origins of the Urban Crisis: Race and Inequality in Postwar Detroit*. Princeton, NJ: Princeton University Press, 1996.

Suskind, Ron. *The One Percent Doctrine: Deep inside America's Pursuit of Its Enemies since 9/11*. New York: Simon & Schuster, 2006.

Szasz, Ferenc. *The Day the Sun Rose Twice: The Story of the Trinity Site Nuclear Explosion, July 16, 1945*. Albuquerque: University of New Mexico Press, 1984.

Taylor, Bryan C. "'A Hedge against the Future': The Post–Cold War Rhetoric of Nuclear Weapons Modernization" *Quarterly Journal of Speech* 96 no. 1 (2010): 1–24.

———, ed. *Nuclear Legacies: Communication, Controversy, and the U.S. Nuclear Weapons Complex*. Lanham, MD: Lexington Books, 2007.

———. "Nuclear Weapons and Communication Studies: A Review Essay." *Western Journal of Communication* 62, no. 3 (1998): 300–315.

———. "'Our Bruised Arms Hung Up as Monuments': Nuclear Iconography in Post–Cold War Culture." *Critical Studies in Media Communication* 20, no. 1 (2003): 1–34.

Teller, Edward, Wilson K. Talley, Gary H. Higgins, and Gerald W. Johnson. *The Constructive Uses of Nuclear Explosives*. New York: McGraw-Hill, 1968.

Thacker, Eugene. *In the Dust of This Planet*. Vol. 1 of *Horror of Philosophy*. Winchester, UK: Zero Books, 2011.

Titus, A. Costandina. *Bombs in the Backyard: Atomic Testing and American Politics*. Reno: University of Nevada Press, 2001.

Tucker, Robert. "Morality and Deterrence." In *Nuclear Deterrence: Ethics and Strategy*, edited by Russell Hardin, John Mearsheimer, Gerald Dworkin, and Robert Goodin, 53–70. Chicago: University of Chicago Press, 1985.

Turse, Nick. *Kill Anything That Moves: The Real American War in Vietnam*. New York: Picador, 2013.

United States Congress, Senate Committee on Armed Services. *Nomination of Millard Frank Caldwell, Jr., to be Federal Civil Defense Administrator: Hearing before Subcommittee, 82d Congress, 1st Session, January 15, 1951*. Washington, DC: US Government Printing Office, 1951.

Velocity, Max. *Patriot Dawn: The Resistance Rises*. Self-published, 2012.

Waltman, Michael, and John Haas. *The Communication of Hate*. New York: Peter Lang, 2011.

Warren, Donald. "Community Dissensus: Panic in Suburbia." In *A City in Racial Crisis: The Case of Detroit Pre- and Post- the 1967 Riot*, edited by Leonard Gordon, 120–45. Dubuque, IA: W. C. Brown Co. 1971.

Watts, Eric King. "Postracial Fantasies, Blackness, and Zombies." *Communication and Critical/Cultural Studies* 4, no. 4 (2017): 317–33.

Weber, Eugen. *Apocalypses: Prophets, Cults and Millennial Beliefs throughout the Ages*. London: Hutchinson, 1999.

Weinstein, Adam. "VIDEO: Nuke the Oil Spill?" *Mother Jones*, May 24, 2010. http://www.motherjones.com/blue-marble/2010/05/nuke-bomb-oil-spill-cleanup-crazy-russia-gulf-bp.

Wellerstein, Alex. "James B. Conant on Trinity (1945)." *Restricted Data: The Nuclear Secrecy Blog*, July 16, 2012. http://blog.nuclearsecrecy.com/2012/07/16/conant-on-trinity-1945/.

Widick, B. J. *Detroit: City of Race and Class Violence*. Chicago: Quadrangle Books, 1972.

Wiener, Norbert. *God & Golem, Inc.: A Comment on Certain Points Where Cybernetics Impinges on Religion*. Cambridge, MA: MIT Press, 1964.

Wilkening, Dean, Kenneth Watman, Michael Kennedy, and Richard Darilek. *Strategic Defenses and Crisis Stability*. Santa Monica, CA: RAND Corporation, 1989.

Williams, David Cratis. "Nuclear Criticism: In Pursuit of a 'Politically Enabling' Deconstructive Voice." *Journal of the American Forensic Association* 24 (Winter 1988): 193–205.

Williams, Raymond. *Literature and Marxism*. Oxford: Oxford University Press, 1997.

Wilson, David. *Cities and Race: America's New Black Ghetto*. London: Routledge, 2007.

Winkler, Allan. *Life under a Cloud: American Anxiety about the Atom*. Oxford: Oxford University Press, 1993.

Winner, Langdon. *The Whale and the Reactor: A Search for Limits in an Age of High Technology*. Chicago: University of Chicago Press, 1986.

Woolsey, James. "Hearing of the Senate Select Committee on Intelligence Subject: Nomination of R. James Woolsey to Become Director of Central Intelligence." *Federal News Service*, February 2, 1993.

Wright, Patrick. *Tank*. Penguin Books, 2000.

Yudkowsky, Eliezer. "Cognitive Biases Potentially Affecting Judgment of Global Risks." In *Global Catastrophic Risks*, edited by Nick Bostrom and Milan Ćirković, 91–119. New York: Oxford University Press, 2008.

Žižek, Slavoj. *The Plague of Fantasies*. London: Verso, 2008.

Zukin, Sharon. *Landscapes of Power. From Detroit to Disneyworld*. Berkeley: University of California Press, 1991.

Index